CD ROM

VOLUME TWO

OPTICAL
PUBLISHING

A practical

approach to

developing CD ROM

applications.

EDITED BY SUZANNE ROPIEQUET
WITH JOHN EINBERGER AND BILL ZOELLICK

MICROSOFT
PRESS

PUBLISHED BY

Microsoft Press
A Division of Microsoft Corporation
16011 N.E. 36th Way, Box 97017, Redmond, Washington 98073-9717

Copyright © 1987 by Microsoft Press
All rights reserved. No part of the contents of this book may
be reproduced or transmitted in any form or by any means without
the written permission of the publisher.

Library of Congress Cataloging in Publication Data
CD ROM
Includes bibliographies and indexes.
Contents: v. 1. The new Papyrus   v. 2. Optical publishing.
1. Compact discs.   2. Optical storage devices.
I. Lambert, Steve, 1945-   . II. Ropiequet, Suzanne, 1954-
TK7882.C56C3   1986   004.5'3   86-2369
ISBN 1-555615-000-8

Printed and bound in the United States of America.

  2 3 4 5 6 7 8 9 FGFG 8 9 0 9 8

Distributed to the book trade in the
United States by Harper & Row.

Distributed to the book trade in
Canada by General Publishing Company, Ltd.

Distributed to the book trade outside the
United States and Canada by Penguin Books Ltd.

Penguin Books Ltd., Harmondsworth, Middlesex, England
Penguin Books Australia Ltd., Ringwood, Victoria, Australia
Penguin Books N.Z. Ltd., 182-190 Wairau Road, Auckland 10, New Zealand

British Cataloging in Publication Data available

CD\ROM

OPTICAL
PUBLISHING

Acknowledgments

Making a book out of the words of more than a dozen different authors is not a simple task. It not only requires the efforts of many copyeditors, typists, proofreaders, artists, and typesetters—the unsung heroes of any publishing company—but in this case, it also involved a few other people to whom I owe special thanks:

Bill Zoellick of the Alexandria Institute and John Einberger of Reference Technology, Inc., for their support, contributions, and commitment to this project; Dale Callison, for keeping me awake late at night, buoying my spirits, and doing a fine job of copyediting; the entire CD ROM Group at Microsoft, especially Gene Apperson, Dan Newell, and Gordon Griesbach; and last, but not least, Buzz Shaw, for standing by me and un-wittingly making this book a part of his life too.

Suzanne Ropiequet
Seattle, Washington
1986

Contributors

This book was shaped by the expertise, insights, and words of the following people:

Rich Bowers
AITRC, Columbus, Ohio

Bill Zoellick
The Alexandria Institute, Boulder, Colorado

Anne Armstrong
CD Data Report, McLean, Virginia

Rick Doherty
CMP Publications, Seaford, New York

Joe Bremner
Database Development, Milwaukee, Wisconsin

David Roux
Datext, Woburn, Massachusetts

Brian Martin
The Library Corporation, Charlestown, West Virginia

Marilyn Winokur
Leonard Rann
Micromedex, Denver, Colorado

Gene Apperson
Microsoft Corporation, Redmond, Washington

Mike Befeler
Ray Bridge
Greg Colvin
John Einberger
Jerry Fand
Jamie Morin
Bill Thornburg
Reference Technology Inc., Boulder, Colorado

Leonard Laub
Vision Three, Los Angeles, California

CONTENTS

Changing the Publishing Paradigm

This book is a handbook for publishers, librarians, authors, and other people who need to know about publishing on optical discs. It is also a guide to some of the key ideas driving a revolution in the way we distribute and use information.

The publishing industry is changing rapidly. Optical discs, most notably CD ROM discs, are one primary agent of this change. They are accompanied by other important technological developments, such as more powerful, less expensive microcomputers, improved networking capabilities, and less expensive, higher resolution monitors. This book describes these technological developments, but we do not make the mistake of equating the new publishing industry with the hardware it uses. The most revolutionary changes taking place in publishing are not related to hardware, but to *ideas*. People are *thinking* about publishing in a new way. This book describes the nature of this thinking and the publishing processes it implies, rather than focusing solely on the hardware required to make it all happen.

Amazing But True

Computers dominate the publishing industry, since most type is "set" with one, but the final goal still is a printed product. The computer is being used as a sort of high-tech Linotype machine; it is, most assuredly, fast and flexible, but ultimately it achieves nothing more than hot lead can do. The outcome remains a product printed on paper.

Within the past 25 years, many printed products have been collected into electronic databases. Incredibly, this collection process sometimes requires "capturing" the printed data—that is, returning it to the electronic form from which it started. Other times, a publisher can write conversion software that reformats the electronic typesetting tapes allowing them to build a database. But this kind of conversion, when possible, is expensive. It is so expensive that retyping the data can be faster and more reliable.

2

Why is database building so difficult? Because it is being treated as an afterthought, as a secondary outcome. Most publishers still see their business as that of creating printed products. As Nick Alter of University Microfilms explained it:

> Traditionally publishers have rushed to format information on a page, and in the process, have in effect fenced the information in. Then later when they have tried to database the information, they've had to strip out all the formatting that they put in when they paginated it.

Moreover, databases require different information than print products require. To print a journal article we need to know what it looks like—which type fonts, type sizes, indention, and other *physical* characteristics it will have. To place a journal article in a database, we must identify search words, distinguish the article's title from each section of its body, and label copyright dates and authors' names. To do this, we need to view the article structurally, or *logically*. An article's structural characteristics are conveyed by different information than its physical characteristics.

The Paradigm Shift

The solution to these problems is at once simple and radical: Reverse the process. Build the database first and then extract the information needed for printing from the database. Reversing the process not only makes it easier to build databases, but it makes it possible to publish using media other than paper. You greatly simplify publishing on CD ROM, for example, if you start with a logically organized database rather than a set of formatting instructions for electronic typesetting.

When we speak of the publishing revolution as one driven by ideas rather than solely by technology, this notion of reversing the publishing paradigm stands out as an archtypical example of this revolutionary power. Information that is stored electronically and organized logically is a transportable and searchable commodity. You can repackage, subdivide, and rearrange it to suit a variety of purposes. Articles can be printed on demand, as needed, rather than printed in batches, distributed, and stored in expensive, bulky paper form as we do at present.

Like all revolutions, this paradigm shift to producing electronic databases rather than printed products requires new tools and new ways of thinking. For example:

- Current copyright law protection is inadequate for information distributed on networks and printed on demand. We need to find new legal models for protecting the rights of those who create information and for compensating authors and publishers for the information's use.

- When we collect hundreds of thousands of pages of information on a single disc, old methods of finding the information, such as browsing through books on a shelf, no longer apply. We must introduce new retrieval and index-building tools in delivering documents.

- New delivery mechanisms require that we develop new standards for storing and interchanging information. When we want to distribute and interchange electronic products on a medium such as the CD ROM, we need to agree on ways to compress, index, and arrange the information on disc.

- New kinds of workstations, using high-resolution display devices, image-decompression hardware, faster communications links, and other new tools for delivering information, must be developed to give the user easier access to the information.

This book surveys these problems and explores both the solutions systems provide today and those we anticipate in the next few years.

About the Book

The contributors to this book are actively involved in CD ROM publishing. Some are publishers. Most have worked with publishers directly, helping them to create their first CD ROM products. Others have tracked the industry from its infancy, guiding and advising publishers and manufacturers alike with insights gained through their observations. Yet others are developing new ways to work with information so that it can be stored and retrieved more efficiently on CD ROM.

We have molded the diverse experiences and opinions of these people into 16 chapters, each chapter building on the next to paint a picture of disc publishing. We begin by presenting an overview of the CD ROM hardware and software environment. In Chapter 2, "Information Delivery Systems," Leonard Laub describes the workstations that will read and display CD ROM information. And John Einberger, in Chapter 3, "CD ROM Characteristics," explains the nature of CD ROM, its physical makeup, and its strengths and weaknesses.

Section II, "Text Preparation and Retrieval," describes the issues publishers face when preparing text applications. Chapter 4, "Preparing Text," by Ray Bridge and Jamie Morin, explains the important, and sometimes difficult and expensive, problems of capturing textual data for publication. Since distributing data on CD ROM gets a publisher into the

4

electronic document retrieval business, publishers working in this area will succeed only if they understand something about indexing and retrieving electronic data. Bill Zoellick in Chapter 5, "Selecting an Approach to Document Retrieval," gives a high-level view of fundamental ideas and options associated with document retrieval systems. In Chapters 6 and 7 we focus more closely on the retrieval strategies and indexing techniques common to two basic data structures — "Full-Text Retrieval and Indexing," by Jerry Fand, and "Database Retrieval and Indexing," by Greg Colvin.

Many publishers successfully store microfiche documents and other images on CD ROM. As CD ROM publishing becomes more acceptable to the publishing industry, we will begin to see products that integrate text, images, and perhaps sound. Section III, "Image and Sound Preparation," considers some of the technical aspects of these two information formats. Chapter 8, "Displaying Images," by Gene Apperson and Rick Doherty, explores image technology and describes many of the current methods of preparing and processing images for CD ROM and CD-I. Bryan Brewer delves into some of the properties of digital audio in Chapter 9, "Using Audio," explaining how sound is prepared and integrated into CD ROM and CD-I products.

After the database is built and the images and sound are prepared, it is time to make the CD ROM disc. In Section IV, "Disc Production," we discuss the role the CD ROM publisher takes in the final stages of data preparation and manufacturing. Chapter 10, "Disc Origination," reviews the processes involved in combining data files and preparing the "disc image" for the disc manufacturers to record on CD ROM. John Einberger and Bill Zoellick explain the importance of the proposed "High Sierra" disc format in Chapter 11. Anne Armstrong concludes the section with the final step of CD ROM production in Chapter 12, "Premastering and Mastering," in which she ensures that readers have basic "CD ROM literacy" by briefly guiding them through the steps involved in mastering and replicating CD ROM discs.

The entire business of publishing presumes that the rights of the authors and publishers who create and distribute data can be protected. Publication on CD ROM discs and associated electronic technologies such as delivery over networks and "on demand" publishing tax the current copyright law's ability to guarantee authors and publishers compensation. Chapter 13 explores this important problem, providing a much-needed overview of this complicated and rapidly evolving intersection of law and technology with Joe Bremner's essay, "Data Protection."

Just as books are reprinted periodically, so will CD ROM publications be remastered. In Chapter 14, David Roux explains the updating options available to publishers and some of the design considerations involved in choosing an updating strategy.

The work of those pioneers who have brought CD ROM products to market can teach a great deal. Section VI contains two case studies that share the insights of two pioneering CD ROM publishers. Brian Martin, in Chapter 15, tells how he and others in The Library Corporation brought BiblioFile, the first CD ROM publication to market. Marilyn Winokur, Leonard Rann, and Bill Thornburg follow with the story of how Micromedex, a microfiche company specializing in medical information, began publishing on CD ROM.

This book is a survey of problems and issues encountered in CD ROM publishing; it is not meant to be a definitive reference. As is the case with any good survey, we include a comprehensive list of references and resources that readers can turn to for more information. We also include an extensive glossary; to be "literate" in this field, we must understand the terminology of optical disc publishing.

Since the CD ROM industry is still in its infancy, developers have not yet achieved consensus on which words to use to describe the various CD ROM publishing processes. We have suggested a few terms in this book in hopes that all of us can begin using the same language to describe the things we do. We are fully aware, however, that language evolves. If the words we use seem appropriate to you, adopt and use them. If you have a better, more descriptive way to say the same thing, tell everyone you know and see if they agree. The sooner we all begin speaking the same language, the easier it will be to communicate our ideas.

Scylla and Charybdis*

As publishers begin to chart their course and explore the potential of the CD ROM industry, they will undoubtedly confront obstacles. Two stories exemplify the hazards through which we must steer the CD ROM publishing industry in the coming years.

---

*Scylla and Charybdis are rocks in the Strait of Messina off the Italian coast. In ancient times they were thought to be monsters set by the gods to guard the strait. Scylla, a six-headed, man-eating beast, guarded one side of the strait. Charybdis defended the other side, creating a huge whirlpool every time she drank the strait's water and spat it out. Ancient mariners were well advised to chart a mid-course between the two rocks.

6

The first was told to me by a friend who writes for *Infoworld*. A library staff decided to experiment with CD ROM databases. They bought a database they thought their patrons would find useful. They also, of course, bought the CD ROM drive that the database vendor supplied.

At the end of the fiscal year, the staff found a few hundred dollars were left in the budget and decided to purchase a second CD ROM database distributed by a different vendor. At first this seemed to be an advantage: They not only would bring in a second optical disc database, but would also learn a different vendor's approach to delivering the information.

Imagine their surprise, disappointment, and, ultimately, their incredulity when they learned that, even though this second product, like the first, was published on a CD ROM, it could not be read with the CD ROM drive they had originally purchased. Each product required a different manufacturer's drive. This is equivalent to needing one brand of floppy disk drive in your computer to use Lotus 1-2-3 and a different brand to use Framework. Both discs were designed for one drive, but both lacked a standard format that would allow them to be interchangeable.

Charybdis, the whirlpool on one side of the market straits, then, is a failure to develop standards for interchanging information, thus encouraging the problems experienced by the librarians in the previous story. Developing such standards depends, in part, on our thinking about information in different terms. Rather than thinking of information as printed pages, we need to begin thinking of it as structured, organized documents in a database. We need to use standard languages, such as the Association of American Publishers' Electronic Manuscript Markup Standard, to define such structures. We also need to arrange the information on the disc in a standard way, as proposed in the High Sierra Proposal and in the international standards for a disc format expected to emerge in the coming year. We probably even need to guarantee at least minimal data indexing standards for many of these databases to ensure that all software can perform at least basic retrieval operations on any published database.

But too much standardization can also lead us to the other side of the strait. This extreme is best described through another story that I gleaned at a recent optical disc conference. A panel of experts were discussing vendors' diverse approaches to giving users access to the information on CD ROM discs. After listening to product descriptions and arguments over differences among query languages, browsing techniques, and so forth, one audience member (another journalist) observed that there was a lot of "reinventing the wheel" going on. Different firms were working on the same problems, coming up with solutions similar in many respects. At the same time, the products differed subtly. It all seemed complicated and confusing. Wouldn't it be simpler if we all decided on *one* approach, or if some large firm could set a de facto standard?

That journalist was, unwittingly, pointing the way toward the rock opposite the whirlpool. Failure to standardize fundamental, underlying data organization is dangerous, but so is standardizing too completely. CD ROM involves a software hierarchy that extends from the system software on up to the user interface. Standardizing too high in this hierarchy, too close to the user interface, will stifle innovation. If we are not innovative and do not find ways to make using electronic information easier, the CD ROM industry will founder.

As the articles in this handbook show, this is an exciting time in a young industry. Currently, a lot of innovation is taking place; things are moving fast. We need this rapid movement to create the critical mass of products that will make CD ROM publishing attractive and economically viable. The question is whether we can sustain the movement while steering between the whirlpool, the failure to ensure the interchangeability of information that a universal publishing medium requires, and the rocks, the stasis of settling too soon for too little. It is an interesting business. The scope and the depth of the articles in this book attest to that.

About the Author

Bill Zoellick is Director of Technology for the Alexandria Institute, a nonprofit organization dedicated to making CD ROM information retrieval systems more widely available to users through libraries and other resource centers. Before joining the Alexandria Institute, Bill was Manager of Software Research at TMS, Inc., where he designed and implemented information retrieval software and lower level, file system software for CD ROM. He was a key participant in the High Sierra Group, playing an active role in producing the CD ROM logical format proposal. He has written and spoken widely about a broad range of CD ROM publishing issues and is co-author of a major new textbook on file structures.

THE CD ROM ENVIRONMENT

Information Delivery Systems

The small, shiny, rainbow-colored plastic discs called CD ROMs are so captivating that people can be excused for not realizing that these little wonders only *carry* information. Unlike books, the discs cannot deliver that information directly to people. As you might expect in this day of long but implicit names, that job falls to something commonly known as a *delivery system*.

In its simplest form, a delivery system contains:

- A drive, which reads the digital data stored on the CD ROM disc.

- A controller, which gives directions to the drive.

- A search engine, which consists of a microprocessor, memory, and software. This system interprets the user's requests and responses and generates instructions for the controller.

- An input device, which receives the user's requests and responses.

- An output device, which displays information taken from the disc for the user.

Such delivery systems can be part of larger systems and include familiar computer applications such as word processors and spreadsheets. They also can be dedicated to special purposes, such as instruction or research.

This chapter introduces those interested in publishing or distributing information on CD ROM to the sorts of delivery systems people are building and describes what the systems can do.

The Concept of a Workstation

This chapter uses another new-age term, *workstation*. The term usually refers to a high-end personal computer tailored to perform a specific task such as data retrieval or engineering design. Here, workstation refers to a computer system designed to search for and find information stored on a

CD ROM disc. A CD ROM workstation can be a shared mainframe, a general-purpose microcomputer, or a dedicated delivery system.

A CD ROM workstation must contain, or have unrestricted access to, all elements of a delivery system. The concept of a CD ROM workstation goes hand in hand with the idea of individuals working on whatever interests them, at whatever time and rate, and with whatever emphasis makes sense to them.

Although large, centralized systems that process big batches of queries can use CD ROM discs, this discussion concerns applications that are basically "one person, one disc." Here, we don't presume that the user, although possibly skilled in other fields, is a computer specialist or a librarian. We presume the delivery system can respond correctly, appropriately, and clearly to casual, vernacular requests.

CD ROM is a low-cost medium, usually using low-cost hardware of moderate performance. The drives and the ways they attach to computers are appropriate for a low-cost computer environment. It is thus not surprising that a PC is today's most frequently used general-purpose host for CD ROM delivery systems.

Most PC-based delivery systems are designed for use by one person at a time. Such a system typically contains:

- A PC-XT, PC-AT, or compatible, depending on how much computing the search engine or graphic display requires.

- A floppy disk or hard disk drive to store either the system software (device driver) the PC needs to find and control the CD ROM drive or the application software needed if CD ROMs store only data and indexes. If the CD ROM is bootable and stores the application software, magnetic disks still are needed to temporarily store file directories and indexes downloaded from the CD ROM.

- A CD ROM drive.

- A CD ROM drive controller or SCSI (Small Computer System Interface) host adapter.

- Some type of input device.

- A video card and CRT display (usually).

- A printer.

- A hard disk to store indexes for the CD ROM application, data, system software, and other applications.

We now examine major components of such a CD ROM workstation. Multiuser and more specialized workstations are addressed later.

CD ROM Drives

In consumer electronics, machines that record information usually are called *recorders*. The machines that play CD audio discs are called *players*. In the computer world, these machines are called *drives*, partly because they both play back and record information and partly because that's just what they're called.

Freestanding drives. Many CD ROM drives come with their own power supplies and housings. Such a freestanding drive gets its power directly from a wall socket. It plugs into the rest of the delivery system (usually a microcomputer) through a standard external interface or through a special device interface card that plugs into an expansion slot of the host computer.

The initial popularity of freestanding drives comes from:

- Availability, since these drives usually are based on commercial CD players.

- Simple interfacing.

- Freedom from problems of limited power supplies and available slots.

Built-in drives. More recently, manufacturers began supplying CD ROM drives that can be connected inside microcomputers in the same manner as floppy disk and Winchester drives. The first generation of built-in CD ROM drives uses the standard, full-height, 5¼-inch design, but newer models fit into half-height packages for use with the newer, smaller desktop and portable computers.

As with their magnetic counterparts, built-in CD ROM drives take direct current (DC) from the host computer's power supply; eliminating a separate power supply and package saves money. At this writing, OEM prices of such drives already are less than $500, with some quotations less than $250 in large volume, and prices are expected to continue dropping as production increases.

Jukeboxes. The consumer CD market has become interested in multidisc machines to reduce the need to get up and change discs. Some machines hold six discs; others hold 100 or more. These all have been adapted for CD ROM use and provide direct, online access to tens of thousands of megabytes of data.

Audio CD jukeboxes take as long as 10 seconds to swap discs, which may seem like a long time to the user of a highly interactive computer. A powerful technique for reducing this swap time is to incorporate several CD ROM drives in the jukebox so that you can load discs containing data likely to be called soon in anticipation of the request. Such multidrive jukeboxes are not yet available.

The jukebox is itself a data-storage device. Just as a disc drive is directed to a track or sector of data, a jukebox must be directed to a disc. So the jukebox requires a device interface and software to communicate with the operating system and application software in the host. Jukebox manufacturers can provide information about specific requirements.

Specialty drives. One of several refinements in CD ROM drive design recognizes the great similarity between CD ROM and CD audio, providing decoders for both data and audio. This hybrid is achieved by adding the Digital-to-Analog (D/A), low-pass filtering, and audio output stages of a standard CD player to a standard CD ROM drive. Thus, the microcomputer can control audio programs, and audio can accompany data presentations. OEM prices of the first generation of such drives are similar to those of standard CD ROM drives, in the range of $500 to $1000.

The focus and tracking servos of all optical disc drives provide a degree of shock and vibration protection, but CD ROM applications destined for moving vehicles require even more protection. These *severe environment* applications call for rugged drives, obtained either by repackaging standard drives (producing "ruggedized" drives) or by redesigning them from the ground up. Both methods were used in designing the CD players that were recently introduced commercially for automobiles. Because of this consumer product base, rugged CD ROM drives will also probably cost less than $1000.

Consumer CD players usually take several seconds to move between nonadjacent tracks. This access time is too long for most computer applications, so CD ROM drives move faster. Most CD ROM drives have an average access time in the range of ½ to 1 second, or 500 to 1000 milliseconds (msec). The heads of some newer drives are slightly lighter and their head positioners more powerful, enabling average access times of less than 300 msec. Future drives probably will be even faster and will not cost significantly more.

The Controller

Magnetic disk drives, particularly those made for microcomputers, contain little of the electronics that make them work. All dialogue between the drive and the computer about commands and status, and most of the error detection and correction of digital data recovered from the disk, are processed by a separate package of electronics called a *controller.*

CD ROM drives contain most of the functions associated with magnetic disk controllers, including data separation, error correction, and simple data buffering. But a data connection still must exist between the CD ROM drive and its host computer. This connection consists of a host adapter printed circuit card, device driver software in the host computer, and a cable that connects the CD ROM drive to the host adapter. The host adapter card converts the bus signals of the host computer to a series of signals known to the CD ROM drive; the cable is the electrical link between the two. Connectors on each end of the cable mate with connectors on the host adapter card and the drive. Electrical signals exchanged between the CD ROM drive controller and the host computer are sent through a *device interface.*

Many newer CD ROM drives contain their own controllers, which talk to standard high-level interfaces such as the IEEE 488 or SCSI (Small Computer System Interface—pronounced "Scuzzy"). Both SCSI and IEEE 488 are drive-independent interfaces, and both are configured as buses. This means, for example, that a single SCSI interface can deal with as many as eight devices, among which might be CD ROM drives, Winchester drives, writable optical disc drives, and, soon, printers and other peripherals. All the system developer needs is a software device driver that tells the operating system how to find and communicate with each device attached to the SCSI bus.

The SCSI bus is said to be *intelligent* because it can partially process the information coming from the CD ROM drive. This processing takes time. The time required to execute a command is known as *command latency.* Although command latency decreases the performance of SCSI interfaces, having the interface do this work removes a portion of the burden from the host computer.

SCSI is a high-performance interface and can move data at rates of a maximum of 32 megabits per second (Mb/s). This rate satisfies the system developer's desire to attach several drives, such as a Winchester disk (5 to 10 Mb/s), writable optical disc (1 to 5 Mb/s), or CD ROM (1.2 Mb/s), to the same interface.

16

The Search Engine

CD ROM discs store enormous amounts of data, but most people are concerned only with answers to their immediate questions. In addition, most people do not know (or really care) how the information is organized on the disc. They probably will pose questions in their own terms. The job of interpreting such questions and determining which information to take from the disc to gratify them belongs to the *search engine.*

Search engine, yet another new-age term, refers to the combination of:

- A scheme for indexing and organizing information on the CD ROM disc, carried out during premastering by (or for) the publisher.

- Software that interprets queries and generates citations (listings of where relevant information can be found on the CD ROM disc).

- Processor hardware, which runs the software, receives queries from the input device, sends requests to the CD ROM drive device interface, processes the information as needed, and sends the information to the output device.

Many types of search engines are available, but, as with other technologies, none can be called "best" out of the context of an application. The most prevalent search engine designs in CD ROM applications are described elsewhere in this book.

Input Devices

Most CD ROM delivery systems are designed to retrieve information. The user enters a request for information by means of an input device. The most common input devices are:

Keyboards. To the delight of touch-typists everywhere, keyboards have become the most common input device for general-purpose computers. In CD ROM delivery systems, keyboards make sense when the user's queries involve large amounts of text.

Touch screens. In simple delivery applications such as point-of-sale kiosks in retail stores, the user indicates choices by touching menu selections. When a finger, pencil, or other rod-shaped object touches the surface of the screen at a certain location, the program compares this location with those of the names or symbols for the various current choices. It then selects the one corresponding to the touched location.

Touch screens can be constructed by means of several technologies, including:

- A yoke of LEDs and photocells that surround the screen. Touching the screen breaks some of the beams, and special circuitry calculates the horizontal and vertical locations of the touch.

- Ultrasonic transducers that launch sound waves across the glass faceplate. The touch causes sound waves to be reflected. Location is calculated from the delay times that occur when the reflected sound waves return to the source.

- A pair of transparent plastic membranes with conductive coatings that are stretched over the screen. Where touched, the coatings contact each other. Location is calculated from the resulting electrical resistance.

These methods require that you add components either to a standard monitor or to a TV screen or that you use a special monitor with a circuit card added to the host. All three options cost several hundred dollars. They also lead to "messy faceplate" as fingerprints build up. And all three suffer from poor resolution (pointing accuracy), because fingertips typically are large and people point them in a casual way.

A related method, the use of a *light pen* (a wand with a photocell at the tip that picks up the light from the phosphor as the scanning spot moves by), doesn't mess up the faceplate and can provide better resolution, but the user must play with a valuable and fragile object. Light pens also require special circuit cards to talk to the host, and they may cost several hundred dollars. However, light pen hardware and software drivers generally are cheaper than touch screen systems.

Mice, joysticks, and trackballs. In environments in which users can be trusted with something valuable and fragile, any of several cursor positioning devices can perform the function of a touch screen with much greater reliability and resolution.

The *mouse* is a palm-sized box that slides around on a desktop. As the user moves it, the cursor moves in the same way on the screen. When the cursor points to the desired item, the user presses a button on the mouse, selecting that item. After years of obscurity, the mouse now is in common use with general-purpose microcomputers, largely because it is bundled with the Macintosh.

Joysticks are familiar to many people as the control devices for video games. They are wands that you tip to direct the cursor. For delivery systems use, they are inferior to the mouse in resolution, but exceed the mouse in durability and economy. Joysticks are quite inexpensive—sometimes costing as little as $5 for parts.

Hard-core video game people know that serious players use *trackballs*. These are large plastic balls in a housing. The user rolls the ball to position the cursor. A trackball provides resolution at least equal to that of the mouse, doesn't require a lot of clear desk space, and usually is more durable than a mouse.

Most of these pointing devices talk to the host through a serial (RS 232C) port, of which most host computers have only two. Alternatively, they can talk to the PC's bus through a special circuit card. This approach is preferable except when no slots are available and power-supply capacity is spoken for already.

Voice recognizers. For text-based applications with vocabularies that, while small, are too large to fit on the screen as a menu, voice recognition is an attractive alternative for input or selection. These systems currently can handle only a few hundred words, which must be spoken clearly and distinctly (no continuous speech) into a recognition device that has been trained for a specific speaker. Voice recognizers are expensive and may increase the hardware budget by hundreds of dollars.

The user of a voice recognition system need not touch a keyboard or screen (very good for repair or manufacturing personnel with both hands on a machine), but must carry or wear a microphone. Practical systems show the word they think they've heard and ask for confirmation before proceeding. Commercial voice recognition systems include software drivers that let them pretend to be keyboards.

Input Generated by Other (Nonhuman) Devices
As mentioned, an information delivery workstation may also be a more general-purpose computer system. In a growing category of CD ROM applications, the delivery system responds to calls from word processors (dictionary or thesaurus lookup), computer-aided design (CAD) systems (standards, symbol, or template lookup), and file servers on networks (historical or reference information).

In these cases, the other applications input data directly, in digital form. Human input goes to these other applications by the customary means.

Display Equipment

A delivery system can display information it finds and processes in a variety of ways. Common output devices include:

CRT displays. Most TV sets and computer monitors display data on a cathode ray tube (CRT). CRT technology has been improving for decades and, despite its many problems, remains the best method for displaying large amounts of text or images.

CRTs are bulky and fragile. They can consume lots of power. They often don't preserve the exact geometry of images, tending to stretch and bend them. They are hard to read in bright light. If used incorrectly, they can emit radiation. The electronics driving them can make high-pitched sounds. If you consider any of these characteristics an absolute disqualification, investigate one of the alternatives discussed below. Chapter 8 deals at length with display technology and applications, so in this discussion we address functional issues.

Most PCs use CRT displays specially designed to show a moderate amount of text (usually 24 rows of 80 characters) clearly, although with no graphic variety. Such monitors usually can show graphics, provided the appropriate circuit card is installed in the host. Graphics cards treat the screen as a mosaic of dots (called *picture elements* or *pixels*). The more pixels per screen, the more detail (*resolution*) is delivered.

Manufacturers' descriptions of screen resolutions sometimes are reminiscent of olive size nomenclature (the smallest is "giant"). The lowest resolution commonly used is a mosaic 320 pixels across by 200 high (the IBM Color Graphics Adapter low-resolution mode). This is coarse enough for a standard TV receiver to display, but too coarse to be satisfactory in most applications. Other common pixel maps include 640 by 200 (IBM CGA high-resolution), 640 by 350 (IBM EGA), and 720 by 348 (Hercules).

None of these is sufficient to show large areas of maps, business documents, or engineering drawings. For these demanding applications, other graphics standards exist with pixel maps such as 1024 by 800, 1280 by 800, 1280 by 1024, and even 2200 by 1728. Displays and adapters for these standards are available for PCs, but cost from $1500 to $5000. They also usually require the developer to write or buy special application software.

This range of resolutions can be found in monochrome (not necessarily black and white, because many screens produce only green or amber light) or in color. Color costs more because of the more complex CRT, the additional electronics needed to drive it, and the more complex driver card required to address it.

Most color computer displays are limited to a small number of colors at each pixel (for example, 16), poorly suiting them to depict natural scenes. Even if the same pixel counts are specified, monochrome screens usually deliver more detail and sustain their image quality with less maintenance.

The circuit card, sometimes called a *video* or *display adapter card*, is installed in the host computer. This card, which drives the display, consists primarily of semiconductor RAM that stores the brightness and color of each pixel on the screen. The memory organization can be thought of as a map of the screen, hence the widely used term *bit map* to describe pixel-oriented graphics displays.

Television sets and audio output. As CD ROM matures, interest in interactive applications that present TV-quality images overlaid with simple computer graphics and accompanied by sound (ranging from very high fidelity down to telephone squawk) is growing. This idea is at the heart of the CD-I (Compact Disc Interactive) standard, but probably will be implemented by some vendors before CD-I stabilizes.

TV sets are as omnipresent a display device as can be imagined, so it makes sense to tailor the delivery systems for mass applications to use them. Compared with computer monitors, TV sets usually are better at delivering natural images but much worse at showing crisp graphics or lots of letters and numbers.

LCDs. Many portable computers deliver information using liquid crystal displays (LCDs). These are addressed as dot matrices, similar to those in CRTs, and produce somewhat more blurred images and text. Brightness and the direction of light falling on the screen are critical. Recently developed backlit LCDs, however, can be read under less stringent lighting conditions.

LCDs are attractive purchases because they are almost flat (this really means thin compared with a CRT) and draw very little power. Color LCDs are beginning to appear commercially.

GPDs, ELDs, et al. Other "flat" image displays employ gas plasma (GPD) and electroluminescent (ELD) technologies. Their display and usage characteristics are somewhere between those of CRTs and LCDs. Military users like the GPD's ruggedness.

ELDs use a powdery, electrically sensitive material that glows when electronically stimulated. Their colors range from a soft blue to yellow, green, and white. Electroluminescent display brilliance usually is about the same as that of CRT screens. By their nature, ELDs involve none of the glass, vacuum, and high-voltage hazards associated with CRTs; nor do they produce radiation.

Electroluminescent displays at present are monochrome. Displays that are gray-scale capable are rare, and experimental color EL panels are years away from manufacture. Still, these displays are popular with several portable computer manufacturers and may eventually find their way into CD ROM display workstations.

Vacuum Fluorescent (VF) displays are miniature CRT systems. However, like electroluminescent displays, these thin, glass-enclosed displays use point-addressable (bit-image) matrices to create images instead of the raster-scanned electron beam system typical of large CRT displays. Vacuum fluorescent screens operate at lower voltages than do electroluminescent panels and CRTs and therefore are appropriate for portable and hazardous-environment CD reader systems.

Vacuum fluorescent displays usually are monochrome. The normal color for these "fluorescent" displays is a soft blue-green. However, some manufacturers import other colors to the system using colored overlays. Red, yellow, blue, and green can be obtained, but white cannot.

Color VF displays still are experimental. They lend themselves to portable and battery-powered applications, as do EL displays. Vacuum fluorescent display systems' greatest limitation is screen size. The largest VF glass packages are about the size of a 7-inch TV screen. That's a safety measure; it keeps atmospheric pressure from crushing the vacuum glass package. But the total display thickness, less than an inch, still makes color VF displays appropriate for portable CD reader applications.

Printers

A number of reference applications, such as those for air navigation and medical investigation, may require "hard copy" printouts of information. Several types of printers are available commercially.

Daisy-wheel printers produce truly high-quality text at PC prices. These speedy descendants of electric typewriters spin wheels or thimbles covered with molded representations of the characters in a typeface along a ribbon, striking the appropriate character at the appropriate time to make the requested letter. Daisy-wheel printers are rarely used for graphics, and changing their typefaces is a tedious manual operation.

Dot-matrix printers lay down small dots in a fine mosaic pattern to form characters or images. As with pixel-oriented displays, the resolution of dot-matrix printers varies widely. Resolutions are usually expressed in dots per inch (dpi). They range from 72 dpi for the basic printer often attached to a PC, through 120 to 240 dpi for higher quality *near letter quality* or *graphics* printers, through the 300 dpi and higher typical of laser printers, and climbing to 2500 dpi and beyond for phototypesetters and for drum plotters.

Daisy-wheel and dot-matrix printers are mostly mechanical, moving a print head across the paper. The head usually contains an array of pins, which it drives against a ribbon to transfer ink to the paper. This *impact* method is valuable for printing multicopy forms, but the head wears quickly, and it is noisy. Prices for such printers can range from $200 to more than $1000.

Other print head technologies, such as thermal transfer, ink jet, and direct thermal writing, are in the low resolution range. These printers are relatively quiet, but can mark only one surface at a time. Some new models can print in a limited range of colors. The direct thermal writing printer requires special paper and is used widely in facsimile (*fax*) machines working at 200 dpi. These printers are not quite as well developed as the impact models mentioned above, and the least expensive is about $300.

Laser printers make it easy to print a page in a variety of typefaces and to print graphics and are part of the hot new area of *desktop publishing*. And, with potential resolutions of 300 dpi and higher, they are the most versatile hard-copy units for CD ROM applications. Unfortunately, laser printers still cost more than $2000, are evolving rapidly, and require considerable maintenance.

Video printers are a new entry into the market and faithfully reproduce video images. Most rely on some sort of thermal printing technology. Color video printers use either instant camera film packs or color thermal ribbons on smooth paper. The photographic cameras produce color screen images about the size of a snapshot, but the resolution is too poor to recreate text or detailed images. Color-thermal transfer ribbons allow page-sized printing. These systems can reproduce several colors and some shades of gray. Printing an image can cost as much as a dollar per copy.

Additional Components

Many applications require special delivery system components.

Data-encryption devices. Data on a CD ROM disc is often encrypted for several reasons. One is security. Many companies encrypt their private databases for this reason. Another is commercial protection.

Widely distributed publications often are encrypted to ensure that only customers who buy the decoding software can use the publication.

Either way, the delivery system must decode the data. In most systems, after the file manager makes the data available to the operating system, decryption software decodes the data. However, software decryption creates problems with speed and security that can be overcome only by adding a hardware decryptor.

A decryptor may be a plug-in circuit board, but more typically it is a metal box with a key-locked switch, or a card reader. The U.S. government has set very tough standards for these devices' security and dependability, and the manufacturers of government-approved devices are happy to let you know this.

Image compression and decompression devices. Images (such as business documents, engineering drawings, maps, or printed pages) can quickly consume space on a CD ROM. Many system developers use compression techniques to increase the number of images that can be placed on a disc. Compression involves analyzing a stream of data and rewriting it to be more compact.

Images are compressed before they are mastered to a disc. The combination of hardware and software compression techniques is discussed elsewhere in this book. A compressed image must be decompressed to its original form before it is displayed or printed. This requires a software or hardware decompression device.

CD-I (Compact Disc-Interactive)

CD ROM's inherent flexibility enables you to do all sorts of impressive and surprising things with data, and it lets you attach the drives to many kinds of computers and other data systems. But it also requires application developers to learn more about the technology than they might wish to know. In addition, the open format of CD ROM tends to cause incompatible system architectures to proliferate and keeps the minimum cost of a delivery system rather high—typically, the cost is at least as much as that of a PC and CD ROM drive.

Philips and Sony early in 1986 announced a new CD ROM-based standard that outlines a completely self-contained delivery system that should be a low-cost alternative. The standard is called CD-I for *Compact Disc-Interactive.* Commercial availability of such systems, aimed at the consumer market and selling for less than $1000, is expected during 1988.

24

The CD ROM standard tells you how to record 2048-byte *blocks*, or *sectors*, of data on a disc in such a way that each has its own explicit address. This enables you to retrieve data randomly or in big, serial chunks. The standard also provides for error correction and detection sufficient to protect the stored data at least as well as does any other available storage medium. (See the following chapter for more information about the CD ROM standard format.)

That, however, is the extent of the specification. All decisions about system design and packaging are left to the product's author or vendor. These design decisions involve determining such things as:

- A logical file format for the disc (such as the proposed High Sierra format we describe elsewhere in this book).

- The disc's directory and file structures.

- Graphics and audio formats.

- The operating system on which the application will run.

- The type of processor or computer system the application will require.

- The display system to be used.

Philips/Sony's CD-I standard is based on the CD ROM format, but provides a tightly specified software and hardware framework for developing and presenting data, images, and sound. Designed for minimum hardware cost and maximum compatibility of discs and delivery systems, the CD-I standard will specify everything about:

- Digital representation of pictorial and audio information.

- Data organization on the disc.

- Hardware and software system components.

CD-I delivery systems will work as adjuncts to television sets and home hi-fi systems, which will be their output devices. They are intended to have computing power sufficient to support rapid, complex interaction; presentation of good-looking graphics; and information searching. This comes from a dedicated computer based on a 68000 microprocessor and 512 KB of RAM, running a ROM-based variant of the OS9 operating system. Input could be from a keyboard, but more likely will come from some sort of pointing device, because the design calls for simplicity.

People now selling CD ROM systems to professional, technical, and industrial customers look forward to using low-priced CD-I players to broaden their markets—although this may be at the expense of features or performance value that their current products deliver.

Creative people are now developing CD-I multimedia programs for use in the home market. They hope to share in some of the initial success that CD-I's grandfather, CD audio, is experiencing. Time will tell whether CD-I achieves the omnipresence of CD audio and PCs, or whether it will be just another special-purpose information tool like the videodisc.

Specialized CD ROM Systems

Some CD ROM publishers design applications to run only on specially designed hardware. Often they believe that offering a dedicated system makes good business sense. But just as often, developers discover they cannot find the right combination of equipment to satisfy their design specification.

Two commercial systems demonstrated recently are examples of dedicated, portable CD ROM delivery systems. One is a navigation system for cars that uses a form of dead reckoning to determine current position. This information in turn is used to decide which part of a map of the area stored in the system will be displayed on a CRT that the driver views.

Magnetic tape cassettes at present store the digitized map information for this system, but their limited capacity restricts coverage to part of a single metropolitan area. With CD ROM storage, one disc could store maps representing a large part of the United States.

Another system, now in prototype, customizes navigation maps for pilots. The pilot works with the system, either on the ground or in the air, to put in a flight plan and other relevant information, and receives an appropriate map from the system's printer. Since this system must be carried onto small aircraft, it must be small and light.

Multiuser Systems

Most of this discussion of CD ROM delivery systems deals with single-user systems. In several special cases, one CD ROM disc can be shared among many users. For instance, as local area networks (*LANs*) connecting PCs become more common, we can expect CD ROM servers to appear on the networks along with print servers and file servers.

Sharing a CD ROM drive among many users is a dangerous economy, because the CD ROM standard limits performance to a level that will frustrate several users simultaneously requesting information. If many users will be active at once, it probably is wiser to give each a CD ROM drive and a copy of the CD ROM disc containing the information of interest. Regardless of the drawbacks, a CD ROM file server might consist of the following elements.

A specialized *search server* (or *library server,* or *teacher server*) could contain:

- A dedicated hardware search engine.
- A CD ROM drive and device interface.
- A network node.
- A hard disk to store the index temporarily or to buffer requests and responses.

This machine responds to queries by sending back blocks of information (text or, with proper linking of protocols, images) that the user's computer or terminal displays. As with the single-user system, the user can invoke information directly, or another application can do so.

The CD ROM delivery system also can be integrated into a general-purpose file server, letting users call for information that is either on the file server's hard disk or on the CD ROM disc. In this case, the search engine may reside in the user's computer.

Mainframes and Minicomputers

CD ROM can be useful when attached to bigger computers, but the same caution applies here. If a network of users communicates through terminals by means of a central computer that stores all storage peripherals, CD ROM applications will require either multiple CD ROM drives, to avoid head contention, or the transfer of CD ROM data to one or more high-performance hard-disk drives. Under these circumstances, CD ROM becomes purely a distribution medium, rather than one accessed directly.

CD ROM is well suited to deliver system and application software to large computers. Many large system software packages are tens of megabytes in size and are sent out on magnetic tape. Tape is expensive, bulky, and fragile compared with CD ROM and does not allow random access to data.

General Concerns

To this point, we have focused on the components of a delivery system. We will now deal with a few issues you should address when you begin analyzing your delivery system requirements and choosing components.

Frequency of access. CD ROM, a disc medium, can be accessed directly. However, because access and transfer are slow, very active users (or networks of users) will demand more throughput (measured, for example, in records per hour) than a CD ROM drive delivers.

Three remedies (ordered below according to the degree of throughput improvement and cost) are available:

- Provide multiple CD ROM drives, each loaded with a copy of the same disc, controlled to spread access requests among the drives.

- Transfer the database index on the CD ROM disc to a hard disk to support the many accesses typical of a query session. The CD ROM drive then supplies only the relatively large blocks of information called for once the retrieval list has been refined.

- Transfer the CD ROM disc's entire contents to one or more hard disk drives, and let them support the accesses. This can be a costly proposition since one CD ROM disc's contents would require about five 100 MB hard disks, costing about $1500 apiece.

Number of users. Giving many users access to a CD ROM drive can cause the kind of access overload mentioned above. The same remedies are available, but so is the straightforward remedy of distributing CD ROM drives among the users. As the cost of a drive decreases, this will make even more sense.

Updating. At the current state of the technology, CD ROM discs must be mastered and replicated in special facilities. Thus, when a database changes or evolves rapidly, this medium may be inappropriate unless an updating strategy is in place.

Many developers are exploring new ways to update. Some strategies involve periodic reissue of an updated disc. Others require an additional hard-disk drive to store the new information. Still others may require modems, which receive new information by telephone or drives for removable magnetic media. Every method, no matter how simple it seems, also will require software designed to unify the directories and data structures of the updated material and the CD ROM data. Since the subject of updating is rather complex, the options are discussed in more detail in Chapter 14.

Security. Distributing information via CD ROM eliminates the "hacker" vulnerability of networks and telecommunication systems. However, the organization distributing the CD ROMs must deal with unauthorized use of a CD ROM disc. Most commonly, data encryption, building unconventional directory structures and file formats, and keeping the discs under lock and key prevent this.

It is frequently said that pirating CD ROM is impossible because of the difficult technology and expensive equipment needed to replicate the discs. This, unfortunately, is not true. The commercial pressure to find simpler and less expensive ways to duplicate CDs carries over directly to CD ROM, making piracy fairly simple. You can find more information on data protection in Chapter 13.

Building Your Own System

This section is a one-minute guide to putting together a delivery system for resale. It provides a quick look over the shoulder of a database publisher that needs to equip its customers with adequate delivery hardware and that never really intended to be in the hardware business.

What to Buy

Everything you can. Shop hard and flexibly, looking for any way to use what others have designed, put into production, and committed themselves to support.

Hardware design and integration, even at the level of attaching drives to device interfaces and host computers, contain all kinds of technical traps. Getting the hardware fixed in the field usually is something you'd rather someone else did. The hypothetical publisher probably will use a PC with an internal-mount CD ROM drive containing an internal cable to a SCSI host adapter. The choice of SCSI frees the publisher to add Winchester, writable optical disc, or more CD ROM drives to the system without software gymnastics.

Writing and debugging system software (such as drivers for storage devices, displays, or input devices) is more dangerous than designing the hardware. Field support of system software is never effectively provided except by its authors, so buy your system software unless you enjoy traveling to visit angry clients and spending many painful hours fixing bugs. The publisher should choose a CD ROM drive manufacturer that also has a proven driver for the PC's operating system.

What Hardware to Build

For marketing reasons, you may wish to have a custom package designed for your system so it looks like a system and not like something that escaped from a computer store. Designed properly, this package also can make the system easier to use and harder to abuse.

What Software to Write

There are good reasons to write the application *front end* (that is, the software that controls communication between the human user and the heart of the application, be it a database management system (DBMS), full-text search, menu process, or whatever). You want to make your product look special when the user views it on the screen, and, more substantially, you want to suit the product to its targeted user or market.

This technical area, more than any other, is the one in which the publisher can best express its understanding of the market, its needs, and its culture. The perceived difference between a computer (that is, something fragile and scary) and a tool that does **my** job (that is, an ally, something appropriate and useful) lies mostly in this user interface.

How Much Marketing Value to Add

If you've designed (or had designed for you) a good, well-tailored user interface and physical package, they'll be unobtrusive in use, letting your customers feel they're interacting directly with the database you sold them. Drive this point home in your advertising and sales. Semantics are all-important here.

If customers understand that you are selling them a genuinely useful, ready-to-use solution to their very own problems, they'll like you more and pay you a higher price. Otherwise, they may feel you are trying to sell them the same kind of computer they could buy more cheaply through the mail, together with some general-purpose hardware they can't use until they've spent a lot of money on local "consultants" who are trying to finish the job.

Conclusion

Electronic publishing and database distribution are now in their early days. If the subject were cars, development would be at that point during the first decade or so of this century, when mass production of simple, straightforward machines had not yet begun. Inventors still are the main vendors of CD ROM hardware, and major revelations on how to do the job come several times a year.

Many publishers already have put together adequate delivery systems and are making money selling database products to markets that need and benefit from them to a degree that far more than compensates for their cost and awkwardness. Other publishers considered acting now, but decided to wait a bit for the frenzy of delivery hardware development, not to mention program production, disc replication, and all other phases of this technology, to subside as the products mature.

This maturation will involve several steps. Along the way, some publishers will find that they need to act *now* or that their markets oblige them to put together delivery systems with special capabilities (such as very high resolution displays). The key to success remains understanding the market and applying technology judiciously in its service.

About the Author

Leonard Laub studied physics at the University of Chicago, Illinois Institute of Technology, and Northwestern University. In 1965 he began work in the research department of Zenith Radio Corporation where he conducted research in the fields of acousto-optics, signal and image processing, laser system design, and optical videodisc recording and playback. In 1976 he went to Zerox Electro-Optical Systems where he set up a program to develop read/write optical disc systems for computer and office system applications. Laub founded Vision Three, Inc., in 1981 to implement at full-scale the consulting and custom systems work that he has been involved in since 1972. Listed in *Who's Who in Frontier Science and Technology*, Laub is the author of numerous articles and reports, the holder of 12 patents, and a member of OSA, IEEE, ACM, SPIE, SPSE, and the Western Area Committee of the IEEE Computer Society.

3

CD ROM Characteristics

CD ROM technology is derived from CD audio technology and uses the same basic drive mechanisms and disc manufacturing processes. Because of this close relationship, CD ROM player and disc development has benefited directly from the technological advances and cost reductions associated with the rapid growth of the CD audio industry.

The impact of CD ROM's heritage cannot be overstated, but perhaps equally important to CD ROM technology is that, as with CD audio, the CD ROM disc format is an industrywide standard. CD ROM discs, in other words, are all the same size and their data is arranged in exactly the same pattern. This common structure is often called the *physical format*. Having a common physical format ensures that the CD ROMs one manufacturer makes can be read on any other manufacturer's drive.

The CD ROM physical format was devised by Philips and Sony, the developers of compact disc technology, and is described in a document known as the Yellow Book. In the Yellow Book specification, Philips and Sony completely define the physical layout of a CD ROM disc for disc manufacturer licensees.

The Yellow Book defines the size of the microscopic pits that represent data bits (see Figure 1). It dictates that the pits be arranged in a continuous spiral and that this spiral be divided into *sectors* about 2000 bytes long. Each sector is subdivided into fields, one of which is the sector address.

Physical compatibility of discs is a significant achievement. It distinguishes CD ROM from other optical media such as the videodisc and write-once disc, for which no single format has been established. This feature is essential for a publishing medium, because any disc readable only on certain machines will fail as a mechanism for broadly distributing information.

Although a standard physical format is essential for optical publishing, it is not sufficient. The disc must also have a *logical format* to specify how the information on the disc is organized.

32

Users, whether application programs or human beings, do not address a disc in terms of pits, tracks, or sectors; they look for *files*—files being a collection of related information. The logical format, also called the *file format*, of a CD ROM specifies the organization and location of files on a disc. It defines such things as a file's size, the directory structure for all files on the disc, and the number of discs an application includes.

The Yellow Book does not define the disc's logical format. In the past the logical format has largely been determined by the operating system developer, resulting in as many file formats as there are operating systems. Recently, a group of companies interested in read-only optical discs joined forces to propose one standard logical format for CD ROM. This format has become known as the *High Sierra Proposal* (HSP). Details of the High Sierra Proposal are discussed in Chapter 11.

Layout of a Disc

The surface of a CD ROM disc, seen under a powerful microscope, is a spiral of micron-sized pits. The laser and circuitry of the disc player convert these pits to binary data bits, which they process and send to the computer logically divided into sectors (see Figure 1). Each sector contains 2352 bytes of information, of which 2048 bytes are user data. The sector is divided as follows:

Synchronization data	12 bytes
Header data	4 bytes
User data	2048 bytes
Error detection code (EDC)	4 bytes
Unused space	8 bytes
Error correction data	276 bytes

Synchronization data. Sectors are not physically separated. Instead the beginning of each sector is marked with a 12-byte sequence called the *sync code*. The CD ROM drive keeps track of its location on a disc by tallying the number of bytes it passes and by looking for sync information. It uses both tracking methods because the sync data alone is not enough to establish the boundary between sectors, since the same sequence of sync bytes could conceivably exist in the user data.

Header data. The 4-byte *header* identifies the sector. The first 3 bytes contain the sector's address, which the drive uses to locate a sector. The last byte in the sequence is called the *mode byte*. It indicates the presence

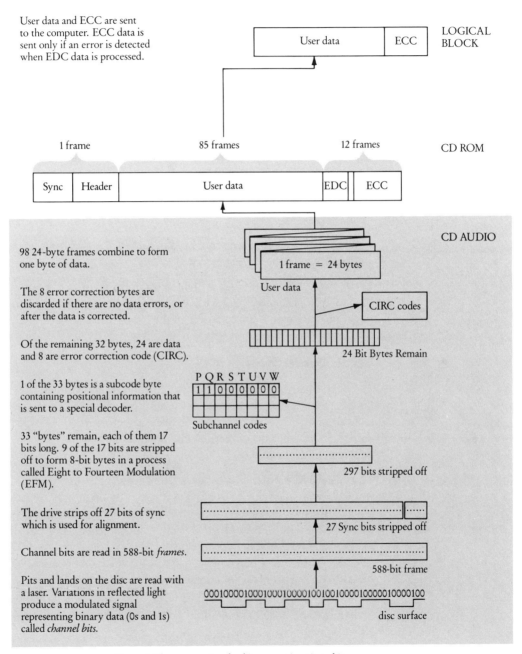

User data and ECC are sent to the computer. ECC data is sent only if an error is detected when EDC data is processed.

LOGICAL BLOCK

User data	ECC

1 frame   85 frames   12 frames   **CD ROM**

Sync	Header	User data	EDC	ECC

CD AUDIO

98 24-byte frames combine to form one byte of data.

1 frame = 24 bytes

User data

The 8 error correction bytes are discarded if there are no data errors, or after the data is corrected.

CIRC codes

Of the remaining 32 bytes, 24 are data and 8 are error correction code (CIRC).

24 Bit Bytes Remain

P Q R S T U V W

1	1	0	0	0	0	0	0

1 of the 33 bytes is a subcode byte containing positional information that is sent to a special decoder.

Subchannel codes

33 "bytes" remain, each of them 17 bits long. 9 of the 17 bits are stripped off to form 8-bit bytes in a process called Eight to Fourteen Modulation (EFM).

297 bits stripped off

The drive strips off 27 bits of sync which is used for alignment.

27 Sync bits stripped off

Channel bits are read in 588-bit *frames*.

588-bit frame

Pits and lands on the disc are read with a laser. Variations in reflected light produce a modulated signal representing binary data (0s and 1s) called *channel bits*.

00010000100010001000010010010000100000010000100

disc surface

Figure 1. The processes involved in converting pits to bits.

of error correction data. Mode 1 includes error correction and detection information. Mode 2 does not include the 280 bytes of error codes and can be used instead to store additional user data.

User data. This is where you store your information, be it text, graphics, sound, or video. The premastering process divides data files into 2048-byte blocks, calculates the error detection and correction codes, and adds sync and header information.

Error detection code (EDC). The EDC is a 16-bit value generated from the values of the sync, header, and user data, which the drive or computer uses to determine whether the user data read from the disc is different from the original data. The EDC is calculated when the disc is premastered.

Unused space. This space is not used in CD ROM, but has been moved and redefined in the CDI standard.

Error correction code (ECC). The bytes in the error correction field are used to correct the user data when an error has been detected. A sophisticated algorithm that is based on the Reed-Solomon code is used to correct erroneous data.

Error Correction

The data density of a compact disc is tremendous, approaching 100 million bits per square centimeter. With densities this high, even a microscopic defect can cause hundreds of errors. To alleviate errors, the CD ROM standard includes an error correction scheme to assure the integrity of the data delivered from the disc.

The CD ROM player has error detection hardware that compares the error detection code value to the data as it passes by on its way to the computer. If the decoder detects an error, it signals the computer system. The computer system uses the error correction codes stored alongside the user data to regenerate lost or "wrong" bits. The codes designed for CD ROM can take the bit stream coming from a disc in which one in every 10,000 bits is wrong, with bursts of more than 1000 bad bits, and regenerate all but 1 bit in every 10 quadrillion, or one in every 10^{-12} bits. This amounts to about one unrecoverable error in every 2000 discs.

CD audio players generally have at best a rate of one error in every 100 million bits (10^{-8}). For CD audio this lower rate is acceptable, because the CD audio player extrapolates for missing bits and the ear tends to compensate for the minute sound imperfections an incorrect bit causes. In CD ROM, however, even a 1-bit error can significantly affect the integrity of the information. For example, an image that is highly compressed from 1 million bytes down to 50,000 bytes could look very different from its original form if 1 bit (representing several bytes of uncompressed data) is not read properly.

For a detailed look at error correction, I recommend that you read "Error Correction Codes: Key to Perfect Data" in *CD ROM: The New Papyrus* (Microsoft Press, 1986).

35

CAV v CLV: The Spin of the Disc

Most magnetic disks record sectors in concentric tracks, each of which holds a specified number of sectors. By contrast, a CD ROM disc arranges sectors in one continuous spiral. The different formats relate to the way the disks spin when recorded and read. A magnetic disk usually spins at a constant rate, or a *constant angular velocity* (CAV). A CD ROM disc spins at a varying rate—faster when reading the inner sectors and slower when reading the outer sectors. The CD ROM disc spins at a *constant linear velocity* (CLV).

Constant Angular Velocity

Anyone who has played the children's skating game Crack the Whip knows that the person at the end of the whip must travel much faster than the person at the center to keep the line straight. The outside person also must travel farther than the inside person. Yet, the whole line actually turns at the same rate.

Figure 2. Concentric circles of CAV disks. Sectors on the outer edge are longer than sectors on the inside, though they store the same amount of data.

This game illustrates constant angular velocity. Most magnetic disks and some videodiscs use CAV formats. A CAV disk spins at a constant rate, but the inside and outside tracks pass the reading mechanism at different speeds, the outside tracks traveling much faster than the inside tracks.

A CAV disk's storage capacity depends on how much data can be stored at the inside radius. Figure 2 shows how sectors on a CAV disk are organized, illustrating the varying densities of data. As you can see, the inside sectors are short, their data densely packed. At the outside radius, the data is stored in longer sectors at a much lower linear density.

Constant Linear Velocity

Unlike a magnetic disk, a CD ROM disc spins at a constant linear velocity. A CLV disc rotates so that the data sectors pass the reading head at a constant speed. A CD ROM drive maintains constant linear velocity by changing the disc's rotational speed as the head moves along the track.

You'll notice in Figure 3 that the CLV format of a CD ROM disc results in sectors having the same length. This kind of format increases the amount of data a disc can store by allowing more sectors at the outer radius, where the circumference is larger.

Although the CLV format is ideal for storing large amounts of data, it is not ideal for retrieving data. For one thing, the long spiral track makes it difficult to find individual sectors. In addition, each head movement to find a particular sector must be accompanied by the mechanical process of speeding up or slowing down the disc. These drawbacks account for a rather slow data access time for CD ROMs.

Addressing

A CLV disc requires a different addressing scheme than does the more familiar track-oriented scheme of magnetic CAV disks. Although an operating system can find a sector on most magnetic disks using just a track and sector number, it needs to know the minutes and seconds of linear "play" time and the sector number to find a sector on a CD ROM (see Figure 4).

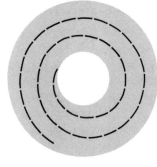

Figure 3. Spiral format of CLV disks. All sectors are the same size.

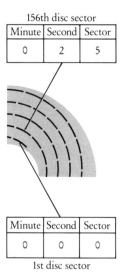

156th disc sector

Minute	Second	Sector
0	2	5

Minute	Second	Sector
0	0	0

1st disc sector

Figure 4. The CD ROM physical addressing scheme comes from its CD audio heritage. A disc can hold 60 "minutes" of data. Each minute is divided into 60 "seconds." A "second" of data is divided into 75 sectors. Therefore, a disc holds 270,000 sectors (60 minutes × 60 seconds × 75 sectors). Since each sector contains 2 KB of data, not including the sync, header, and EDC/ECC codes, a CD ROM's total capacity is 540,000 KB.

An application rarely deals with the physical address of a CD ROM. It views the data as a group of files, each with an associated filename. When the application calls for a particular file, the operating system takes over. It converts the application's logical view of the disc to a physical view, finding the file's location on disc by using the CD ROM's physical address.

Performance Characteristics

Good software design must anticipate the strengths and the weaknesses of CD ROM. CD ROM has its share of both, as do all storage media (see Table 1).

Because of the mechanical characteristics of a CD ROM drive, the access time from one edge of a disc to the other is comparatively slow. Therefore, it is important for a retrieval system to avoid unnecessary accesses. The data transfer rate, however, is respectable in relation to those of other media, and only becomes a concern when transferring large quantities of information such as high-resolution graphics, animation, or audiovisual material.

MEDIA	Small Winchester Disk	Large Optical ROM	Floppy Disk	Magnetic Tape	Large Winchester Disk	CD ROM
Media Cost (in US $)	N/A	15-30	1-5	10-20	N/A	10-20
Drive Cost	500-3,000	7,000-100,000	200-1,500	3,000-15,000	10,000-150,000	500-2,500
Capacity (in MB)	5-50	1,000-4,000	0.36-1.20	30-300	50-4,000	550-680
Media Size (in. diameter)	5.25	12.00	5.25	10.50	14.00	4.72
Access Time (sec.)	0.03-0.30	0.03-0.40	0.03-0.05	1-40	0.01-0.08	0.40-1
Density (avg. bits/in.)	15,000	35,000	10,000	300-6,250	15,000	35,000
Data Rate (avg. KB/sec.)	625	300	31	500	2,500	150

Table 1. Performance characteristics of CD ROM and other storage media.

Access Time

To read a sector, the head moves to its approximate location and then follows the spiral until it finds the appropriate sector. To reread the same sector, the drive must jump back onto the spiral and wait for the sector to come around again. Since the speed of the disc at the outer radius (200 rpm) is less than half its speed at the inner radius (530 rpm), reading the outer spirals takes longer than reading the inner spirals. Hence, CD ROM access time is also a function of the radius where the read occurs.

The term *access time* is a measure of the time required to locate a particular piece of information on a disc. The term is frequently misused and abused. Its most widely accepted definition includes three events:

Seek time. The time it takes to position the head assembly at the desired radius.

Settling time. The time the head takes to settle into position at the desired location.

Rotational delay. The time the disc must rotate to get the desired sector under the read head.

Seek times on CD ROMs range from 200 milliseconds (ms) for short distances to 800 ms for longer distances. The seek time of a good 5¼-inch Winchester disk may be about 30 ms or less. *Settling times* are more modest, and with CD ROMs depend almost entirely on the drive's ability to position the read head accurately the first time. *Rotational delays* for CD ROMs range from 60 to 150 ms, compared with 8.3 ms for Winchesters rotating at 3600 rpm. Thus, the average access time for a CD ROM drive might be anywhere from 400 ms to 1 sec.

Transfer Rate

Transfer rate refers to the speed at which the host computer reads data from a disc once the data is found. The transfer rate does not include access time, but is merely the speed at which data moves from the disc to the host computer.

The CD ROM's transfer rate is somewhere between that of a floppy disk (31 KB/sec) and a Winchester (625 KB/sec)—a very acceptable rate. The Yellow Book fixes the maximum transfer rate at 176.40 KB/sec. This rate is calculated for the time to read and transfer the sector's 2352 bytes of sync, header, user data, and error correction codes. The more widely quoted rate of 150 KB/sec involves only the time for transferring the user data, which amounts to 2048 bytes per sector.

Data errors can slow down the overall data transfer rate. If the EDC detects errors, the hardware stops data transfer and initiates the error correction process. Only after the data has been successfully corrected will the drive once again begin reading data.

Logical Characteristics

Ensuring that CD ROMs can distribute information to a broad range of users requires more than just a physical format; it also requires a *logical format,* as discussed earlier. The logical format, or *file format,* allows applications to view a CD ROM as a collection of files. This format is constructed from the simpler, sector-oriented view of the disc.

By viewing a disc as a group of files, the application can find data by calling a filename, such as FILE1.DOC. The operating system's file manager looks up the filename in the disc directory and uses associated information to locate the file. Without this higher-level view of the disc, the application would have to know the physical location of each sector related to the file. Instead, all it has to know is the filename; the file manager does the rest.

What Is the Logical Format?

A logical format is broken into two distinct structures: the *volume table of contents (VTOC)* and the *directory structure.* The VTOC contains information about the disc as a whole, including the location of the disc directory. When the file manager begins reading a disc, it reads the VTOC before anything else. The *directory structure* specifies the exact locations of the files on the disc.

Early Proprietary Formats

In the short history of CD ROM, several companies have developed their own logical formats. Some developers tried to adapt the *hierarchical file structures* of magnetic disk operating systems (such as MS-DOS, VMS, and UNIX) to CD ROM. Others assumed the average user was more interested in running the application than in exploring the filenames on the disc and used the *hash* method to organize files, opting for fast access over the ability to conduct generic directory searches. Still others assumed few files (fewer than 100) were likely to be placed on a single CD ROM and organized the files into *tree directories.* (These methods are defined in the glossary at the end of the book.)

Many of these early CD ROM file formats reflect an attempt to design a structure well suited to the unique characteristics of CD ROM.

Characteristics Affecting File System Design

CD ROM is a read-only medium and does not need the complex file allocation tables required by read/write media. In fact, this characteristic greatly simplifies the design of a logical format, since files need to be organized only once to be read thousands of times. Below are some of the major characteristics that affect file format design.

The file system does not need to track deletion or modification of files. Unlike magnetic media, once a CD ROM disc is mastered, the data cannot change. When a file manager deletes data on magnetic media, it can reuse the freed space (that is, the sectors) to store new data. Consequently, when the file manager frees disc space, it must update its record of available sectors. And when it adds a file, the file manager must also map the new data's location on the disc. Since CD ROM discs cannot be changed, the file system need not incorporate a bookkeeping mechanism to record the locations of used and empty sectors.

Read-only media allow you to determine disc layout in advance. Many applications perform better when certain elements of the data are stored together. For example, a drive can traverse a series of indexes faster if the indexes are arranged on the disc sequentially rather than randomly.

Carefully laying out the disc also prevents unnecessarily fragmenting files across the disc, which causes poor performance when reading them. Often, locating duplicate data at diverse addresses can also improve performance by minimizing the distance over which the drive must seek.

The file system software must account for slow access time. The single largest disadvantage of CD ROM is its slow average seek time (about 1 sec). In traditional magnetic-disk-based systems, access time has not been a prime consideration. These designs assumed a fast seek speed and made little attempt to minimize the number of seeks required to perform directory operations. A good CD ROM design, however, keeps the number of seeks to the absolute minimum. (Table 1 shows the seek times of various storage devices.)

You must design around the disc latency period. Another important consideration when designing CD ROM systems is the *disc latency period*. This is the average wait of two disc revolutions between the time that one read ends and the time when the next sequential sector can be read. Because of this lag, if the application must read sequential sectors, it is quicker to read them all at once rather than to request successive reads.

Converging on a Standard Format

The Yellow Book standard format for CD ROM does not include a specification for a logical format. Only the physical format of a disc is standardized, which means that all CD ROM drive manufacturers agree on what a sector is and how to address it. For example, if you know that some particular data exists on a disc at Minute 33, Second 20, Sector 5 (33:20:05), you can find and read that data. At this physical level all discs are interchangeable from one drive to another. However, when you move beyond the physical format to the logical view of the disc, this guarantee of interchangeability evaporates.

From the time the CD ROM industry began in 1985, software houses and data-preparation services used their own logical formats. Each competitor's format was unreadable by the other's file management system. As more discs appeared, users' confusion over formats made it clear to a number of firms in the optical disc industry that they should converge on a common, standardized logical format. For CD ROM to be a true publishing medium, it must have a logical format that is accessible to all in the public domain.

It was clear the process of adopting formal standards would take three to five years and that was too long to be without a standard. In the fall of 1985, Chris Hamlin of XEBEC and I invited all known players in the CD ROM field to a meeting at the High Sierra Casino and Hotel in Lake Tahoe, Nev. Our intent was to determine whether industry leaders would cooperate in submitting a common logical format proposal to the accredited standards organizations. The result of this first meeting was a resounding "Yes," and together we formed a committee that became known as the High Sierra Group. The first group consisted of people from Apple Computer, Digital Equipment Corp., Hitachi, LaserData, Microsoft, 3M, Philips, Reference Technology Inc., Sony Corp., TMS Inc., Videotools, and XEBEC.

The committee set out to formulate a proposal that met the group's requirements. Its design objectives included:

- Develop a file format that compensates for the relatively slow seek time of the CD ROM drives.

- Maintain compatibility with Compact Disc Interactive (CD-I).

- Provide for easy use with the most popular operating systems (MS-DOS, UNIX, VMS, and Apple DOS).

- Optimize the design for read-only media.

For the next six months the group met monthly, working steadily. On June 17, 1986, the group announced that its work was complete and formally presented its proposal to national and international standards organizations.

The High Sierra Proposal (HSP), as the group's recommendation became known, is now in the formal standards process. An international standard based on the proposal is expected in late 1987 or early 1988. The next chapter contains a description of the features and functions in the High Sierra Proposal.

A Logical Format for Everyone

Some designers object to a standard format, believing each CD ROM should use a unique logical format that maximizes the application's performance. They also think the security benefits in designing a proprietary format can be worthwhile, especially if the data is extremely valuable. However, discs designed in this way require special hardware and software to read them and for this reason are not interchangeable among various host computers and operating systems.

Fortunately, CD ROM is a versatile storage medium, and it can accommodate standard and nonstandard formats. This is part of what gives CD ROM its great potential both in the mass market and in specialized market arenas.

About the Author

John Einberger, vice president for software development for Reference Technology, Inc., in Boulder, Colorado, is responsible for the development of software products optimized for use with read-only optical data systems. He was instrumental in forming and chairing the High Sierra Group, which has proposed a logical format standard for CD ROM discs. He has more than 18 years in the computer industry, has taught at the university level, holds many patents, and is the author of many publications. His degrees are in Electrical Engineering, Computer Science, and Business.

Resources

Zoellick, Bill. 1986. File System Support for CD ROM. In *CD ROM: The New Papyrus*, ed. by S. Lambert and S. Ropiequet. Redmond, WA: Microsoft Press.

TEXT PREPARATION AND RETRIEVAL

Preparing Text

As CD ROM technology develops, we gradually will see applications that incorporate various combinations of text, images, and sound. Since most developers tend to view applications in terms of these three data types, we deal with each one separately in this book. Since text-oriented applications are likely to predominate, we discuss text first, dealing with the initial stage of data preparation in this chapter, then with document retrieval (Chapter 5), and then the indexing of full-text databases (Chapter 6). Discussions of preparing images (Chapter 8) and sound (Chapter 9) follow.

Text as Characters and Text as Images

A publisher can deliver data on a CD ROM only if the data is *machine-readable*. This means the data must be transformed into binary digits, or *bits*. In general, you can do this in two ways. You can either pass the pages through a sophisticated *optical scanner,* which produces a *bit-mapped image* of the document, or you can capture each individual letter of text, transforming the letters into binary representations to produce *character-coded text.* The first method creates a *digitized* picture of the page. The second produces a sequence of characters similar to the files a word processor produces.

Bit-Mapped Images

Most optical scanners "read" a printed page by passing a light-sensitive grid over it, each grid element recording an area of the reflected light. This process creates a mosaic pattern of dots, or *pixels,* measuring from 100 to 400 dots per inch. The scanner converts each pixel to a bit value based on the intensity of its reflected light. A bit-mapped image is the string of bits this process produces. The more pixels and bits an image contains, the more closely the displayed image resembles the original.

Storing these bits requires a great deal of disc space. To be readable, a typewritten page must be stored with about 300 bits per vertical and horizontal inch, a total of about 8 million bits, or 1 megabyte (MB), per image. Compression schemes such as those that compress data for facsimile transmission can reduce this storage requirement; even so, storing the compressed image of a typewritten page usually requires 100 kilobytes (KB, or ¹⁄₁₀ MB). A CD ROM can store about 5500 such pages.

Character-Coded Text

Rather than storing a document as a series of pixels, computers traditionally have stored text in character form, using 7- or 8-bit codes in different combinations to represent alphanumeric characters, punctuation, and a few other miscellaneous symbols. These codes are stored on disc as a string of bytes, and the computer's display hardware translates them into the characters the screen displays. For example, the 7-bit code shown in Figure 1 is a bit representation of the letter *A*.

ASCII code for
the letter "A"

0	1	0	0	0	0	0	1

Image produced
on screen

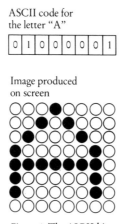

Figure 1. The ASCII bit representation of the letter A.

The most familiar coding methods are ASCII (American Standard Code for Information Interchange) and EBCDIC (Extended Binary Coded Decimal Interchange Code). The ASCII coding system, which predominates in the United States, consists of 128 codes for letters, numbers, and punctuation. This basic set usually is extended to provide 128 additional characters containing various foreign-language letters, characters for creating simple line graphics, and so forth. No standard extended character set has been established, although in the realm of personal computers, the extended character set of the IBM PC family and its clones form a de facto standard. The EBCDIC coding system contains 256 characters. Developed by IBM, it is used primarily with IBM mainframe computers and minicomputers. Since delivery systems and retrieval software most commonly use ASCII codes, text stored in EBCDIC format usually is converted to ASCII before mastering data to CD ROM. From this point on, we will refer exclusively to ASCII character codes, even though the same information may apply to both formats.

ASCII-coded text offers several advantages over bit-mapped text:

- ASCII codes are accepted almost universally in the computer and data-processing industries, providing a generally understood and usable standard for information exchange. Machines manufactured worldwide can decode and process them.

- A vast literature of programs and algorithms is recorded in ASCII.

- Storing ASCII-coded text requires much less space than does storing bit-mapped images. The typewritten page described earlier, if stored in ASCII code, consumes only 2 to 3 KB, compared with the 100 KB the compressed, scanned image requires. Thus, a CD ROM coded in ASCII could store about 220,000 pages of coded data, as opposed to 5500 page images. Material that can fit on one disc in ASCII form fills about 40 discs in digitized image form.

- The individual words, letters, and numbers in ASCII-coded text can be identified, indexed, and retrieved. ASCII characters provide the same subdivisions as print media—letters, words, lines, sentences, paragraphs, and pages. Character codes enable a publisher to organize and index data in the same familiar ways.

Choosing a Method for Storing Text

Your choice of a text-storage method depends on what you intend to do with the data. If your customer will need to search for individual words or jump to specific sections of text, you'll need to store the text in character form so each letter, word, or number can be retrieved. If you want to display the document in its original physical form, and if searching for specific words is not important, you'll want to store it as a bit-mapped image.

Bit-mapped images and character-coded documents both have their place in CD ROM applications, and the same application may use them together. For example, capturing abstract and index data in ASCII form so that you can search and retrieve it term by term often is useful. You then can package the abstract and index data with digitized images of the articles it references. Each format is stored and prepared differently, of course. We focus on character-coded text for the remainder of this chapter and will discuss bit-mapped documents in Chapter 8.

An Overview of Text Preparation

The goal of text preparation is to convert your original material to a form that indexing and database-building programs can interpret. Figure 2, which outlines the process of publishing a CD ROM containing text, shows this fundamental first step.

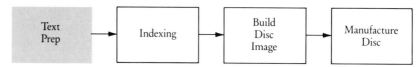

Figure 2. The role of text preparation in the CD ROM publishing process.

Preparing text for CD ROM applications involves more than simply placing a string of characters on a disc. Along with the characters must be a structure—the structure that was implicit in the form of the original printed pages may have been lost in converting them to an electronic format. Titles, headers, footnotes, and even italicized words are all examples of print structures that are desirable elements in electronic publications. The character-coded text that the text-preparation process produces must include codes that reflect these structures, as well as codes that tell the display system how to format the document for display.

Structural Organization

Text usually has some kind of hierarchical structure. It is often broken into chapters, sections, subsections, and paragraphs. Within each chapter or section, you usually can distinguish a title from the body of the text. Some other common structural elements are authors' names and affiliations, publication dates, and abstracts.

Indexing software must be able to find and index a document's structure so that the retrieval software can retrieve each item individually. The indexing software does this by searching for codes embedded in an electronic document and then indexing the text that they mark based on the codes' meaning. For example, if a code such as <<01>> indicates a title, the indexing software places the text that follows it in a title index.

Electronic documents may or may not contain codes that mark the different structural elements, so embedding codes that are intelligible to the indexing software in the appropriate places throughout a document is up to the text-preparation software. This task often is formidable. Publishers or service bureaus must write or modify programs that can read a document and either add codes based on structural cues or convert existing codes into codes the indexing software understands.

Formatting Instructions

Text that is displayed on a screen or printed usually must be formatted in some way. For example, titles often are centered or boldfaced for emphasis, words might be italicized, or lines indented. The data you generate for CD ROM must somehow be able to communicate these display formatting instructions.

Some systems insert explicit formatting characters as they prepare text. For example, they insert spaces to center or indent lines of text, set specific line lengths with hard carriage returns, and add codes for special effects such as highlighting or underlining. This approach places a minimal processing burden on the display system, since the hard work is done in advance. However, the publisher must know which display system the customer will use, since characteristics and formatting codes of each display system differ.

Other text-preparation systems insert general formatting instructions into the text, leaving interpretation of codes to the display system. This approach enables the display system to tailor and optimize the format for the output device. For example, a laser printer encountering a boldface or typeface code can print the text to specification; a display unable to show special text characteristics ignores codes it can't handle and uses the ones it can handle.

A third class of systems uses a *style sheet* or *lookup table* to determine how to format each structural element (that is, author's name, title, section heading, and so forth). This approach provides maximum flexibility, because it lets the publisher tailor a procedure to the needs of the customer's delivery system, which interprets the codes in the text.

Finding a Starting Point

The goal of text preparation is to produce a file containing all letters to be displayed, along with information about structural organization and format of the text. Possible ways of achieving this goal depend on the original form of data. A survey by the Association of American Publishers (AAP) found that about 80 percent of the book and periodical manuscripts published in 1985 were originally produced on a computer. The association estimates that in scientific and technical publishing virtually 100 percent of the manuscripts being published start out in computer form.[*]

---

[*]Electronic Publishing Business 4 (September 1986): 5.

It would seem, then, that publishers should begin by working with authors' original electronic documents. This approach indeed is sensible, and in the long run it probably will be the most practical and economically feasible. But at present the practice is not common. Instead of preparing an author's files, electronic publishers usually begin either with printed manuscripts or with the electronic data that typesetting or microfilm systems produce.

Converting Printed Data

Transforming a printed page into a machine-readable document requires either a fast typist or optical character recognition (OCR).

Keyboard Entry

The most obvious method for converting a textual or numeric database into useful, machine-readable form is to type it. This is usually the last method seriously considered, although it should be the first. Typing is low-tech, unimaginative, and has the distasteful effect of making obvious just how much money you spend entering data that has already been typed once. However, this method is often the most cost-effective, particularly if you use inexpensive labor pools or contract services. The typist can enter special structural and formatting information along with the main text. And a publisher can easily budget, schedule, and plan keyboard entry accurately. Managing such a project, though less glorious than supervising more exotic solutions, is a known art. All project managers worth their salt should be able to handle such a task within budget and on time, a rare phenomenon when converting printed materials with techniques such as OCR.

Optical Character Recognition

Optical character recognition is conceptually one of the most attractive methods for converting printed text to machine-readable character codes. An optical character reader scans, or "reads," a typewritten or printed document, stores it as bit-mapped images, and then converts the letter shapes into ASCII codes. OCRs have had a long, but until recently not a particularly successful, history. Innovators tried to manufacture them long before digital computers became common, and a number of companies have made serious attempts to use them in production. Unfortunately, many of these early attempts failed because the technology had not been sufficiently developed to make the job easy. Only recently has OCR technology advanced far enough to make this alternative practical.

Character-Matching Templates

Some of the most advanced OCR systems available read only selected fonts, using a system of character-matching templates that are stored in memory. This approach normally samples a line of text using a fixed character size and assumes that each character occupies the same amount of space (it is *monospaced*). Although most typewritten characters are monospaced, nearly all typeset material is proportionally spaced. This means that the typesetter allots less space to narrow letters such as *i* and *l* than to wider letters such as *m* and *w*. Template-based optical readers often have difficulty reading proportionally spaced characters because they expect to see characters spread evenly across a line. Frequent font changes, ligatures, and kerning—common features of typeset characters—also cause trouble for many OCR systems. *Ligatures* are letters that run together, such as Æ, and *kerning* is respacing of individual letter combinations for more pleasing display, such as moving the *o* in *To* under the cross-stroke of the capital *T*.

Pattern-Matching OCR

The recognized standard in OCR scanning is the Kurzweil 4000. Kurzweil developed its technology while building a reading machine for the blind. In the process, Kurzweil confronted and solved many issues associated with reading the different fonts and proportional spacing encountered in normal typeset material—problems the developers of many OCR systems ignored.

The Kurzweil machine uses a pattern-matching algorithm instead of comparing a scanned letter with an image in memory. Thus, an *s* is viewed as a character with a west-convex curve above joined with an east-convex curve below. The machine learns a specific font, character by character, when it begins scanning a document. An operator also "teaches" the machine during this stage, resolving ambiguous characters or sets of characters. Eventually the machine builds on this information, compiling the pattern-matching rules as it learns, requiring fewer operator interventions as the process progresses—and ultimately less error correction and proofing when the process is complete.

Error Rates

Scanning and translating a printed page can take as long as a minute even with the best of equipment. However, even at this rate OCR often can convert a document more quickly than can a typist. Thus, OCR seems fast and promising until you fully examine its implicit error rate. A good OCR system may have an error rate of about 1 percent—about 25 characters per page. Obviously, you must examine and correct each unrecognized character individually before the conversion process is complete. This task may seem trivial until you think about converting a 100,000-page document—25 errors per page means 2,500,000 errors. Correcting these errors might add hours and considerable expense to a project. This OCR drawback often makes retyping documents more cost-effective.

Potential Problems with OCR

The OCR process requires the careful design of scanning procedures and quality-control checks. Managing the scanning haphazardly can cause delays and frustration. For example, if you insert a page into the scanner slightly skewed or rotated, the OCR system may not be able to read it at all—or, if it does, it may misinterpret the characters. Or, if your original document is printed on both sides of thin, see-through paper, the image may be unclear. The scanning equipment records every variation in light intensity, so it will try to record both front and back of the transluscent page simultaneously, making accurate character recognition difficult at best.

As we said earlier, you must capture structural information as well as the characters within the text. "Training" an OCR system to recognize codes or other structural cues can be time-consuming, and recognizing these cues is often beyond the system's capability. If the system can't recognize a structure, then structural information must be entered manually at the keyboard.

All these problems add to the expense and difficulty in using OCR. However, you can avoid many of them if you pay close attention to detail while choosing and using the equipment.

Equipment Prices

Prices of some OCR equipment range from $1500 to more than $25,000, with quality and reliability generally ranging accordingly. Most template-based systems are less expensive than pattern-matching systems, but as the technology develops, this price distinction is fading. You may find the low-cost systems adequate for your needs, especially if your documents are written in a common typewriter font such as Courier or Courier Elite.

Anyone planning to use OCR equipment should learn about the state of the art and research the production problems that publishers typically encounter. This is particularly important if you are investing in some of the less expensive scanning equipment, which, although adequate for some jobs, sacrifices important capabilities of the more expensive equipment. OCR technology is developing rapidly, and major improvements and price reductions certainly will occur during the next few years.

Starting with Data in Electronic Form

Many publications are available in electronic form. Clearly, starting with character-coded text eliminates the need for using OCR or retyping the text. However, starting with data already on tape does not necessarily simplify text preparation. Remember, the prepared text must contain all the formatting and structural information that subsequent processes require; simply capturing the actual characters within the text will not suffice. The difficulty in uncovering the structural content of an electronic text file is closely related to the nature of the data. In general, you will find text databases in one of three electronic forms:

- Photocomposition tapes

- Structured, record-oriented data

- Word-processing data

Photocomposition Tapes

Virtually any publication typeset during the past decade has been put on some kind of *photocomposition tape*. A photocomposition tape is a character-coded computer tape read by a machine that photographically generates printing plates. This process has essentially replaced setting lead type into a galley and then composing pages from the unpaginated text.

Photocomposition tapes most frequently consist of ASCII character codes combined with additional codes that represent special characters, font changes, page format changes, type size changes, and so forth. Codes differ for every typesetting system, and frequently the same operation can be coded in several different ways, even on the same system.

For example, this book was typeset using a Computer Composition International (CCI) composition system and a Mergenthaler Linotron typesetter. You can see some of the codes used to structure Chapter 4 in Figure 3. The code %CH stands for chapter head, %NP stands for non-indented paragraph, and <MC> stands for *merge copy*—a code that instructs the composition system to momentarily escape from the foreground (text mode) to reference additional coding instructions in the background.

The major problem with using photocomposition tapes as source material for a CD ROM publication is that they are coded to produce a specific *page* format. A CD ROM tape must be coded to produce a structure that can be indexed and that can adapt to a variety of displays and printers. Often the tape's formatting data gives clues to a document's underlying structure, but sometimes you can't translate the formatting codes. Trying to uncover structural content within formatting specifications might raise questions such as: Does a change to 10 point boldface roman type always indicate the start of a new section? Do sections ever begin some other way? Is this type font used to do other things, and will it therefore fool the software into marking the start of a section where there is none?

Figure 3. Typesetting codes used in Chapter 4 of this book. The code %CH stands for chapter head, <MC> stands for merge copy, %NP stands for new paragraph, and <EP> stands for end paragraph.

The rules for placing "tags" such as %CH, %NP, and <MC> in the text of a photocomposition tape define a special kind of language called *markup*. Different markup schemes use different languages, each containing a unique set of tags (the language's "words") controlled by a unique set of rules (the language's "grammar").

Some markup languages are embedded in the text. They spell out exactly how many spaces to indent a line, which type font or type style to use, and so on. Such languages are called *procedural markup* languages because they delineate explicit instructions or procedures within the text.

Other markup languages describe the text-formatting characteristics stored in files outside the text called *code files*. These languages, called *descriptive markup* languages, embed simple codes in the text, much like the ones shown in Figure 4. The code files contain formats and text styles, defined for a particular book, that are called when the typesetting equipment encounters markup coding in the text of that book. For example, Figure 4 shows the formatting routine that is called when the system processes the %CH code shown in Figure 3. This file actually produces the type style

```
<SF30>••%CH--chapter head, 2 merges••
<GD100,120><EP><EL6><CFFB><CP11>
<CL11><CC41.6><IT23.6,2.6><IF0>
<CS3,4,4,0,4><T2><RR><AH><XL><AF>
C<EI18>H<EI18>A<EI18>P<EI18>T<EI18>E<EI18>R<EP>
<IT38,0><CFU47><CP48><CL25><MC><QR><EP>
<EL64><CFFXK><CP20><CL20><CC41.6><IT15.6,0>
<IF0><CS3,5,4,0,4><T2><RR>
<XH><XL><AF><MC><QT><EP><UF6><EF><QT>
```

Figure 4. The formatting routine that the %CH code in the chapter heads of this book calls. This routine specifies the type style, spacing, and location of the word "Chapter" at the beginning of each chapter.

and format that begins each chapter of this book. With code files, a typographer can more easily use a standard coding scheme for all publications and still specify format characteristics that are unique for each book. Understanding and deciphering the %CH code clearly is far easier than deciphering the formatting codes it represents.

Photocomposition tapes are much more useful for the CD ROM publisher if they use a descriptive markup language. First, structural elements such as the beginnings of sections and subsections can be identified much more easily if a simple code marks them. The alternative, identifying the sections by interpreting a sequence of elaborate formatting and type-style codes, can be inaccurate and sometimes impossible.

Second, descriptive markup languages enable CD ROM publishers to define their own formats. Most CD ROM publications are destined for screen display rather than for printed pages. The explicit instructions characteristic of procedural markup languages often are inappropriate for screen display, whereas descriptive markup leaves the precise nature of the formatting undefined and therefore flexible.

Common Difficulties with Photocomposition Tapes

We have stressed that not all photocomposition tapes are equally easy to use as input in preparing text for a CD ROM. The prospective CD ROM publisher needs to understand the characteristics of the tape's markup language before planning a production schedule. Other considerations are:

- A publishing company needs to determine its tapes' coding consistency before converting them. A large and interesting database on photocomposition tapes is a valuable asset because the format is already machine-readable. But because companies may use a variety of typesetting systems, a single database often will contain several different formats. Moreover, even tapes from a single typesetting system are often formatted differently.

- Traditionally, pasteup artists and typesetting system operators probably have been the single most common reason for format inconsistencies in a single-system company. When a book enters the production phase, layout problems often force a "quick fix"—a block of text will be moved, deleted, or reformatted. A typographer may solve the problem by resetting an entire page, while a pasteup artist may cut and paste only blocks of corrected type into the page by hand. Thus, photocomposition tapes that a publisher converts for CD ROM often do not represent a final document—and most likely the embedded codes will offer no clues to the status of the tapes.

- Phototypesetting tapes that specify formatting characteristics via code files often cause problems during format conversion, mainly because they often don't specify which code file a document uses. This information usually is stored in someone's desk drawer or memory.

No matter how simple or clean a publisher's photocomposition tapes are, converting them to a format that the company's development software can index may require custom programming. This conversion has yet to be automated and often is the most expensive and time-consuming part of a project. The product manager must give these prospects some serious thought before assuming too much about the effort, money, and time that converting a pile of photocomposition tapes into a format useful for CD ROM will require.

Structured, Record-Oriented Data

Photocomposition tapes are not necessarily organized reliably, nor do they always contain the structural information that systems require to prepare CD ROM documents. But sometimes a product is stored as a highly structured, record-oriented database—a set of data that is divided into groups of identically formatted *records*, which are further divided into *fields*. The fields contain such information as the document title or author's name, and the field structure and organization is repeated throughout the database. Working with structured databases is a much more predictable, orderly process than is dealing with photocomposition tapes.

Some publications actually are record-oriented databases that were converted to photocomposition tapes for printing. For example, many abstract and index publications, such as *Dissertation Abstracts International* or *The Reader's Guide to Periodical Literature,* start out as databases. Although you can use the photocomposition tapes these databases generate, preparing text for CD ROM is far simpler if you use the original structured data. This is not surprising. The photocomposition tapes were derived from the database to produce printed products; CD ROM publishers need to extract a different kind of data stream from the database to produce electronic products.

Online databases are another source of highly structured, record-oriented data. Typically, the fields within the records on these tapes contain a variety of data types. Some contain ASCII or EBCDIC text characters; others contain numeric data, and still others contain information about how other fields are to be processed. The format of an online database generally is predictable. The only inconsistencies occur when the database's structure or the requirements of the online retrieval system have changed drastically from one product generation to the next. These structural or programming changes can slow data conversion, especially if they are not well documented.

We discuss structured databases in more detail in Chapter 7. For the purposes of this chapter, note simply that although converting online database tapes can involve a significant programming effort, the data's predictable structure makes it much easier for a programmer to anticipate problems and design a conversion routine that will work on all the data. After a programmer analyzes the data and designs the program, the conversion process is fairly routine. Because of this predictability, a publisher working with fielded data usually can concentrate on other aspects of the project, confident of the time and money allocated to data conversion.

Converting Word-Processed Data

Word-processed data is another common form of machine-readable information. In many ways, the problems associated with this kind of data are similar to those encountered when dealing with photocomposition tapes, although they frequently are more severe. Again, you typically find ASCII text peppered with embedded specialized codes that vary from word processor to word processor. What's worse, as far as the CD ROM publisher is concerned, is that word-processed data often contains even fewer structural cues than do photocomposition tapes. This is not surprising, since when we use a word processor, we don't identify a title as a title; all we care about, for example, is that it is centered and boldfaced.

Another problem is that applications developed from word-processed files may well involve thousands or tens of thousands of small, poorly documented files with different internal formats. Authors and clerical personnel are notorious for arranging titles and section headings in "their own way," making it difficult to devise one program to convert every variation to a common format. In addition, the information may be recorded on media readable only by special, perhaps obsolete, equipment. Many floppy disks contain valuable information that only word processors made years ago can read—the means of reading these disks, much less transferring the data, may be hard to come by. Finally, many text formats such as tables and footnotes may have been typed in rather than coded—a fact often not obvious. If no formatting codes specify such structures, you must add them, either by hand or by finding a structural cue in the text and writing a program that inserts the code at the cues.

The challenge of figuring out how to make a silk purse out of a 10,000-floppy-disk sow's ear should not be underestimated. Although, in principle, converting typesetting or word-processing formats is not difficult, most standard tape service bureaus seldom do these jobs, so they can't accurately estimate the costs. Most important, they can give little advice on difficulty or cost during the early stages of your project, a critical time in product planning.

The AAP Standard

At the start of this chapter, we noted that more than 80 percent of all books and periodicals published today originate in electronic form and that this trend is on the rise. We described the methods you can use to recapture text once the original electronic manuscript has been transformed into print. We also cataloged the sometimes severe difficulties encountered in trying to start from electronic text forms in which information about a document's structural organization is not explicit.

This picture suggests an obvious solution to all these problems: Ensure that the original electronic manuscript contains the structural information we need, using a markup language that all conversion systems understand. This would enable publishers to use the author's original electronic manuscript to produce either a printed product or a CD ROM.

But how do we form a standardized markup language from the Tower of Babel that exists among electronic data-formatting languages? This is a question the Association of American Publishers addressed during the past three years through their Electronic Manuscript Project. They produced a document entitled "Standard for Electronic Manuscript Preparation and Markup," which we will simply call the AAP Standard. It describes a powerful descriptive markup language that publishers can use to organize the information in books and articles.

The AAP Standard has enormous potential for making CD ROM text preparation and all forms of electronic publishing more straightforward and economical. Authors would provide basic structural information about their manuscripts in a useful form that requires no conversion. Publishers, during the editing process, would refine and complete this structure, storing the manuscript as part of a database of publications in a general, flexible form. A publisher could print specific documents or could publish a CD ROM database simply by extracting the desired material from the database and then converting the data to the appropriate form in an orderly, predictable process. Because of the defined, established coding schemes, the data-preparation team would not have to write special conversion programs for every product. Publishers and software houses could create standard conversion software to accomplish most steps in the publishing process.

Making this vision a reality will require that several conditions exist. First, publishers must recognize the nature of the problem and accept the necessity of beginning work on its solution with the author's original manuscript. Authors will need access to word-processing software that produces coded-character output conforming to the AAP Standard while still being user-friendly. Software vendors must create products such as database-indexing programs or photocomposition software that use the AAP Standard as an interface at the "front end" of the process. Authors and publishers must shift their focus from the physical format of the printed product to the internal structure of the electronic product. For the project manager trying to bring a current database to CD ROM product status, the AAP standard provides no immediate help. It will make the job easier in the future, but only after databases exist that conform to the standard.

Text Preparation in Review

This chapter describes the fundamental alternatives for preparing text to be indexed and structured for CD ROM publication. It also identifies some problems typically encountered during this process. We will conclude with a summary of steps that this initial stage involves.

All data on a CD ROM that will be retrieved using the same method must share a common format. This aspect of data preparation is sometimes called *data normalization*. The process includes the following steps:

1. Reformat nonstandard record formats. You must convert all data records with different formats to the record format that the targeted delivery system can interpret. This conversion process might include removing padded blanks from records or removing noncontent characters to cut back on required storage space.

2. Convert characters from EBCDIC to ASCII codes. ASCII is the accepted character-encoding scheme in the United States. Most microcomputer software is designed to work with ASCII characters rather than with EBCDIC characters.

3. Convert graphics or any characters not present as part of the ASCII standard character set into a form the targeted delivery system can read and display.

4. Strip out all symbols that cannot be translated into or have no equivalent form in either the ASCII standard character set or the extended character set that the delivery system specifies. Most nontranslatable characters will reside in photocomposition data.

After all data is in the same basic format, you will identify and mark the data's structural components. Often, you will translate one kind of structural cue or identifier into the structural coding that the indexing software uses. Occasionally, you will have to mark these structural elements manually. In general, this process includes these steps:

1. Strip out all data not pertinent to electronic displays. For example, OCR scanning often will pick up page numbers and running heads in addition to the main text. You may wish to remove page numbers and running heads, since they clutter the display unnecessarily.

2. Identify document boundaries. You must mark each document's beginning and end with the special codes that the search and retrieval software requires.

3. Convert structural clues in the original data to a code or format the display software will understand.

4. Recognize and mark fielded data. For example, if you want to extract particular sections of data to collect into a topical index for a database, you must find a way to mark them. This process usually is automatic. You or the service bureau probably will have to write a program that recognizes

and marks certain predictable features of the data structure. For example, if all article titles are unmarked and appear on the third line of the article's first page, you could write a program that searches for that point in an article and inserts a mark, enabling the indexing software to find the title.

5. Error checking and correction are the final steps. Publishers and service bureaus always are well advised to carefully examine all aspects of a document's structure and organization. If the data structure is inconsistent, some of the automatic formatting routines probably will either fail to index the data at all or will index it improperly. Finding these errors at this stage of data preparation is far better than waiting until the data is indexed or, worse yet, mastered to disc.

As noted, these steps are only the first stage in preparing text for a CD ROM. The next steps involve building indexes, which we describe in Chapter 6, "Full-Text Retrieval and Indexing."

The art of electronic publishing is relatively new, and even the experts are still learning new ways to speed up this laborious and often expensive process. As standardized tools become available, we should begin to see this process become easier and far more economical.

About the Authors

Raymond Bridge is a Systems Engineer at Reference Technology in Boulder, Colorado, where he has been responsible for production of more than a dozen read-only optical discs. He worked in Engineering and Technical Management at a number of high-tech organizations before joining Reference Technology in 1982. He is an avid mountain climber, kayaker, and cyclist and is the author of numerous technical articles and nontechnical books.

James Morin has a B.S. in applied mathematics and computer science and is currently studying for an M.B.A. at the University of Colorado. Morin joined Reference Technology in 1984 as a systems software engineer and was responsible for designing and developing their CD ROM data mastering software. In his current position as Systems Support Engineer, he also helps customers structure their data to meet retrieval and mastering requirements.

Selecting an Approach to Document Retrieval

Distributing documents on a CD ROM puts a publisher in the electronic document retrieval business. There just is no other way to get the documents back off the disc. For many publishers this means learning about an entirely new discipline. This chapter gives publishers the framework they need to evaluate document retrieval options and select an approach that will work for their products.

The Nature of Document Retrieval

Before you can intelligently evaluate a document retrieval system, you need to understand what it does. An essential distinction must be made between retrieving *documents* and retrieving *data*. In a 1984 article, David Blair suggested four important differences:

1. Document retrieval systems answer inquiries less directly than do data retrieval systems.

   A *data* retrieval system returns the information we seek. For example, if we ask for the population of Stillwater, OK, the system answers 38,268. A *document* retrieval system, on the other hand, responds with a list of documents likely to contain the information. The same inquiry might produce a list of census documents.

2. Document retrieval is probabilistic and nondeterministic.

   In a data retrieval system, there is a direct relationship between the request and the correct answer. If we ask for the population of Stillwater, there is only one correct answer. On the other hand, if we use a document retrieval system to find documents containing the terms "Stillwater" and "population," we do so because it is likely that documents containing these terms will tell us Stillwater's population. The relationship between our request and the answer is nondeterministic:

○ Several documents may satisfy a request.

○ Documents containing "Stillwater" and "population" may not provide the number 38,268.

○ Some documents that contain Stillwater's population may not include the requested terms.

3. Success in document retrieval is measured in terms of utility rather than in terms of correctness.

Because data retrieval is deterministic, it is possible to judge success in terms of correctness. Did the system retrieve the correct population for Stillwater? Such an objective criterion makes it simple to tell how effective a system is.

Judging the effectiveness of a document retrieval system is harder, particularly if the inquiry is about a subject such as "methane gas production from municipal solid waste" rather than the more straightforward matter of "the population of Stillwater." The documents the system retrieves are not simply right or wrong, but must be judged in terms of utility. In comparing systems, a user must decide which retrieve the most useful sets of documents. Clearly, this decision is much more subjective than whether or not the answers are correct.

4. The user's time, not the machine's response time, determines retrieval speed.

Because a one-to-one relationship exists between inquiry and answer in a data retrieval system, performance can be measured in terms of "How long does the machine take to get the answer?" Physical performance measures such as this are much less appropriate in a document retrieval system, where the process is nondeterministic, requiring that the user decide which information is relevant. A system that retrieves document lists rapidly, but includes many irrelevant documents, can be slower for the user than one that spends more time retrieving a smaller, but more relevant, set of documents.

The design and evaluation of document retrieval systems are more challenging because they involve making judgments under uncertain conditions. Just as there is no right answer in a document retrieval environment, so is there no single right approach to the design and structure of document retrieval systems. The systems, like the documents they retrieve, must be evaluated in terms of utility. Utility implies a context: Different document retrieval methods are more or less useful for different kinds of users and different kinds of document collections.

The Two Fundamental Approaches to Document Retrieval

Document retrieval systems can be distinguished by whether they rely primarily on searching or on browsing. Searching begins with a term or set of terms that we believe occur in the documents of interest on a particular subject. When we look for the population of Stillwater by retrieving all the documents containing the terms "Stillwater" and "population," we are searching for documents. Searching is like using a book's index: We start with a term and find the pages where it is discussed.

In browsing, we open the database to a particular document and then read what is there. Browsing is like using the table of contents of a book. If we open *CD ROM: The New Papyrus* to its table of contents, we find that Chapter 3 is about retrieval software and that it begins on page 131 with an article by Gregory Colvin entitled "The Current State of Text Retrieval." We turn to page 131 and page through Colvin's and the following articles, discovering what is there. That is browsing; some CD ROMs allow us to do the same thing.

Another useful way of distinguishing between browsing and searching is to view electronic document retrieval as a matter of locating some particular content at a particular place in the document collection. The content is the *what* of the retrieval operation; the place is the *where*. Searching moves from what to where. We know the terms associated with what we want, and the system finds where they occur. Browsing moves in the opposite direction, from where to what. We open the database to a location and find what is there.

Browsing is the mode of document retrieval that we usually use when we are dealing with printed information. Consequently, people at first find browsing the most familiar and therefore the easiest way to retrieve documents electronically. This familiarity also makes users view browsing as less sophisticated and useful than searching for documents on disc. Searching seems somehow more "computer-like" and therefore more powerful.

The notion that electronic searching, unaided by browsing, is the "real" way to retrieve electronic documents is one of the greatest impediments to the success of CD ROM publishing. Searching has been the most common retrieval mechanism because, until now, retrieval has been primarily "on-line." It has therefore been limited by the slow data transfer rates available over telephone lines. A CD ROM can connect a large database directly to a personal computer. We can afford the luxury of moving through data bases with the freedom we use in reading a book: We can jump to a place of interest, read awhile, then scan backward, forward, or jump again, searching for terms as necessary.

Browsing is an important tool in electronic document retrieval systems. To fully appreciate browsing, however, we must look at research on document searching. We need to understand what searching does well and what it should not be expected to do.

Why Is Searching Done at All?

An article by Blair and Maron (1985) received a great deal of attention because it raised fundamental questions about the usefulness of many contemporary document retrieval systems. Part of the article's notoriety, no doubt, is due to its closing sentence:

> Full-text searching is one of those things, as Samuel Johnson put it so succinctly, that " . . . is never done well, and one is surprised to see it done at all."

Robert Carr expresses the same sentiment, though less radically, in a 1986 article:

> There is no doubt that keyword searches of CD ROMs will be a standard tool. But unassisted, the user exploring the CD ROM with only a keyword search facility is left in the position of an ice fisherman dangling his line through a small hole in the ice: He must guess what fish might be in the water below, set the appropriate bait, cast through the small hole in the ice, and hope to hook a fish.

These reservations are not new. As early as 1960, Don Swanson, in a *Science* magazine article, concludes:

> The effectiveness of all information search techniques tested on the model was found to be rather low. Text search by computer was, however, significantly better than a conventional, nonmechanized subject-index method. Thus, even though machines may never enjoy more than partial success in library indexing, a small suspicion might justifiably be entertained that people are even less promising.

This is hardly a ringing announcement of the start of a new era. What characteristics of document searching caused Swanson's caution? Why would Blair and Maron voice such a negative view of searching? Is it really that bad?

Precision and Recall

The question of retrieval effectiveness is central to the debate over searching. Effectiveness is typically measured in terms of *precision* and *recall*.

Precision measures the extent to which a search retrieves only relevant documents. If a search retrieves N documents and R of these are relevant to the user's question, precision is calculated as R/N—the proportion of relevant documents to all documents retrieved. Precision also can be viewed as the probability that a retrieved document will be relevant.

Recall is a measure of thoroughness. If a database contains TR documents relevant to the research question and a search retrieves R relevant documents, recall is R/TR. Figure 1 summarizes these definitions.

$$\text{Precision} = \frac{\text{Number of relevant documents retrieved}}{\text{Total documents retrieved}}$$

$$\text{Recall} = \frac{\text{Number of relevant documents retrieved}}{\text{Total relevant documents in database}}$$

Figure 1. Definitions of precision and recall.

Ideally, we would find every relevant document, and *only* relevant documents. In this exceptional case, both recall and precision would have a value of 1. But perfect performance is rare. Researchers have found an inverse relationship between recall and precision. They have also found that the sum of recall and precision values usually ranges between about 1.0 and 1.4 (Salton, 1986; Blair and Maron, 1985; Salton, 1970; Salton and McGill, 1983; Colvin, 1986). Figure 2 shows a typical graph of the relationship between recall and precision. Recall is gained at the expense of precision.

This trade-off makes intuitive sense. Suppose we want to find legal documents to help us prepare a product liability suit involving the failure of a seat belt. We can get reasonably high precision by restricting our search of a legal database to documents containing the terms "product liability" and "seat belt." But since suits involving other products may provide important precedents, such a restrictive search probably will have poor recall, omitting many useful documents. Searching for *all* documents containing "product liability" will improve recall, but reduce precision. We will retrieve many irrelevant documents with the additional relevant ones. Such is the trade-off between recall and precision.

PRECISION

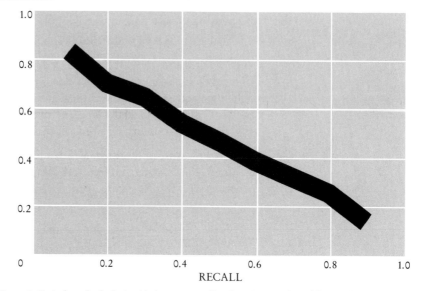

RECALL

Figure 2. Typical graph of relationship between recall and precision. Adapted from Salton, 1970.

The Futility Point and Output Overload

In deciding the relative merits of recall and precision, we must consider a database's size and the number of documents retrieved by searches that have high recall. Suppose we decide recall is more important than precision in our seat belt liability search and request all documents containing the phrase "product liability." The system tells us that 3912 documents contain the term. Do we begin looking through the 3912 documents? Probably not. We are beyond what Blair calls our "futility point" thanks to "output overload." The results of the search are hardly more useful than not having searched at all; we are no more willing to look through 3912 documents than we are to look through the entire database.

The usual response to output overload is to restrict the search by specifying that documents contain some additional terms. We might, for example, request only those documents that also contain the word "vehicle," "automobile," or "automotive" with the phrase "product liability." The system tells us 1423 documents contain these words. We can then further restrict our search to include only cases tried since 1980. We keep restricting our search until we pare the set of documents to manageable size, finally retrieving some number below our futility point. Though we would like high recall, we are unwilling or unable to handle the proliferation of documents and are pushed toward increased precision.

The Blair and Maron Study

We began our discussion of searching by quoting the last sentence from the much discussed article by Blair and Maron. This article reports on the effectiveness of a system called STAIRS in retrieving information from a collection of 40,000 legal documents, representing about 350,000 printed pages. The database would fit on a couple of CD ROMs, so their results are relevant to CD ROM publishers.

Blair and Maron drew a number of conclusions from their study:

1. Unavoidable output overload results in low recall on this size database.

   Searches monitored by Blair and Maron on average retrieved only 20 percent of the relevant documents. The lawyers who ordered the searches stipulated that they find 75 percent of the relevant documents. Interestingly, the lawyers had no idea the system's recall was so low; they thought they were getting the 75 percent recall they required.

   Precision, on the other hand, was quite high. On the average, 79 percent of the documents retrieved were useful.

   Blair and Maron assert that this bias toward high precision and low recall is in part created by output overload: By the time the researchers pared down the document set to an acceptable size, they had thrown away many useful documents along with the irrelevant ones.

2. Users often cannot come up with a set of terms that occur in relevant documents and only there.

   The system Blair and Maron studied uses automatic indexing. This means that the search terms must occur within a document for it to be retrieved. The alternative is manual indexing, in which index terms are assigned to each document. The limitation of automatic indexing is that the researcher must be able to make good guesses about the precise terms that will occur in the sought-after documents. An example from the Blair and Maron study illustrates the problem nicely:

   > In the legal case in question, one concern of the lawyers was an accident that had occurred and was now an object of litigation. The lawyers wanted all the reports, correspondence, memoranda, and minutes of meetings that discussed this accident. Formal queries were constructed that contained the word "accident(s)" along with several relevant proper nouns. In our search for unretrieved relevant documents, we later found that the accident was not always referred to as an "accident," but as an "event," "incident," "situation,"

"problem," or "difficulty," often without mentioning any of the proper names . . .. Those who were personally involved in the event, and perhaps culpable, tended to refer to it euphemistically as, inter alia, an "unfortunate situation," or a "difficulty." Sometimes the accident was referred to obliquely as "the subject of your last letter," "what happened last week was . . .," or, as in the opening lines of the minutes of a meeting on the issue, "Mr. A: We all know why we're here. . . ."

3. Manual indexing is preferable to the automatic indexing used in full-text retrieval.

By *full-text* retrieval, Blair and Maron mean document retrieval based on automatic indexing of the full text of documents. Hence, when they say they are surprised that full-text retrieval is used at all, they are not really renouncing the idea of keyword document searches; they are panning a single, albeit commonly used, approach to document indexing. They recommend that systems rely on manual indexing instead of automatic indexing for these reasons:

○ Manual indexing would, in their opinion, circumvent the problem of guessing at terms that will lead to the relevant documents. Taking the example that we quoted from the Blair and Maron article, the presumption is that a human indexer would assign the same keyword to all documents relevant to the accident.

○ The entire text of documents must be entered into a system for full-text searching. That is the only way that all the terms can be captured in an index. An average document in the system Blair and Maron studied was about 10,000 characters long. With manual indexing, a document record would consist only of a document reference and some keywords—perhaps 500 characters. The construction of the index of manually selected keywords does not require entry of the full document text. Blair and Maron suggest that the cost of entering the full text is greater than that of manual indexing.

○ Storing entire documents costs more than storing the smaller records required for manual indexing.

○ Since fewer terms are associated with documents in a manually indexed system, the index is smaller.

The Manual v Automatic Indexing Debate

A number of Blair and Maron's arguments for manual indexing don't apply to most CD ROM databases. CD ROMs do more than simply provide indexed access to a document collection; they contain the actual documents. Consequently, matters such as the amount of effort required to capture the text of documents or the amount of space required to store them are not valid considerations when comparing manual with automatic indexing on a CD ROM.

From the point of view of a CD ROM publisher, then, the principal concern raised by Blair and Maron is whether automatic indexing can be as effective as manual indexing. In an excellent 1986 article, Gerard Salton, a widely published authority on automatic indexing and full-text retrieval, pointedly observes that Blair and Maron's study does not, in fact, compare manual with automatic indexing systems; it evaluates a single automatic system. Assertions about the superiority of manual indexing, Salton says, are "unsupported by any data submitted to the reader—outside the alleged poor recall performance exhibited by the STAIRS system in the legal case."

In fact, Salton says, comparisons of automatic with manual indexing show that "properly designed text-based systems are preferable to manually indexed systems." He cites two studies. In 1968, Lancaster found that the MEDLARS system's manual indexing did not necessarily make guessing keywords easier. And in Clarendon's 1977 experiments, conducted using a large NASA document collection, automatic indexing of terms extracted from titles and abstracts produced better recall than did the use of a controlled set of terms assigned manually.

Salton closes his article with a review of mechanisms that improve automatic indexing and a "blueprint" for using them to build more effective document retrieval systems. The simpler suggestions include:

- Restrict indexing to terms extracted from titles and abstracts. This can be a very effective strategy for CD ROM collections of digitized images of journal articles and other source documents. The digitized image collection can be coupled with machine-readable, searchable titles and abstracts.

- Use a stop list to exclude high-frequency terms that do not usefully distinguish between documents.

- Store only the roots of keywords so that a search for a term such as "indexing" also will retrieve documents containing "index," "indexed," "indexes," and so forth.

Salton also describes more complicated strategies that rely on statistical analysis to discover the terms that best discriminate between documents. One such procedure, *term discrimination analysis,* is used to build a thesaurus of terms referring to similar documents. With the thesaurus, a user can improve recall, broadening the search to include a larger set of documents. The additional documents have a high probability of being related to those retrieved in the original query. *Term discrimination analysis* also can improve precision. Terms that occur frequently in the collection are replaced with narrowly focused phrases consisting of several terms.

These suggestions for improving the performance of automatic indexing are important, and should get close attention from CD ROM publishers. The high costs of moving large reference collections from print to CD ROM necessitate automation when possible. Projects requiring a great deal of manual analysis not required for print products will not be attractive CD ROM publishing opportunities. We need to make the best possible use of what automatic indexing has to offer.

It is interesting to note that, at present, CD ROM systems' document retrieval capabilities are usually relatively primitive, using only the simplest elements from Salton's blueprint. One can only speculate about the reasons. Certainly, the high cost of preparing data for the CD ROM, often involving substantial reformatting, translation, marking, and indexing, is an inducement to keep matters as simple as possible for these early products. It will be interesting to see whether lower costs or better performance drives the market. This will determine whether automatic indexing becomes more sophisticated.

The Question of Retrieval Effectiveness

Although Blair and Maron focus on the use of full-text retrieval, implying automatic indexing of entire documents, their study raises general questions about term searching as a document retrieval tool. Significantly, in Salton's response to the Blair and Maron article, he never questions the validity of perhaps the most striking result of their study: Experienced searchers familiar with the subject area retrieved only 20 percent of the relevant documents. Salton, in fact, says:

> In this chapter we will argue that not only is this level of performance typical of what is achievable in existing operational retrieval environments, but that it actually represents a high order of retrieval effectiveness.

This must astonish publishers taking their first look at document retrieval systems. How could an ability to find only 20 percent of the relevant documents be acceptable? There are several answers:

1. Not all users need high recall.

   The lawyers using the system Blair and Maron studied wanted to retrieve at least 75 percent of documents relevant to their queries. But lawyers' recall demands are unusually high: They need to be aware of every fact relevant to a case.

   Other users often have different needs. Typically, an engineer, scientist, or academic researcher uses keyword searching to find the "handles" in a new area: to uncover the core of essential critical documents that define and shape a subject. These researchers often are more interested in precision than recall. Finding a dozen or so key documents, they use references, authors' names, and other information to set out on a research trail. They would consider the performance of the STAIRS system in the Blair and Maron study to be satisfactory.

2. Higher recall is available if precision is sacrificed.

   As noted, it is possible to broaden a search, obtaining better recall, if one accepts less precision. For all but the most persistent, patient researchers, however, this option is more theoretical than actual; the number of retrieved documents quickly mounts into the hundreds. The futility point for most researchers is well below this.

3. Searching is not the only means of document retrieval.

   Searching for terms and phrases is only one approach to document retrieval. Unfortunately, in an online system as was studied by Blair and Maron, it is the only practical approach available. But when the documents are available locally on a CD ROM, searching can be supplemented with browsing capabilities. Browsing makes it easy to use searching in the manner we described above when we characterized the needs of many document system users: They need searching only to find fertile starting places for research. Working from a core of documents found through a high-precision search, they can use the system's browsing facility to follow references to other documents.

   It's not surprising that full-text searching is "done at all." It is the most economical mechanism for searching most document collections suited to CD ROM distribution. If the index is prepared carefully, following at least some of Salton's guidelines, searching on an automatically indexed CD ROM can be as effective as on a manually indexed one. Although the.

recall effectiveness of searching large databases will disappoint lawyers and others who require high recall, searching will be useful to many researchers and professionals. Automatic indexing can be particularly useful with CD ROMs, on which the documents can be coupled with a retrieval system that allows the user to combine searching with browsing.

Browsing

At the outset, we distinguished browsing from searching by saying that browsing moves from where to what, from place to content, while searching moves in the opposite direction, from what to where. Now that we know more about searching, we can make finer distinctions between these two very different views of a document database.

● Browsing presumes a document collection is structured in some way.

In searching, we view retrieved documents as discrete, independent entities. Browsing, on the other hand, places documents in the context of a larger structure. The simplest structure that suffices for browsing is a document sequence. To the extent that the sequence is a meaningful arrangement which groups related documents, browsing from document to document is useful. If, however, the sequence is without meaning (for instance, documents arranged in order of entry, without regard to content), browsing is also without meaning.

Browsing systems can use structures that are much more complex than a document sequence. Documents can be grouped into subchapters, and subchapters into chapters. Or they can be broken into sections, subsections, and so forth. Browsing can be designed to support entry at the start of any of these divisions.

● Browsing does not necessarily deal with documents.

The concept of a *document* is central to searching: Searches retrieve documents. Browsing, on the other hand, can dispose of the idea of documents completely. The database is viewed as a structure with certain defined entry points. Some entry points may be the beginnings of documents. But, with a hierarchical structure in which documents are grouped in chapters and subchapters, and further divided into sections and subsections, we can browse to the start of a chapter or subsection as readily as to the start of a document.

● Searching produces a list of documents; browsing opens the database to a single location.

Consequently, the index that supports browsing is usually simpler and smaller, requiring less storage space.

- Preparing a database for browsing is often more difficult than preparing one for searching.

Although the indexes for browsing are smaller than those required for searching, their preparation is often more difficult. The difficulty arises from browsing's need for a view of the structure of the document collection. The problem is one of recognition: The indexing can proceed only if we can recognize and differentiate between the collection's structural components. Frequently the input data (such as photocomposition tapes) does not contain enough information to permit automatic generation of this higher-level view of the database. *Linked browsing,* which is described below, is especially likely to present data preparers with complex recognition problems.

A Taxonomy of Browses

Browsing can refer to several kinds of document retrieval activity. For some systems, browsing means scrolling around in the text. For others it means opening to a specific document, just as we open an encyclopedia to the article on Abraham Lincoln or one on the moon. In yet other systems, browsing involves jumping from one place to another in the document collection. It is useful to distinguish among four browsing methods.

Sequential Browsing
Sequential browsing is moving forward or backward through a document collection. It is like paging forward or backward through a book or journal. If you page forward to the end of one document, you encounter the beginning of the next one.

Structural Browsing
In *structural* browsing, you enter a document collection at points related to its structure. You might, for example, enter at the table of contents, Chapter One, or Paragraph 3.1.2. The usefulness of structural browsing depends on how rich a structure is recognized when the database is prepared for indexing.

Access to the database's structure can be implemented in a number of ways. One method consists of extracting the titles of the major access points to create a database table of contents that summarizes the structure. For example, if we treat this chapter as an entire document collection, we might make each of its headings an access point. Figure 3 shows the table of contents that would be created. A retrieval system could display this table, letting the user browse by using a mouse or some other pointing device to select a line from it. The system then opens the document collection to the selected heading.

Selecting an Approach to Document Retrieval
The Nature of Document Retrieval
The Two Fundamental Approaches to Document Retrieval
Why Is Searching Done at All?
Precision and Recall
The Futility Point and Output Overload
The Blair and Maron Study
The Manual v Automatic Indexing Debate
The Question of Retrieval Effectiveness
Browsing
A Taxonomy of Browses
Sequential Browsing
Structural Browsing
Keyed-Access Browsing
Linked Browsing
When Is Browsing Useful?
Combining Searching and Browsing
Conclusion

Figure 3. A database table of contents that could be created from this chapter. Each header represents an access point to the entire document.

Keyed-Access Browsing

Another way to provide access to the document collection is to associate a specific entry point with a unique identifier, or *key*. Clearly, keyed access can be related to the document collection's structure. Assuming a database structure like that in Figure 3, our system might allow us to type in the key "A Taxonomy of Browses" to open the database to the start of that section.

The problem with this mode of access is that the user must know the key. Structural browsing, on the other hand, gives the user an outline of the database's structure, allowing the user to select entry points rather than having to name them. Even so, keyed-access browsing is useful for some applications. TMS, Inc. found, for example, that accountants who use its Internal Revenue Code database often know the number of the section of the code they wish to reference. An accountant preparing an application for nonprofit tax-exempt status, for example, would know that section

501(c)(3) contains the relevant information. In this instance, keyed-access browsing is the quickest way to find the desired information.

Linked Browsing

Technical documents, government regulations, and literature reviews often contain references to other documents. Consider, for example, this excerpt from section 110(i) of the 1977 Clean Air Act:

> Except for a primary nonferrous smelter order under section 119, a suspension under section 110 (f) or (g) (relating to emergency suspensions), an exemption under section 118 (relating to certain Federal facilities), an order under section 113(d) (relating to compliance orders), a plan promulgation under section 110(c), or a plan revision under section 110(a)(3) . . . .

One browsing feature that consistently excites users is being able to point to such internal references and automatically open the database to the cited location. To look at section 118, you simply put the cursor on that reference and press a button. This capability has been called, among other things, *sideways browsing, point-to-point browsing,* and *associative linking.* We refer to it as *linked* browsing because it follows links between points in the database.

Linked browsing is related to the concept of *hypertext* originated in 1980 by Ted Nelson. Viewed as *hypertext,* a document collection is part of a broader *literature.* By *literature* Nelson means "a system of interconnected writings." The researcher follows these connections, or *links,* between documents until the corpus of the literature is extracted. A true hypertext system allows the researcher to create, as well as follow, links, making new connections and extending the literature.

Exciting as the capability is, enabling the user to create links is not nearly so difficult as the prosaic matter of automatically recognizing implied links already in the text. Let's consider the Clean Air Act excerpt further. The user wants to be able to point to the reference to section 110(f), push a button, and jump to it. For the user to do this, the system must recognize that "110(f)" is a section reference and must find a link leading to the point where the section begins. What happens when the user points to the "(g)" in "section 110 (f) or (g)"? What happens when the word *section* does not precede a section number? What happens when the user points to a number that is not a section number? Solving these recognition problems can add significantly to the cost of preparing the document collection for electronic retrieval.

Linked browsing is not limited to linkages between text documents. CD ROM products such as University Microfilm International's INSPEC/ IEEE abstract/image database use links between text documents and digitized images. It is easy to envision links between text and video sequences, images and sound, and so forth.

When Is Browsing Useful?

We opened this discussion with the observation that browsing is tied to the structure of the document collection. To the extent that the structure is rich, as is usually the case with text databases such as technical manuals and collections of scholarly articles, browsing can be an important access mechanism. Structural and keyed-access browsing are most useful when a rich hierarchical organization is coupled with internal tables of contents and other finding aids.

These browsing methods are less effective in document collections that are organized sequentially, such as a chronological series of daily newspapers; however, sequential browsing usually is important for such collections.

Linked browsing is very useful for any document collection in which it is economically feasible to recognize the linkages. This is true even if the document collection lacks any other structural organization. If it is possible to discover links between the documents in a *core set* that make up a *literature,* then document retrieval is a simple matter of following the links. Finding the core of documents relevant to a subject area is, after all, what document retrieval is all about. When the input data structure is such that creating links is economical, linked browsing is one of the most exciting tools available in an electronic document retrieval system.

Combining Searching and Browsing

In discussing searching, we carefully considered searching's effectiveness. Because browsing is so sensitive to the document collection's structure, it is more difficult to generalize about the effectiveness of browsing as a retrieval tool. However, in recalling the general observations about document retrieval that we began with, we can conclude that access to both browsing and searching improves a document retrieval system. We said that designing effective document retrieval systems was difficult because:

1. A document retrieval system doesn't answer inquiries directly.

2. Document retrieval is probabilistic and nondeterministic.

3. Success in document retrieval is measured in terms of utility rather than in terms of correctness.

4. The user's time, not the machine's response time, determines retrieval speed.

With this emphasis on indirection, nondeterminism, and utility, we can expect to increase overall system performance by providing a user with additional flexibility. Combining searching and browsing enhances flexibility, allowing the user to look at the document collection in many ways.

Suppose we design a document retrieval system for library patrons. These users are often unfamiliar with sophisticated keyword search strategies. Often they are also unfamiliar with subject areas they inquire about. If a document collection has a well-defined hierarchical structure, structural browsing from a table of contents is the fastest, simplest way for them to begin their investigations. Browsing quickly takes them to documents that provide an overview of the subject area. They can browse sequentially through these documents, uncovering important terms, names, and phrases. If the system allows it, the users then can look for other documents that include these terms and phrases. Browsing introduces the subject and key concepts; searching helps fill out the subject area.

In a document collection that supports linked browsing, the research often takes the opposite direction: Searching leads to browsing. High-precision, low-recall keyword searching uncovers a handful of key documents. Following links in the hypertext, the researcher can expand the collection of relevant, important documents. This is a powerful, proven method for conducting research: Find a core set of documents, then follow citations and references to uncover the entire literature in an area. We are not introducing a new research paradigm; we are importing a very successful approach from the world of print media into the realm of electronic document retrieval.

Conclusion

Document retrieval is not a simple matter of asking a question and getting an answer; it is an exploration, seeking a set of writings that connect to form the literature surrounding a research question.

Document retrieval systems used on large computers rely on searching to find the literature. Certain words and phrases, it is assumed, will occur in the writings that are sought, but not elsewhere. But research over the past 25 years has shown that this assumption is not true in any absolute, satisfying sense. Language is not so simple. By the time a user develops a collection of terms restrictive enough to exclude most irrelevant documents, more than half of the desired documents may have been excluded as well.

Consequently, document retrieval is never a fully automated process; the researcher always must make judgments, rejecting some documents and seeking others, shaping the set of writings to represent the desired body of literature.

The CD ROM can give researchers some tools that make this shaping and judging easier and more profitable. A document collection on CD ROM coupled with a personal computer greatly expands the interaction between researcher and writings. No longer restricted to searching, the researcher can browse through the document collection, getting a different view of the writings. Thus, the researcher can better judge and select data.

Browsing's potential is most exciting when related documents contain a network of links. This hypertext view of the writings frees the researcher from relying on the weak assumption that related writings will use the same terms. Connections between related writings are now explicit, rather than probabilistic. The researcher can browse through the links, reaching out to the boundaries of the literature.

In combining searching with linked browsing, we fuse a computer's power to impose order with the trained researcher's judgment, a combination that will change the whole nature of document retrieval.

About the Author

Bill Zoellick is Director of Technology for the Alexandria Institute, a non-profit organization dedicated to making CD ROM information retrieval systems more widely available to users through libraries and other resource centers. Before joining the Alexandria Institute, Bill was Manager of Software Research at TMS, Inc., where he designed and implemented information retrieval software and lower level, file system software for CD ROM. He was a key participant in the High Sierra Group, playing an active role in producing the CD ROM logical format proposal. He has written and spoken widely about a broad range of CD ROM publishing issues and is co-author of a major new textbook on file structures.

Resources

Blair, David C. 1984. The data-document distinction in information retrieval, *Communications of the ACM*, 27(4):369-74. An excellent discussion of the difference between document retrieval and data retrieval. Blair explores the recall problem resulting from the need to keep the document list size below the user's *futility point*, suggesting a search optimization procedure that might provide better results than does the simple addition of terms to the query.

Blair, David C., and M.E. Maron. 1985. An evaluation of retrieval effectiveness for a full-text document-retrieval system, *Communications of the ACM*, 28(3):289-99. This is the "Blair and Maron" study discussed at length in this paper and elsewhere.

Carr, Robert. 1986. New user interfaces for CD ROM. In *CD ROM: The New Papyrus*, ed. by S. Lambert and S. Ropiequet. Redmond, WA: Microsoft Press. A discussion of the problem of providing an interface that gives the user convenient access to the large amount of information on a CD ROM. Carr argues for the use of hierarchical structures and browsing to assist the user in finding information.

Cleverdon, C.W. 1977. *A Computer Evaluation of Searching by Controlled Language and Natural Language in an Experimental NASA Data Base*. Report ESA 1/432. Fascati, Italy: European Space Agency. A series of experiments comparing automatic with manual indexing is described. The report is cited in Salton (1986).

Colvin, Gregory. 1986. The current state of text retrieval. In *CD ROM: The New Papyrus*, ed. by S. Lambert and S. Ropiequet. Redmond, WA: Microsoft Press. A brief survey of approaches to document retrieval, including a discussion of some newer strategies using fuzzy sets and expert systems.

Fox, Edward A. 1986. Information retrieval: Research into new capabilities. In *CD ROM: The New Papyrus*, ed. by S. Lambert and S. Ropiequet. Redmond, WA: Microsoft Press. A survey of recent research into document-searching techniques. Like Colvin's article, this is a very high-level survey aimed at readers with technical backgrounds. One valuable feature is an 8-page bibliography, which, unfortunately, is not annotated.

Lancaster, F.W. 1968. *Evaluation of the MEDLARS Demand Search Service*. Report. Bethesda, MD: National Library of Medicine. Cited in Salton (1986).

Nelson, Theodor H. 1982. A new home for the mind, *Datamation*, 28(3):169-80. This is a more conversational, less formal discussion of hypertext and Project Xanadu than the 1980 paper. It is also easier to find in most libraries.

Nelson, Theodor H. 1980. Replacing the Printed Word: A Complete Literary System. In *Information Processing 80*, ed. by S.H. Lavington. New York: North-Holland Publishing Co. This paper presents a clear, complete description of Nelson's thinking on hypertext, literatures, linkages, and other matters encompassed in his Project Xanadu. It is the best short description of Nelson's viewpoint.

Salton, Gerard. 1986. Another look at automatic text-retrieval systems, *Communications of the ACM*, 29(7):648-56. This reply to the Blair and Maron article also serves as a brief review of the literature on document retrieval by searching. It closes with a blueprint for automatic indexing.

Salton, Gerard. 1970. Automatic text analysis, *Science*, 168(3929):335-43. An excellent, readable survey of research in document retrieval before 1970. Reports the results of using some more sophisticated approaches to automatic indexing.

Salton, Gerard, and Michael J. McGill. 1983. *Introduction to Modern Information Retrieval.* New York: McGraw-Hill. A relatively recent and very important textbook on information retrieval. The focus is almost wholly on automatic indexing and searching. Provides detailed descriptions of term weighting and other indexing strategies.

Swanson, Don R. 1960. Searching natural language text by computer, *Science*, 132(3434):1099-1104. An important early study comparing manual indexing with automatic indexing. The document collection used in the experiment was quite small. This historically important paper is a well-written discussion of the same issues confronting those working in document retrieval today.

Weyer, Stephen A., and Alan H. Borning. 1985. A prototype electronic encyclopedia, *ACM Transactions on Office Information Systems*, 3(1):63-88. A description of a prototype electronic encyclopedia implemented through extensive use of browsing. This is an interesting source of ideas on browsing techniques.

Yankelovich, Nicole, Norman Meyrowitz, and Andries van Dam. 1985. Reading and writing the electronic book, *Computer*, (IEEE):15-30. A report on some of the thinking on and implementations of hypertext going on at Brown University. Brown is currently among the most active centers of work in this area. Much of this work extends hypertext to hypermedia, linking the text to images and sound.

Young, Jeffrey S. 1986. Hypermedia, *Macworld*, 3(3):116-21. This brief, readable overview of the major work exploring hypertext and hypermedia is a good introduction to the subject.

Full-Text Retrieval and Indexing

The two basic data storage structures that publishers contend with when they create CD ROM applications are full-text documents and record-oriented databases. Full-text documents are often thought of as a relatively unstructured assortment of characters that are loosely organized into words, sentences, paragraphs, and sections, just like a book. Often called *free-text* documents, they generally have no predictable form, since the length and the content of sentences and paragraphs change throughout the document.

By contrast, record-oriented databases have a distinct structure that is consistent throughout the database. They consist of one or more files that are divided into groups, or *records,* of similar data. Records are divided into *fields,* which are organized in the same way inside every record.

These two basic data storage formats can have many variations, depending on the nature of the data and the application. Each structure has different storage requirements and performance characteristics. In addition, the way the data is organized and the method by which the user will access it help determine which storage method you should use. For this reason, we will discuss the two basic data structures in separate chapters. This chapter deals with the characteristics and index requirements of full-text databases, and the following chapter considers the characteristics and index requirements of record-oriented databases.

Full-Text Retrieval

The publishing industry is gradually moving from the printed word toward the electronic word. This transition alters the way we, as readers, find and retrieve information.

The underlying cognitive skills we take for granted when searching through an index or finding references in a library are similar to those we use to find information electronically. However, since we cannot physically leaf through text on a disc, we request information through a computer and rely on computer programs to do the search and retrieval work.

Programs that search through documents are generally known as full-text retrieval programs. This chapter explores the basic retrieval functions common to most full-text programs. It also discusses the storage structures of full-text documents, describes how they are indexed, and includes methods for efficiently indexing documents.

The Software Components

A full-text document on CD ROM is more than just data. Two other types of information are inextricably tied to it: the search and retrieval software and the indexes. Together the structure and design of these components determine the precision and efficiency of a search procedure.

The Search and Retrieval Software

Search and retrieval software provides the query methods we need to reach information on the disc. When we request data, this software searches for it. To locate a particular word or phrase on a disc, the software can use one of two methods. It can search through the entire document collection from beginning to end, or it can search through an index and collect the locations of each occurrence of the information.

Although a linear search may be appropriate for a small word-processed document, it is not appropriate for CD ROM documents. Even with special hardware that performs high-speed linear searches through large bodies of text, CD ROM's slow data transfer rate undermines the hardware's efficiency. For example, at the standard CD ROM transfer rate of 150 KB/sec, reading 300 MB of text would require 2000 seconds, or well more than a half hour.

Consequently, most full-text retrieval programs made for CD ROM applications use indexes to search for data. Special indexing software creates the indexes before the disc is mastered. The resulting indexes are designed to work exclusively with the search and retrieval software.

The Index

In its simplest terms, a full-text index lists the location of every meaningful word on the disc. The most common indexing process is known as *full inversion*, and the index file that contains the word locations is called an *inverted index file*.

An inverted index file actually consists of several levels of indexes. The top level is a word lookup index, which is usually called a *dictionary*. Instead of a definition, however, the dictionary entry for a word contains a pointer to another index at the second level. This index, called the *occurrence list*, contains the document location and position within the document of every occurrence of that word throughout the entire disc (see Figure 1). The index that contains the occurrence lists for every word in the dictionary is sometimes called a *concordance index* or *reference index*. Each word's occurrence list is generally stored as a variable-length record (see Chapter 7 for an explanation of variable-length fields).

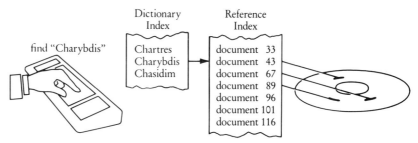

Figure 1. The two-level indexing structure of a fully inverted index. The retrieval software looks up the requested word in the dictionary index. This index points to a reference index, which contains a list of all the documents in which the word appears. Then the retrieval software creates a search list of all the documents containing the requested word, and you select the ones you want.

When looking for specific information, typically you ask for a particular word that best describes it. When a retrieval program searches, it looks up each word in the dictionary and follows the reference pointer into the reference index. This action locates a number of occurrence lists, one for each word in the search request. The lists are then compared. Any document that contains one or more words in the search query is placed in a list of documents that satisfy the search criteria.

As Chapter 5 explained, full-text searches generally produce extraneous as well as pertinent documents. Even if you want to examine all retrieved documents, there may be far more than you can review in one sitting.

Most programs build a result list of document names or topics that is fairly easy to scan, but quite often these lists do not provide sufficient information to give the user a clear picture of the document contents. As a result, many packages include a brief descriptive summary in the result list—a feature many users view as essential.

After the user selects a document from the result list, the retrieval program searches an additional index to find the location of the selected document.

Search Methods

The main way to search a full-text index is by requesting words using simple search phrases such as

FIND sculpin

But in an electronic search environment, not all search words will find information. The words you can use are strictly determined by the indexing programs that perform the file inversion. If you choose search words the index doesn't include, you won't be able to find them. Some systems use hard-and-fast indexing rules; others are more lenient and let the system operator define the rules.

For instance, some indexing programs may consider any transition from alphabetic to numeric characters a word break. But if your documents contain alphanumeric part numbers, this indexing system won't work. A part labeled *ab12* would be indexed as two separate words, *ab* and *12,* and no search would ever find it.

Similarly, if your application uses punctuation in a non-standard way, you would want to define indexing rules to allow for the unique usage. For example, a period usually terminates a sentence, and yet it is an integral part of a decimal fraction such as 1243.25, or an abbreviation, such as U.S. Without special indexing rules, these "words" would very likely be split at the period. Parentheses also present problems. Some parentheses are essential, such as those appearing in legal citations, for example, 405(a)(1). Others are not essential, such as those appearing as a part of a parenthetical phrase (like this).

Exceptions are the rule in most applications. It is important that the indexing software accommodate these exceptions to make data retrieval as accurate as possible.

Phrase Searching

An extension of single-word searching is *phrase searching.* This is just what it sounds like: the ability to search for phrases within a document.

The fundamental principle behind phrase searching is similar in all retrieval systems. Since a phrase is simply a sequence of words, the retrieval software searches for each word in the phrase and compiles a list of all occurrences. Then the software examines the position of each word in the document and checks to see whether any words located next to each other match the exact word order of the phrase. (Positional information is usually stored with the word in the index. A word's position is measured in terms of the number of characters or words from the beginning of the document to the word itself, as shown in Figure 2. This is called the character or word *offset*.)

The manner in which retrieval programs search for phrases varies. Among the more widely used approaches are:

87

Performing exact phrase matching of indexed words. This method is acceptable if you know exactly which words were indexed. Frequently, often-used words such as *and* or *the* are removed to save index space. If you include these words in a search phrase and they haven't been indexed, the retrieval software won't find the phrase.

Allowing imbedded punctuation or noncontent words. If you are searching for a phrase that has unindexed words or punctuation, this type of program lets you include these words or symbols in your query, but it ignores them, matching by other criteria, such as phrase length.

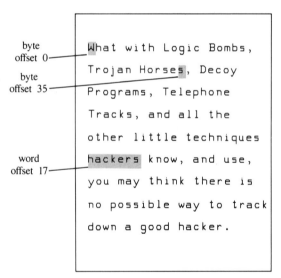

byte
offset 0

byte
offset 35

word
offset 17

```
What with Logic Bombs,

Trojan Horses, Decoy

Programs, Telephone

Tracks, and all the

other little techniques

hackers know, and use,

you may think there is

no possible way to track

down a good hacker.
```

Figure 2. A word's location in a document is usually determined by its character offset, or the number of characters between it and the beginning of a body of text. Its location might also be determined by the word offset.

Discounting blanks within phrases. Some programs ignore the blanks between words, attending only to the nonblank character order. Phrases with an extra blank or two would still be retrieved.

Phrase searching usually doesn't respect sentence or paragraph boundaries. In other words, in the remote instance that your phrase is a composite of the end of one paragraph and the beginning of the next, the retrieval software will retrieve it. This is one reason that extraneous documents are often retrieved.

Proximity Searching

Searching by phrases can be thought of as a type of word-proximity detection. Some programs offer a more general proximity search tool that searches for occurrences of words within larger defined areas. A proximity search may involve two or more words, which can appear in any order within the text.

Depending on the indexing and retrieval programs, sometimes you can restrict a proximity search to sentences or paragraphs instead of entire documents. This feature is extremely useful, but it does add to the index size since you would have to include the sentence and paragraph locations along with the word location. We will discuss the drawbacks of larger indexes later in this chapter.

Boolean Searching

Boolean operators are perhaps the most powerful tool used in full-text searching. They can help to refine search expressions, thereby making retrieval more effective.

Almost every retrieval program on the market offers at least three Boolean operators: AND, OR, and AND NOT. The AND operator dictates that more than one term (a term is a word, phrase, etc.) be in a document for the search to retrieve the document. The OR operator selects all documents that contain any one item from the query. The AND NOT operator excludes documents containing any terms that follow it in the query. Some programs require that NOT be used only with other operators.

Most user interfaces let you formulate a query that contains several terms connected by Boolean operators, such as

> (architecture AND environmental) OR (Frank Lloyd Wright AND design)

The Boolean OR tends to enlarge a search result list. This query would retrieve documents containing the words *architecture* and *environmental* together, and it would also retrieve documents containing the words *Frank Lloyd Wright* and *design.*

Using the Boolean AND generally shrinks a search result list, because the documents would more likely contain one word or set, but not both words or sets, as in

89

> (automobile AND front-wheel drive) AND (Japanese AND American)

This expression would retrieve documents only if they contain all four words: automobile, front-wheel drive, Japanese, and American.

The Boolean AND NOT is usually used in conjunction with the AND operator, as in

> money AND (NOT philanthropy)

When used in this manner, the AND NOT operator acts like the AND—shrinking the result list even further. This example would retrieve documents with the word *money* in them only if they didn't also contain *philanthropy.* Some packages allow use of AND NOT by itself, such as

> AND NOT construction

This usage is dangerous, because it tends to produce very large result sets. If allowed, its use is advisable only if the researcher has detailed knowledge of the text and can avoid retrieving too much.

Use of Wildcard Characters

Another search tool in the basic searching repertoire is the single or multiple *wildcard character.* These are characters that substitute for letters or numbers in a search query. By using them within words or phrases, you can find more than one word in the dictionary index.

The single wildcard character is often used to search for spelling variations or alternate word forms. For example, the word *wom?n,* which uses a ? as a single wildcard, would retrieve both *woman* and *women.*

The multiple wildcard character usually is allowed only at the end of a word root and therefore is often called a *root expansion operator.* Since many words have a common root, root expansion tends to retrieve many undesirable words as search terms unless the root is distinctive. The following queries, in which * is the multiple wildcard character, illustrate this:

head*
undesirable usage

chiropract*
reasonable usage

In the first example, such a query would retrieve every word containing the root *head,* conceivably a very large and diverse list ranging from head to headshrinker. The second would retrieve only the words *chiropractor* and *chiropractic,* a far more manageable selection.

Field Searching

Text often is structured so certain parts of the document can be indexed separately. Such structures within a document are called *fields,* and they are the basic unit of structured databases, which we will discuss in Chapter 7. Fielded documents usually offer faster and more precise retrieval than do unfielded documents. Many publications include fielded data such as abstracts, authors' names, titles, or copyright information. If users know they want to find a particular author's article, they can specify the author field in a form such as

FIND John Smith, Author

For indexing software to properly index fields, the fields must be located at a fixed position within each document or, preferably, marked by non-display character sequences in the text. (The markup procedure you follow to mark fields is described in Chapter 5.)

Regardless of how they are marked, the words within each field are indexed separately and merged into a single reference index that contains the words and their field addresses. At search time, the full-text retrieval program provides the user with a way to specify which field or fields to search for each query term. Some programs display a list of the field's contents in every document on the disc, while others specify a field name with which to search for specific data. For example, you might search for a particular author's writings by entering a phrase that includes the field name *authors.*

FIND AUTHORS EQUAL TO "J. Gordon Coogler"

This would retrieve all documents written by anyone whose name is J. Gordon Coogler.

Nesting Search Tools

A final tool in the basic search toolbox is called *nesting*. In nesting, you combine the elementary search features by using one search feature to construct a query term used in another feature. For instance,

electro* properties

performs a root expansion within a phrase and thereby looks for any of the following terms:

electron properties

electron's properties

electronic properties

electromagnetic properties

The following expression looks for any one of these terms within the current proximity range of the phrase "solid state physics."

PROXIMITY ("electro* properties", "solid state physics")

Nesting enables the user to construct very complex searches and is often extremely useful.

Enhanced Search Capabilities

In this section we describe some additional features that many full-text retrieval programs offer. These advanced features enable the user to expand and yet simplify queries to fine-tune searches.

Query Expansion

Searches often fail to retrieve many desired documents because they contain different spellings for words in the query expression. The user must list all spelling variations unless the retrieval program can help in some way. Some programs help by automatically adding an *s* to form plurals of the search nouns. Others go a step further and use a complicated set of automatic pluralization rules for words that don't follow the norm, such as knife and knives. Yet another level of query expansion techniques includes *depluralization*, or *general stemming*, which looks for a word's root and all expansions of that root. The more query terms that automatic expansion generates, the more complex the search. As a result, the search will take longer. This trade-off between function and performance is inherent in full-text searches.

Thesauruses

Databases are often tailored to a profession that uses a particular jargon or uncommon abbreviations. Certain words may have a set of frequently occurring synonyms. For instance, the legal profession would use these terms as synonyms:

D.A.

district att.

district attorney

These types of databases may have retrieval programs that use a custom thesaurus containing the specialized vocabulary to perform automatic expansion of any query word with listed synonyms. In this case, the word plus all of its synonyms would be Boolean OR'ed together in the query wherever the word appears. Another use for this type thesaurus is to expand queries to include common misspellings.

Back Referencing

A query's length or complexity may be limited by the number of terms you can enter on a line or the amount of Boolean logic you can use without rendering the query unintelligible. In addition, when at the outset of a search, you may not choose the best combination of terms. You may need to refine the search expression several times before retrieving what you want. Both of these situations argue for using the results of one or more previous searches to build the current query. This feature usually is called *back referencing*.

Retrieval programs that perform back referencing record the results of each search and often identify them with a special code. You can include this code in your query to refer to previous search results. Some programs allow you to replace query terms with a back referencing code, while others stringently limit its use and its placement within a query expression. Most allow you to make back references to more than one previous search. This lets you break down a query into a number of easily understood steps without retyping them every time.

Special Function Operators

Full-text retrieval systems can employ a variety of special function operators.

Range searching. An additional operator that full-text programs may provide is a *range operator*. These operators search for ranges of words, numbers, or dates within a document, and select only those documents that satisfy the criteria. For example, if you want to search for all documents about CD ROM published between November 1986 and January 1987, you might enter a query similar to this one:

> CD ROM AND (copyright GREATER THAN 11/86 AND LESS THAN 1/87)

This query would only work if you indexed a field labeled *copyright* during document preparation. As with any other kind of search term or operator, you can use range searching with other search terms as part of a larger search strategy.

Retrieval and indexing programs have different strengths with regard to range searching. Some allow only positive integers and words, while others may allow signed integers or even decimal values.

Proximity operators. Some retrieval programs allow you to specify that search terms fall within a sentence or paragraph, or within a certain number of sentences or paragraphs. These operators diminish performance unless the index contains information about a word's location relative to sentence or paragraph boundaries. This information enlarges the index, but adding it is necessary to improve performance. We previously saw the trade-off between function and performance. Now we see the additional trade-off of indexing overhead versus function.

Cross-Referencing

Any survey of advanced searching features would not be complete without mentioning *cross-referencing.* Rather than an additional type of query operator, this is part of a totally different search strategy called *browsing,* which is based on the premise that you can only determine your information needs by reading the documents.

Cross-referencing lets you branch from one document to another either by selecting a specially marked reference in the text or by constructing a temporary query. In its most useful form, a cross-referencing mechanism allows you to move about from document to document without keeping track of your movements.

Both the retrieval and indexing software must support cross-referencing if you intend to include it in your product. During data preparation you will need to insert marks in the text that indicate a link to another document (or you might simply place all cross-references at the end of a document, as a book does). The cross-reference mark itself may contain the location of the reference, or it may refer to an index that contains the name and location of the reference. Either way, the retrieval software must have some displayable feature indicating to the user that a particular word or phrase is linked to another document. When the user selects a cross-referenced word, the software looks up the value of the embedded code, finds the location of the reference, and retrieves the document.

Audit Trails

Another important feature of a retrieval program is the ability to save a history of your search path. Earlier we discussed back referencing as a method for constructing queries based on the results of previous searches. We also discussed cross-referencing as a method for linking a series of documents containing related information. Some retrieval programs save an *audit trail* of your search activities so you can retrace your steps or review and perhaps modify a previous query.

Saving an audit trail and the search results also lets you quit a search session and resume it later. Future sessions can be much shorter, less tedious, and more effective if the search environment provides this type of *save and restore* mechanism.

Overhead to Support Full-Text Retrieval

Each of the various index files discussed earlier in this chapter contributes to the overhead (storage space) necessary to implement full-text retrieval. The amount of overhead, usually expressed as a percentage of the original text, directly affects the size of database that can fit on a CD ROM disc (or any disk, for that matter). You may need to embed field markers and other indexing marks for cross-references or display features in the text, which also adds to the document's size. In this section, we will briefly discuss each type of overhead and its expected size.

Dictionary Index Overhead

The size of a dictionary index is directly proportional to the number of distinct indexed words in a database. If the database is primarily English text with very few numbers or special strings (such as legal citations), then the total vocabulary tends to level off and stop growing as the text is processed during indexing.

Typically, a large document database of more than one million words contains about 100,000 unique words. The dictionary index for such a database would contain roughly 100,000 entries. If you calculate the number of characters in an average word, and add a few bytes for pointers and positional information, you find the entire index is 1 to 2 MB in size. For large databases, this is well under 1 percent of the amount of text—relatively negligible overhead. If, however, the text contains more than the average number of unique words or numbers, the index overhead would be more substantial.

Typographical errors ("typos") in the original text also drive up the dictionary's size. The indexing software can't distinguish a correct spelling from a misspelling. So it indexes every misspelling as a new word. Not only does this add to the index overhead, but it also affects recall efficiency. Total recall of relevant documents is almost impossible in a large database that contains misspelled words—unless you and the authors misspell them the same way. This fact also endorses a strong recommendation: Always proof your material or run it through an automatic spelling checker program *before* you index it.

Reference Index Overhead

As we said earlier, the *reference index* is the second-level index that contains an occurrence list for every word in the database.

The reference index usually is by far the largest of the indexes. Its size is proportional to the amount of indexed text. If every word in the database is indexed, then every word has an entry in the reference index. You can calculate how much space this will take using this formula:

$$\text{reference index entry size} \quad x \quad \frac{\text{amount of indexed text}}{\text{average text word size}}$$

Storage requirements of a reference index typically range from 30 percent to 100 percent of the total size of the database. This immense range exists because of the size and nature of index contents.

The size of reference index entries varies greatly, depending on which full-text retrieval program you choose. Different programs allow different amounts of information. At a minimum, the index entry will provide space for pointers to the location of the word within each document in which it appears. Not every word in the database will be listed, because you don't index every word—you index only *content* words. *Noncontent* words such as *and* or *the* usually are not indexed, because they have no meaning, or content, by themselves. Other factors affecting the size of the reference index include:

- The number of fields per entry.
- The compactness of index design.
- The degree of index compression.

If the program supports proximity searches by sentence or paragraph, the index also must contain relevant positional information—how many sentences and paragraphs from the beginning of the file, and so forth.

Field Index Overhead

Earlier we discussed fields, describing them as text that is indexed separately and labeled so you can search it apart from the main document. At times you will want to combine fields into one *pseudo* field so you can search several fields with a single query. For instance, if your application is divided into fields that contain author, title, and copyright information, you may wish to search two or all three fields as often as any one of them.

One approach to this is to create multiple indexes within the reference index: one for each separate field, one for a combination of two fields, and one for all fields. Multiple indexing clearly increases the size of the index, but it also enhances search performance. If space is no problem, go ahead and build the extra indexes. They can only add to the product's success because they will improve search performance. If space is of concern, look around for retrieval software that can combine fields at query time.

Structural Coding Overhead

Embedded coding is one additional item you should always consider when analyzing index size. Embedded codes are hidden markers (they aren't displayed) that tell the indexing software about certain structural characteristics. Often called *text flags,* they mark such things as:

- The beginning of a document, fielded data, special display characteristics, nonindexed data, and much more.

- Any field of data that will be searched (and indexed) separately from the main document but will be located inside the document. A title might be an example of this kind of field.

- Any field of data that will be searched (and indexed) separately and will also be stored outside the document. A document abstract would be in this catagory.

- Numeric or date fields for separate indexing. You would search these fields using numeric range searching operations.

- The beginnings or ends of paragraphs and sentences if the retrieval and indexing software support proximity searches. The location of a paragraph marker denoting the paragraph in which the word resides is stored in the reference index entry with each word.

- Display control characters that mark highlighted, boldfaced, or under-lined text. These generally are placed at the beginning and end of the affected text string.

- Image markers within the text that are indexed and contain pointers to image files on the disc.

Although the characters that mark these within the text usually aren't displayed, they still take up disc storage space. If the documents are small, with a great deal of fielding and formatting codes, these characters add more overhead than in large documents with fewer formatting codes. We will not attempt to size this overhead item, since it is strictly data dependent and its impact could range from negligible to substantial.

Techniques to Reduce Overhead

You may have noticed that we distinguish between the amount of *indexed text* and the amount of *text*. Most full inversion programs associated with full-text retrieval products permit some control over what gets indexed.

Searches can only access indexed words. Text usually contains many words that provide reading continuity but add little or no meaning. The articles *a, an,* and *the* are examples. Certain other words refine meaning but aren't significant for queries. Prepositions, pronouns, and some adverbs and adjectives typically are in this class.

These types of words occur frequently in most text. You can save a great deal of disc space if you don't index them. In fact, this can reduce the size of a reference index by 50 percent to 70 percent.

Stoplists

To prevent the indexing of a word, you include it in a *stoplist;* words in this list are known as *stopwords.* If you are judicious in choosing stopwords, you can usually significantly reduce the size of the final index. The most frequently occurring stopwords save the most space.

If you can, perform a word frequency count on a representative sample of your document. If not, references exist that list word frequency statistics for the English language (and probably just about any other language). Figure 3 on the following page shows a partial stopword list for the Bible and the word frequency count it contains.

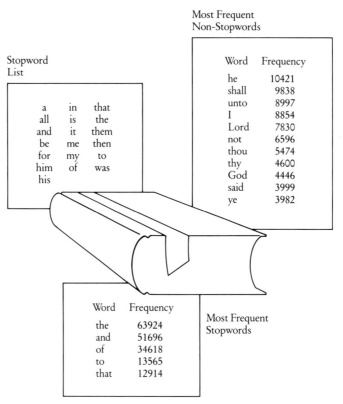

Figure 3. Some sample indexing statistics, extracted from a full inversion of the Bible, including Old and New Testaments.

Excluding Text

Another way to reduce the amount of text indexed is to exclude portions of the document important for display but not for searching. For example, you may not want to index the actual contents of tabular data. It might be better simply to label the table and index the label.

To turn off the indexing process so it skips over a section of text, you must insert special nondisplayable codes at the beginning and end of the section. Not all full-inversion programs permit this. When possible, this technique can greatly reduce the quantity of text to be indexed, with huge savings in reference index overhead.

Text Compression

Once you have shaved off as much overhead as possible by using multiple indexes, stoplists, and on/off indexing controls, you can compress your data. *Text compression* is a process that converts text to a form that requires less space. To be compressed, data must have some repeating pattern that you can replace with a shorter representation such as a code. If there's little or no repeating data, not much will be gained by compressing it. See Figure 4 for a simplified example of a text-compression technique.

You must compress text *after* you index it so the byte location of the compressed word in the text will be properly recorded in the index. For the retrieval software to find the indexed reference to the word, it must know the compression scheme so it can decode the word upon retrieval. Therefore, you can only use data-compression techniques if both the inversion program and the full-text retrieval program understand the scheme.

Compression can slow down displays, because the retrieval system must expand the compressed text before displaying it. The degree to which this affects display time depends on the compression method, the amount of memory available for decompression, and the horsepower of the computer system used to process the data before it is displayed. Compressing the document text does not, however, adversely affect the amount of time it takes to retrieve a document. Retrieval time depends on the indexing structure design, the data transfer rate, and the clock rate of the supporting hardware—no matter which compression technique you use.

The words in this sample of text show one very simple text compression method. To save the most space you will compress long or frequently used words. To compress them you will replace them with numeric codes. To decompress them the software will execute a code expansion routine.	Uncompressed Text				Compressed Text #1 #3 in this sample of #6 show one very simple #6 #2ion method. To save #1 most space you #4 #2 long or #7 used #3. To #2 #1m you #4 replace #1m with #8 #9s. To de#2 #1m #1 #5 #4 execute a #9 #10 routine.
	code	word	# of occur-rences	# of saved spaces	
	1	the	6	8	
	2	compress	4	24	
	3	words	2	6	
	4	will	3	6	
	5	software	1	6	
	6	text	2	4	
	7	frequently	1	8	
	8	numeric	1	5	
	9	code	2	4	
	10	expansion	1	7	

Figure 4. A much-simplified example of a text-compression method that replaces frequently repeated and long words with codes.

Some full-text indexes store words as numeric codes—the original ASCII value, the pointers, and the positional information are all stored as numbers. Compressing these numeric codes usually saves little space, since numbers already use a minimum amount of space. Unlike document compression, index compression causes longer retrieval times, because the indexes must be expanded to restore them to a usable form.

Common Compression Methods

Below we discuss some common text-compression methods, including the expected space savings—assuming each method is used by itself. If the compression technique you use involves more than one of these methods, space savings will not be strictly additive, but these estimates still can serve as a general guide.

Remove trailing blanks on each line of the original text. If all lines in the original document are padded out to 80 columns, you can achieve tremendous savings by removing them. If the average length of a line of text (allowing for blank and partial lines) is 60 characters, this yields a savings of 33 percent.

Defer expanding tabs into blanks until display time. The usefulness of this technique depends strictly on the number of tabs in the text and how they are actually encoded (some tab marks are only one character long). Savings vary from relatively minor to significant and are completely data-dependent.

Encode the most frequent words based on English or database-specific statistics. This method saves space by replacing words with short codes. It can trim 10 to 20 percent from the original text, depending on word lengths and frequencies. A compression scheme such as this uses the same translation table to encode and decode the words.

Encode the most frequent phrases. This method works much like the previous method, replacing multiple-word terms or phrases with a short code. It is a highly data-dependent method, and its impact is difficult to assess.

Encode prefixes and/or suffixes. This method replaces common letter combinations with a short code and saves 20 to 30 percent.

Encode consecutive blanks, repeating characters, or repeating character patterns. The main savings here is from blanks embedded within a line of text, as in large indentions or column alignment. Again, the potential savings will be very data-specific. Highly formatted data such as tables are well suited for this type of compression method; it may not be as effective on regular text.

Encode the most frequent character strings, disregarding word breaks. This method is often referred to as a *Huffman code*. The Huffman encoding routine counts all character strings, from those having the highest frequency down to the strings with the lowest frequency. It then assigns a code to represent each, the shortest codes representing the most frequent data. Savings using Huffman codes can be very impressive—from 25 to 50 percent of the original text.

Many other compression methods are available, but they are too complex and esoteric to discuss here. The critical thing to remember when choosing a compression scheme is that all parts of your system follow the same compression rules. No amount of compression will help if your indexing and retrieval software can't decipher the compression method.

Even with significant text compression, current databases are pushing beyond the storage limits of a single CD ROM. Therefore, compression should not be viewed as a way to fit ever larger databases on a single disc. But it can make the difference with a database that is borderline in size, or it can reduce the number of discs a very large database requires.

Conclusion

Full-text retrieval programs are based on a very imprecise premise: that words alone can approximate meaning. They can't always. Retrieval tools such as Boolean operators, structured data fields, and other advanced search features help compensate for this basic shortcoming and improve precision, but they are never perfect—almost always retrieving far more irrelevant data than you need.

Many full-text retrieval programs are hard to use. Very often you must learn special skills to find what you want—and the most popular retrieval tools, Boolean operators, are not intuitively easy to use. For this reason, some retrieval programs bury the Boolean logic in special templates that prompt you for your request. This approach seems to help, but some designs are limiting and even confusing to some users.

Structuring the data into smaller, well-defined fields can help refine the search process immeasurably, allowing the user to sift through masses of data by subject, title, or author. This feature is critical for most full-text applications, because it enables the user to search for specific types of information. Producing useful fielded data in an otherwise unstructured full-text document requires extra coding and data preparation, an added but worthwhile expense.

In addition, full-text retrieval requires a great deal of disc space, especially when it allows indexed access to every word—involving more trade-offs among overhead, retrieval performance, and usefulness.

But despite its drawbacks, full-text retrieval is the best way to access huge stores of unstructured text. Companies continue to find new ways to access information, making retrieval programs ever easier to use and more efficient. Databases will continue to grow, which eventually will drive up disc capacity and make it possible to store several times the amount we now can store on a single disc. Looking back 10 years from now, we will view the retrieval methods we use today as cryptic and complex. Right now, they're better than ever. We are truly at the dawn of a new era.

About the Author

Jerry Fand is a member of the technical staff at Reference Technology, Inc. He is involved in system integration, software evaluation and design, and data preparation, working with RTI's full-text search software to optimize full-text search on CD ROM.

Resources

Bourne, C.P. 1977. Frequency and impact of spelling errors in bibliographic databases. *Information Processing and Management*, 13(1):1–12.

Burket, T.G., P. Emrath, and D.J. Kuck. 1979. The use of vocabulary files for on-line information retrieval. *Information Processing and Management*, 15(6):281–289.

Devlin, K.J. 1979. *Fundamentals of Contemporary Set Theory.* New York: Springer-Verlag.

Gerrie, Brenda. 1983. *Online Information Systems.* Arlington, Va.: Information Resources Press.

Held, Gilbert. 1983. *Data Compression: Techniques and Applications, Hardware and Software Considerations.* New York: Wiley Heyden.

Kraft, D.H. and T. Lee. 1979. Stopping rules and their effect on expected search length. *Information Processing and Management*, 15(1):47–58.

Maron, M.E. and R.M. Shoffner. 1969. *The Study of Context: An Overview.* Los Angeles: University of California, Institute of Library Research.

Swanson, D.R. 1977. Information retrieval as a trial-and-error process. *Library Quarterly*, 47(2):128–148.

Verhoeff, J., W. Goffman, and J.Belzer. 1961. Inefficiency of the use of Boolean functions for information retrieval systems. *Communications of the ACM*, 4(10):557–558, 594.

Database Retrieval and Indexing

CD ROM data structures fall into two major classes: full-text databases and structured, record-oriented databases. As we discussed in the preceding chapter, full-text databases are large collections of unstructured text from which you can retrieve entire documents with a single request. Structured databases are highly organized collections of data from which you can retrieve specific information stored in a record.

Large structured databases that can be placed on CD ROM require indexing and retrieval software that brings the functionality and performance of mainframe computer record management systems to personal computers. But even these tried and true systems are not adequate for the unique characteristics of CD ROM. CD ROM's read-only nature, its vast capacity, and the drive's relatively slow seek time require new approaches to system design. In these new systems, data indexing is key. In this chapter, we discuss the most common methods for retrieving and indexing record-oriented, structured databases for CD ROM.

The Database Structure

The typical structured database on CD ROM consists of large files, made up of similarly structured data *records*. Each record is divided into *fields*.

The easiest way to describe such a database conceptually is as a grid of rows and columns. A data record, which represents a set of associated information, can be thought of as a row. The fields in each row can be thought of as columns, each column containing the same type of information throughout the database.

Figure 1 shows a simplified, fictional stock market database represented in this row-and-column format. The data records are arranged alphabetically in the sequence of their ticker tape symbols. Each contains ten fields of information identified by the labels at the top of each column.

Record	Symbol	Name	Exchange	SIC	Price	Earnings	Dividend	Images	Comment
1	ABC	AgBusCo	N	0112	22	3.50	1.60	1	Corporate farming is the mainstay of this conglomerate; profits are up 20%, threats of divestiture because of irrigated acreage limitations imposed by the Reclamation Act of 1902 have evaporated, and a bright future in land development looms when the company seeds a fast-growing second-home and planned-subdivision subsidiary with some of the profits cropped from the sale of its implement dealerships.
2	BAC	Tobacco	A	0144	15	(.71)	0	5–7	Chewing tobacco products in the popular pouch style provide a favorable contrast to the lagging sales of smoking products; the company's strong marketing to teenagers and children using sports personalities and rock stars should position it to take a big bite of future market share.
3	CAB	Taxico	N	4577	42	6.57	.45	8–12	This taxi company is running on a high-test mixture of the traditional co-op membership and modern franchising methods, accelerating its profits more than 30% last year; gearing the dividend down may keep the price climbing as the company cruises into new cities.
4	CAR	Meat, Inc.	O	0218	8		.72	13–19	Meat products for school lunches make up the lion's share of this packing operation; scandals and unresolved regulatory problems about contamination and sales of 4D carcasses have lowered earnings, though not enough yet to take a bite out of the dividend.
5	DDE	Dicers	O	5770	17	1.21	0	20–26	This fast-growing widget-maker has diversified its marketing from the traditional late-night television direct sales campaigns centering on vegetable mayhem, and is slicing through the gourmet cooking market with a new, high-end line of designer enamelware and kitchen arcana.
6	DRI	Realest	N	6344	1	(3.44)	0	27–34	Poor investments in California real estate; Midwestern farm loans backed when the farmers weren't making any more land and they were still reaping a whirlwind of crop subsidies; blue-sky appraisals (Realest is litigating its losses on some of these) and costly blunders in managing foreclosed properties have produced a second year of poor results; we think cost-containment procedures will take effect within 1 or 2 years.

Figure 1. A sample record-oriented database.

(continued)

Record	Symbol	Name	Exchange	SIC	Price	Earnings	Dividend	Images	Comment
7	DST	DenStand	0	5057	34	1.21	0	35–44	Designer jeans, indecent blouses, and a fast-moving corporate commitment to surf the *nouvelle vague* of Valley Girl fashion have cloaked this company's balance sheet with profits as splendid as the Emperor's New Clothes—we hope Denstand can either keep its design genius fertile or engender market loyalty in its notoriously fickle clientele.
8	EBR	EBanks	0	6776	34	5.22	1.60	45–50	Regional banking is nowhere stronger than in the Intermountain West, since oil has never really held much importance in the economies of the Rocky Mountain states; this well-diversified, conservative regional banking power enjoying its 5th year of 15% + growth is testimony to a strong future potential.
9	EST	Clocks	N	5470	22	2.11	72	51–56	Despite its name, this company markets mostly watches; one of the nimblest U.S.-based watchmakers, it exported its manufacturing to the Third World in time to avoid the explosion of last year's temporal time bomb: the flood of cheap, accurate digital watches that nearly stopped the clock for some of our larger, more famous corporate timepieces.
10	FIN	Finbank	0	6776	13	1.86	1.00	57–66	Suspending the dividend in the second quarter was required; no other course was open with defaults in the oil service sector wiping out profits and demanding beefed-up loan-loss reserves, but the resulting price break was devastating (36 to 13); near-term recovery is improbable, though an investor with a long-term perspective (2–5 years) may find these shares attractively priced.

Figure 1. A sample record-oriented database.

Databases will have either fixed- or variable-length records and fields. The size of fixed-length fields (and records) is predetermined, while the size of variable-length fields is determined by the length of data in each field as data is added or deleted. Fixed-length fields generally are easier to access because their length is predictable—the software always knows to read a specific number of bytes for each field. By contrast, the sizes of variable-length fields may differ from one record to the next, requiring that the retrieval software "read" for markers that signify the beginning and end of a field. A provision of the High Sierra Proposal (HSP) lets you identify the size of fixed- and variable-length records.

Fields

Data records typically include *data fields* and *pointer fields*. In the sample database, the Images field is the only pointer field; all others are data fields. Data fields can contain a single value of a specific data type, or they can contain an indefinite number of values of different data types. We will distinguish between these types by calling them *structured* or *unstructured* data fields.

Structured fields contain a single data value of a single type. These might be dates, times, part numbers, prices, or names, for example. In our sample database, all data fields except the Comment field are structured fields.

A structured data field usually is indexed and accessed according to the value of its contents, or its *key value.* For example, the key value for the Name field in the second record is Tobacco. To find this record, the user would simply ask for all records having the name "Tobacco"; the search software would look through an index containing all Name fields and, upon finding a match, retrieve and display the record's contents.

Unstructured fields can contain various kinds of data, but most often they contain long strings of characters. For this reason, an unstructured field is commonly called a *free-text* or *full-text* field. The Comment field in the sample database is a full-text field. Full-text fields generally are indexed and sorted using a method called *full-text inversion*, which enables you to retrieve every value individually.

Pointer fields contain the locations of data not in the record itself but associated with it. Supplemental material—digitized images, audio, or video—may be accessed via a pointer field. The data's location can be specified in many ways: by the image file's identification number, the starting time and duration of a segment of digitized audio or video, the name of a file and byte position of data within that file, and so forth. The Images field in the sample database is a pointer to digitized page images of the company's annual report. ABC's annual report is found in pages 1 through 4 of the image file.

Database Retrieval Operations

Data is divided into fields to organize and define it for retrieval. To retrieve and manipulate data values, the typical database retrieval system must support several operations. It must be able to:

- Locate data records using single key values.

- Locate data records using ranges of key values.

- Locate data records using Boolean search logic on several keys at once.

- Locate information from several databases by performing relational operations.

Searching for a Single Key Value

One approach to record retrieval is to search for a key that matches exactly. For example, by searching the Dividend field in Figure 1 for a key matching 1.00, you retrieve data record 10. Records can also be located by searching for a key that nearly matches using a wildcard character such as *, which matches any character.

Conceptually, the search for a matching key begins at one end of the key sequence and continues sequentially toward the other end until a match or near match is found. If the keys being searched are in ascending order, the first key equal to or greater than the desired key terminates the search. Thus an ascending search of the Dividend field in Figure 1 for 0.5 retrieves 0.72, but a descending search retrieves 0.45. The search usually is not physically sequential, but is accomplished through the use of one of the index structures we'll describe later. Indexes give us the very important capability of treating a single file as though its fields were ordered in several different sequences.

Searching for Sequences of Key Values

When searching a database, quite often you will want to retrieve a sequence of related information that meets certain criteria. For example, if you wanted to find all companies returning dividends in the range of 0.4 to 1.0, you would perform a *numeric range search* of all dividend values between 0.4 and 1.0. The ability to retrieve such a sequence presupposes that the key values are ordered numerically.

By the same token, if the keys are ordered alphabetically, you can perform a prefix, or *word stem,* search. A word stem search of the sample database for all words beginning with the letters *AC* would retrieve *accelerate, accurate, acreage,* and *act.*

Hierarchies can also be represented as ordered sequences. In the sample database, the SIC code is a four-digit number in which the first two digits represent primary hierarchical classifications and the final two represent secondary classifications. By ordering this data numerically, you can perform a *hierarchical search* of all industries with a primary classification of Agricultural Crop Production (0100–0199). In this case, you retrieve 0112 (AgBusCo) and 0144 (Tobacco).

Supporting range, hierarchical, and word stem searching clearly requires that every key field sequence be ordered in a way that is most appropriate for its data type (that is, numbers need to be ordered numerically, words alphabetically, and so on). Once again, indexes enable us to maintain these different views of a single file.

Searching for Boolean Combinations of Key Values

Boolean operators (AND, OR, and NOT) work on *sets* of key fields. They are used to request data records that contain combinations of key values. In the sample database, we could request data records for companies in Agricultural Crop or Livestock Production that paid dividends using a rather cryptic Boolean expression such as (((SIC = "01**") OR (SIC = "02**")) AND (Dividend > 0)). This type of search finds all records that meet each of the key value specifications, and then merges the lists of these records to locate the records that meet the complete specification.

Relational Operations on CD ROM

Relational databases are typically divided into many small files, each file containing fielded data. You will usually use Boolean operators to search relational databases. Based on your request, the retrieval software combines the relevant files, searches them, and then assembles the search results. For example, you might search the database shown in Figure 1 for companies in Agricultural Crop production, then search another database for companies with net profits exceeding $1 million, and produce a combined report including the Price, Earnings, Dividend, and Profits values. Many publishers reorganize relational databases into several large files to facilitate indexing and retrieval.

Indexes

Fundamental database retrieval operations on CD ROM require indexes. We already have alluded to the reasons for this:

● Indexes speed data retrieval by reducing the number of disc accesses. Searching through an index is more efficient than searching through every record in a database.

● Search and retrieval operations are more efficient if the key fields are ordered in some way. Indexing and sorting a set of key values is easier than reordering and sorting a set of data records.

● Indexes let the user view a file within a variety of meaningful sequences.

CD ROM databases use two kinds of index structures: *key indexes* and *inverted indexes*. A *key index* is a collection of single field values, and is the predominant indexing method for structured databases. An *inverted index* is a collection of every word in the database, and is best suited for full-text applications. An application may use both indexing methods for one database if the type of data necessitates this. For example, the sample database contains one full-text field, which requires an inverted index if it is to be really useful, and eight structured fields that require key indexes.

Key Indexes

You will notice that each record in the sample database has a number. This is a common way to organize database records. Retrieval software can locate a record by its number, by the contents, or by the key values of its data fields. It finds the data by searching through a key index composed of these values. Key indexes contain, at a minimum, a copy of each key value and the address of the data record associated with it.

Since you cannot write new data to a CD ROM disc once it is mastered, records are stored in the sequence of their record numbers, and they will always retain that order in the data file. In this way, you need store only one set of data records along with several key indexes—conceivably one for every field in the database, on the disc. The sample database might have eight key indexes, one for each structured field. If we were to look at the Name field's index, we might see something similar to the list in Figure 2. The index is arranged alphabetically by key values rather than by record numbers, because it is searched by key value.

To access a particular data item on the disc, the search software simply matches the requested value with a value in the appropriate index. Since the indexes contain the data record's data address, the retrieval software can usually find the data record in a single seek.

Record	Symbol	Name	Exchange	SIC	Price	Earnings	Dividend	Images	Comment

RECORD	KEY
1	AgBusCo
9	Clocks
7	DenStand
5	Dicers
8	EBanks
10	Finbank
4	Meat, Inc.
6	Realest
3	Taxico
2	Tobacco

Figure 2. A key field index produced from the sample database in Figure 1 using the Name field.

Index Structures

Several index designs exist for keyed data. Describing all of these approaches to indexing is well beyond the scope of this chapter; it is a subject that can easily fill an entire book. Readers interested in more information about indexing should consult the reference list at the end of this chapter. Here we will introduce you to the principles and terminology of three indexing methods for keyed data stored on CD ROM: *balanced tree indexes, hash table indexes,* and *inverted indexes.*

Since indexing procedures are inextricably tied to retrieval software, the indexing strategy is transparent to the publisher. Publishers tend to be more concerned with the retrieval methodology than with the retrieval mechanism. However, the indexing strategy you use can affect your product's performance. Some indexing methods enable retrieval software to access data in a single seek; others can require several seeks. If storage space is a consideration, certain indexing schemes are more frugal than others in using space.

Balanced Tree Indexes

Directly searching a sorted index file of key records is not appropriate for a device as slow as a CD ROM, especially considering the very large files common on such a high-capacity device. One alternative is to build an index that rapidly reduces the search to a small part of the file. A balanced tree index uses this approach.

Consider the Comment fields of the sample database. If we eliminate common words and suffixes, fewer than 256 unique words remain. We can place these key words in key records and then place the key records in file blocks on a CD ROM. If we give each word a 32-byte record, 64 words will fit into a 2048-byte disc sector. Thus, the collection of 256 words will require four 2048-byte blocks. We can avoid searching the entire index file if we store the first word from every block (except the first) in a separate *block index* (we need not store the first block, since any words preceding the second block will be in the first block or not in the file). By searching through the block index, the retrieval software can quickly determine which of the four index file blocks to search. For example, a search for *CALIFORNIA,* which is alphabetically before *EARN,* would occur in the first file block, whereas a search for *MODERN,* which is alphabetically after *MARKET* and before *SLICE,* would occur in the third file block. The relationship between the block index and the key record index is shown in Figure 3 on the following page.

111

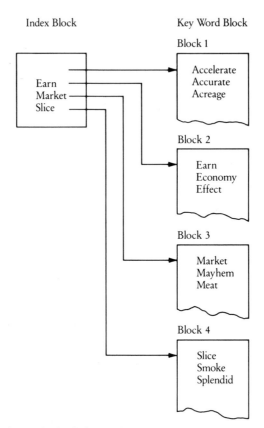

Figure 3. Balanced tree index for the key words in the Comment field.

If the computer has a large memory cache in which to store the block index and the index file, then the retrieval software need only access the disc once to find the database record. In other words, it would search the block index to find the correct block in the index file; search the index file to find the key word and its record address; and, finally, access the stored data record in a single seek. If the index is large and the memory cache small, there's a good chance the entire index file will not fit in memory. Consequently, the retrieval software would have to perform two seeks, one to find the index file and one to find the data.

The index described above is a two-level balanced tree. The tree is "balanced" because the number of levels from the block index to any particular record is the same for all possible search paths through the tree. You can add levels to a balanced tree index, or use larger blocks to store the keys. However, if more index keys exist than can be cached in memory, multiple seeks will be necessary to access the data records.

You can decrease the average number of seeks a balanced tree index requires, but this requires extra planning in preparing the data. For example, if you know some records in your database will be requested more often than others, you can sort the index values according to how frequently they will be accessed. When you block the index to store it on CD ROM, these keys will naturally fall together in certain blocks. Instead of loading the complete index along with all its various levels into memory, you need only load the parts that contain the most frequently used keys. This technique minimizes seeks a good percentage of the time.

Balanced trees on CD ROM can be significantly smaller than on magnetic media. On magnetic disks, key records usually fill the index blocks only partially and contain extra pointer fields so you can update them without rebuilding the tree. Since you can't write to CD ROMs, you can fill their index blocks. Packing almost all blocks of the tree full of key records lets you index many key records in a tree with only two or three levels (Colvin and Perry, 1986; Zoellick, 1986), ensuring that you can locate a key record with a minimum number of accesses.

Hash Table Indexes

The multiple seeks of a multilevel balanced tree index can be avoided if you create a hash table. *Hashing* is an indexing method that uses the key's value to compute its location within an index file. The same hash function used to create the original index is used later to retrieve the record address within the index. A simple example will help explain this concept.

Let's say we want to create a hash table index for the Symbol field in the sample database. The indexing algorithm might replace the characters *A* through *Z* with the numbers *1* through *26*; sum the numbers to produce a unique value representing each ticker tape symbol; and, finally, perform additional calculations on the value to determine its block location within the index file. In this case, we divided each sum by 4 and used the remainder value to distribute the values among four blocks (see Figure 4).

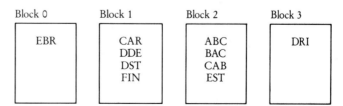

Figure 4. Hash table index of the Symbol field.

You'll notice that the key values are not distributed evenly across all blocks. Such uneven distribution is characteristic of hashing, because very often the hashing function produces values that map to the same block address. In dynamic files on magnetic disks, overflow blocks store the extra values. On the read-only CD ROM, it is better to make the blocks larger, hash to more blocks, or use a different hash algorithm to eliminate overflows (Colvin and Perry, 1986; Zoellick, 1986). When there are no overflows, you can locate any key value with only one disc access.

A powerful variation on typical hash algorithms is to use so-called *tidy functions* (Merritt, 1984). These algorithms distribute keys fairly evenly across blocks while preserving the order of the key values. This makes it easier to search the hash table for partial matches, since the hash algorithm tells which block contains the closest matching values. However, you may be unable to find a tidy function that distributes keys well, especially if the key values are close.

Inverted File Indexes

Inverted files can save index space when used with structured fields that contain repeating key values, and are ideal for full-text fields. For a thorough explanation of inverted files, see Chapter 6. In this section we will describe inverted files in the context of the sample database.

For an inverted file, one copy of each key value is stored in an index along with a pointer to a list of all data record numbers associated with the key.

The Comments field in the sample database is a full-text field—a good candidate for an inverted index. The field as a whole is not useful as a key value, but many words in the field may be. If each word is used as a key in a key record, the same words will occur repeatedly, creating a very large index. An inverted file usually produces a much smaller index, since it stores each word only once to represent all of its occurrences.

Figure 5 shows the result of inverting words beginning with *A* and *B* in the sample database. The index contains a word, the number of times that word occurs in the database, and the record number in a word occurrence list of the first posting of that word. The data pointer records contain the record numbers of each record containing the word.

Key Index			Occurrence List
Word	Count	Pointer	Record #
Accelerate	1	1	3
Accurate	1	2	9
Acreage	1	3	1
Act	1	4	1
Appraisal	1	5	6
Arcana	1	6	5
Attractive	1	7	10
Avoid	1	8	9
Back	1	9	6
Balance	1	10	7
Bank	3	11	8
		12	8
		13	10
Base	1	14	9
Beef	1	15	10
Big	1	16	2
Bite	2	17	2
		18	4
Blouse	1	19	7
Blue	1	20	6
Blunder	1	21	6
Bomb	1	22	9
Break	1	23	10
Bright	1	24	1

Figure 5. An inverted index for words beginning with A and B in the sample database shown in Figure 1. The keywords point to an occurrence list containing the record numbers of each word.

Choosing Which Type of Index to Use

Balanced trees perform best with applications frequently searched for partial matches, because they let you order the index by key value. They also perform well in exact-match applications in which you want to keep the index small. Balanced trees waste almost no space and typically can access any key in the index with only two or three accesses. The Dividend field in the sample database is a good candidate for a balanced tree index because it lends itself to numeric ordering.

Hash tables perform best when your primary concern is with rapidly accessing exact matches. You can usually construct hash tables so exact matches require only one disc access. Because the blocks of a hash table usually are not filled, these indexes are less compact—typically 20 to 50

116

percent of the space remains unused. Also, hash tables perform partial-match searches poorly unless they use a *tidy* hash function. Searching for a partial match in most hash tables is about the same as searching a sequential file. But performing the same search with a "tidy" hash table is almost as fast as searching for an exact match. In our example, the Symbol field might be used primarily for exact-match lookups, so a hash table might best represent the Symbol index.

Inverted files best support Boolean and relational operations on CD ROM. They can be created with either hash tables or balanced trees. Since all data record numbers containing a particular key value are listed together in an inverted file, it must be loaded into a rather large memory buffer to minimize accesses to the CD ROM.

Conclusion

CD ROM offers the database owner low-cost distribution of very large databases. The direct application of magnetic disk indexing technology to CD ROM systems is likely to lead to excessive overhead and slow performance. But by modifying traditional techniques to take into account the CD ROM's high capacity, slow access, and read-only nature, you can get acceptable performance with minimal overhead. Sometimes the CD ROM's extra capacity can be devoted to indexes that locate data values in a single disc access. CD ROM indexes support a broad range of operations, including Boolean, full-text, and relational operations. Today's CD ROM user enjoys the use of inexpensive desktop databases previously available only in hard copy, and can perform operations with a personal computer retrieval system once only available on expensive mainframe systems.

About the Author

Gregory Colvin, a retrieval software specialist, has been with Reference Technology, Inc., an industry leader in laser optic systems for information distribution, since 1984. While with Reference Technology, he has continued research on natural query access to textual data, and has developed methods for optimized access to read-only optical databases.

Colvin received his B.A. in psychology and computer science from the University of Colorado at Boulder in 1977 and his Ph.D. in psychology and mathematics from Cornell University in 1982. He then served as vice president for systems development at Information Access Systems, Inc., where he was responsible for the development of expert systems for text retrieval applications.

Resources

Only the briefest introduction to indexing could be included in this chapter. Fortunately, an extensive literature exists on each topic presented.

Bayer, R., and E. McCreight. 1972. Organization and maintenance of large ordered indexes. *Acta Informatica*, 1(3):173. This is the classic, original paper on B-trees.

Bradley, James. 1981. *File and Database Techniques.* New York: Holt, Rinehart & Winston. Contains a good chapter on hashing.

Colvin, G., and E. Perry. 1986. *Programmer's Guide and Data Preparation Manual.* Boulder, Colo.: Clasixs Key-Record Manager, RTI.

Comer, Douglas. The ubiquitous B-tree. *ACM Computing Survey,* (11)2:121. Perhaps the best brief overview of the entire B-tree family.

Folk, T., and B. Zoellick. 1987. *File Structures: A Conceptual Toolkit.* Reading, Mass.: Addison Wesley. Balanced trees, as described in this chapter, are a general form of a kind of tree structure called a B-tree. This new textbook gives B-trees and closely related structures detailed, extensive treatment. It also explains the theory behind hashing.

Knuth, Donald. 1973. *Sorting and Searching.* Menlo Park, Calif.: Addison Wesley. This is the definitive, classic reference for most issues discussed in this chapter. Even though this book appeared more than 13 years ago, Knuth's discussions of hashing and tree-structured indexes are among the most important resources for anyone working seriously in the area.

Merritt, T.H. 1984. *Relational Info Systems.* Reston, Va.: Prentice Hall.

Zoellick, Bill. 1986. *Byte* 11(5):177-88.

Parts of this article were published previously by Reference Technology, Inc. (Colvin and Perry, 1986).

IMAGE AND SOUND PREPARATION

Displaying Images

Imagine browsing through a CD ROM document on space exploration one day, flipping through photographs of the Apollo missions, and viewing Earth's moon as seen from an orbiting spacecraft. A mark on a large crater on the moon catches your eye and you touch it to get a closer look. Instantly you find yourself at the landing site of the lunar landing module. You touch another mark on the screen, and suddenly you're watching an animated illustration and mathematical analysis of the spacecraft's trajectory as it approaches the Sea of Tranquillity. Another touch reveals a labeled cutaway illustration of the lunar lander—with each removable layer exposing a new part.

Applications such as this are still dreams for most CD ROM developers, but they are possible. CD ROM's ability to store high-quality digital images and computer graphics along with text and sound places it in a league apart from most other audiovisual media. The potential for such richness and texture is driving developers to come up with better, more efficient storage and display methods for the space-hungry images. Imagination is driving others to explore special graphics effects such as animation, zooming, and panning to further enrich applications.

Electronic image technology is complex. You may find it easier to understand how to prepare digital images for publishing on CD ROM if you know something about the display environment—how display systems work and how images are stored. This information is in the first part of this chapter. The second part concentrates on image preparation and processing. Although this chapter is long, it is meant to be an overview. For further information, consult the references listed in the Resources section at the end of the chapter.

The Display Environment

Digital images come in a variety of styles and picture qualities. A delivery system requires special display software and hardware to read, process, and display the different styles, or *formats*. Software transforms image data read from the CD ROM disc to the format the hardware requires. Display hardware uses this transformed data to create the image. The level of sophistication of these components determines the image types and formats a delivery system can produce.

The Display Monitor

The *display monitor* is the part of the display system that presents an image to the user; it also is the only part of the display system the user normally sees. Several monitor technologies are currently in use, including cathode ray tube (CRT) monitors, liquid crystal display (LCD) panels, electroluminescent (EL) panels, and plasma displays. For various reasons, the CRT monitor is by far the most prevalent. Virtually all except a few very small, portable personal computers use CRTs, so the CRT has strongly influenced the design of computer graphics hardware and computer graphics. For this reason, we will spend a little time describing how a CRT-based display system works.

The CRT

CRTs should be familiar to practically everyone alive today, because a television picture tube is a CRT. The tube together with the support circuitry, power supply, and cabinet is called a *monitor*. The monitor converts a signal from some video source (such as a TV receiver, videotape recorder, or computer display electronics) to produce an image on the CRT screen.

The CRT is a glass tube containing an inert gas stored at a very low pressure. In the neck of the tube is an electron gun that emits a narrow, focused beam of electrons. The beam hits a phosphor-covered screen at the front of the tube. The phosphor compound glows where the electron beam hits it.

A monochrome monitor contains a single electron gun, and its screen has a single phosphor coating. Color monitors have three electron guns and three different phosphor coatings—each one glows in a different primary color. As any art student knows, primary colors are the basic colors that are mixed to form all other colors. The primaries that are used when mixing light instead of pigment are red, green, and blue. As the CRT's electron beams emit varying signals, the three phosphors glow at different intensities. The eye averages these colors into a single color.

Color monitors are categorized according to the type of video signal they process. In an *RGB* (Red-Green-Blue) *monitor*, three separate video signals independently drive the three color guns. In a *composite monitor*, a single video signal is decoded to provide the three RGB signals.

Raster Scan Images

All television sets and virtually all computers generate displays using a technique called *raster scan*. In a raster display, a series of horizontal lines drawn across the CRT screen generate the image. As the electron beams trace each line, their intensity is varied, changing the brightness of the spots on the screen to produce the images. This is repeated line by line down the screen until the beam draws the entire image. This raster scan process must be repeated, or *refreshed*, periodically to maintain the display. If it were performed only once, the image would appear for a fraction of a second, then subside as the glow of the phosphor decayed. Refresh rates for computer displays are normally in the range of 40 to 60 times a second. At this rate we can't see the screen being redrawn. However, if the refresh rate drops to around 30 times a second, we perceive an annoying flicker.

Interlaced displays. In the United States, television is broadcast at a standard frequency defined by the NTSC (National Television Standards Committee). The signal produces 262.5 horizontal lines sixty times a second. In technical terms, the signal has a horizontal frequency of 15.75 kHz and a vertical frequency of 60 Hz. (Other countries use the PAL or SECAM standards; both broadcast at different frequencies.)

Unfortunately, 262.5 lines of information is not enough to produce a clear picture, so the display circuitry doubles the amount of displayed information through a technique called *interlace*. This process divides the raster lines for one complete image into two sets, or *fields*. One set contains the even-numbered scan lines, and the other the odd-numbered ones. Even-numbered lines are drawn during one pass down the screen, and the odd-numbered lines are drawn during a second pass. In this way, two consecutive fields draw a single frame of the image, adding another 262.5 lines, for a total of 525 lines. The complete image is refreshed only 30 times a second. We don't notice flicker at this rate because the phosphor maintains its brightness long enough after each field is drawn for our eyes to average the two fields.

Non-interlaced displays. Our eyes easily average the two fields of an interlaced display when both fields contain similar information. This is true for images taken from the real world, but generally not for computer-generated graphics. Consider a horizontal white line drawn on a black background. On an interlaced display, this line would be refreshed only 30 times a second. Without similar information for the eye to average in the adjacent lines, the white line would flicker. This flicker is characteristic of computer graphics on an interlaced display. For this reason, interlace generally is not used in computer graphic displays.

A non-interlaced television display produces the same video signal twice (one for each field) and displays it at 60 Hz. This eliminates flicker, but it cuts in half the amount of information that each frame can display (262.5 lines instead of 525).

The NTSC specification also limits how many points of light the scan lines of televisions and composite color monitors can produce. These points of light are called picture elements, or *pixels*. A scan line produced in a computer-generated composite signal has from 300 to 400 pixels, enough to show about 40 columns of text characters.

The picture quality of televisions and composite monitors is not suitable for high-quality computer displays, so high-end CD ROM delivery systems generally use either monochrome monitors or RGB color monitors.

Resolution

The number of pixels and the number of scan lines together determine the spatial *resolution* of an image. Resolution is a measure of the level of detail an image can represent. A high resolution image has greater detail and better quality than a medium or low resolution image. In computer graphics, discussions of resolution can be somewhat confusing because the word is used in several ways.

Display resolution refers to the number of pixels the screen can display. A display device might have a resolution of 640 by 480 pixels, meaning the screen is divided into 480 horizontal scan lines, each containing 640 pixel positions. The total rectangular grid would contain 307,200 pixel dots. The more pixels a screen can display, the higher the resolution. For computer graphics, the higher the display system's resolution, the better the displayed image.

Image resolution refers to the number of pixels and scan lines in the stored image. Images stored with fewer pixels or scan lines than the display hardware allows will only fill part of the screen. Images with more pixels than the display hardware can handle will exceed the screen boundaries.

Figure 1 shows the difference between three resolution levels. As you can see, as the image resolution decreases, the image quality degrades.

Original Image
512 x 400 Resolution
8 bits per pixel

512 x 400
4 bits per pixel

128 x 80
8 bits per pixel

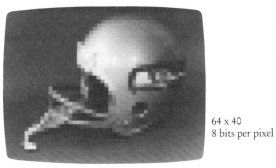

512 x 400
2 bits per pixel

64 x 40
8 bits per pixel

512 x 400
1 bit per pixel

32 x 20
8 bits per pixel

Example showing spatial resolution

Example showing pixel depth

Figure 1. A comparison of different levels of spatial resolution (left) and pixel depth (right).

High-quality computer display monitors can display anywhere from 320 by 200 pixels to 1600 by 1280 pixels. Currently, for personal computer displays, 640 by 350 pixels is considered high resolution, and 640 by 480 pixels will become common in the next year or two. In all cases, the more pixels, the better the display, and the more expensive the hardware will be.

In addition to spatial resolution, *pixel depth* is another measure of resolution. Pixel depth is the number of bits stored for each pixel. It determines how many colors or gray levels (in a monochrome display) a pixel can have. The more bits a pixel has, the more colors it can represent—and the greater its pixel depth. As you can see in Figure 1, pixel depth affects image quality. As the pixel depth, and therefore the number of possible pixel values diminishes, the image looks coarse and unnatural.

Aspect Ratio

Another characteristic of images and displays you need to consider is *aspect ratio.* An object's aspect ratio is the ratio of its width to its height. For example, the NTSC defines the aspect ratio of a TV picture to be 4:3; that is, a TV picture is a rectangle four units wide by three units high. Many computer monitors have the same 4:3 aspect ratio.

In computer graphics, however, it isn't the aspect ratio of the display, but that of the pixel grid, that matters. The rectangular grid of pixels on the display forms a coordinate system, and the unit of distance in this coordinate system is the pixel. In the real world, the units we measure distance with are the same size regardless of the direction in which we measure. An inch is the same distance whether measured vertically, horizontally, or in any other direction. In the pixel coordinate system, though, 10 vertical pixels are the same length as 10 horizontal pixels only if the pixels are square (their aspect ratio is 1:1). For example, if you draw a "square" 100 pixels by 100 pixels, it will appear square only on a display device with square pixels. On other systems it will be rectangular, and the degree of its elongation will depend on the aspect ratio of the display system's pixels. The process of making a square come out square (and circles round rather than elliptical) in a display that doesn't have square pixels is called *aspect ratio correction.* It's been driving graphics software people crazy for years.

When you digitize an image, you will create geometric distortion in the display if you don't match the aspect ratio at which you digitize it to that of the display. You can change the aspect ratio of an image to match that of a particular display, but this requires a great amount of computation and generally is much too time-consuming for the user's system. So if you plan to display an image on several makes of display devices that have different aspect ratios, you may need to store multiple copies of the image, each with a different aspect ratio. Matching image types and display systems is an important consideration when designing an application.

Display Adapters

A monitor produces an image when it receives an appropriate video signal, but what generates the video signal? Computers cannot send signals directly to a CRT monitor. They need a *display adapter* to process the computer's data into the video signal the system's display monitor requires. This display adapter circuitry is built into some computers, such as the Apple Macintosh. For others, such as those in the IBM PC family, a separate circuit card is added to provide display-adapter functions.

As mentioned, the monitor produces the display by drawing a series of scan lines down the screen, each line made up of hundreds of pixels. Thus, the screen display is a rectangular grid of pixel positions some number of pixels wide and some number of scan lines high. For a given image, each pixel is set to a certain brightness level for a monochrome display or a certain color and brightness for a color display.

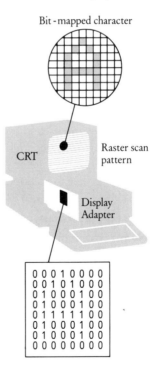

Figure 2. Conversion of a binary representation of the letter A *to a pixel, or* bit-mapped *image.*

The binary value that defines each pixel must be stored somewhere. Display adapters contain memory (called the *display buffer* or *frame buffer*) for storing the pixel values. The computer can create or modify images for display by writing or changing values in this memory. The amount of memory an image will require depends on the total number of pixels and the number of bits stored for each pixel. For example, a display adapter that can display 640 by 350 pixels with 4 bits per pixel (which allows 16 simultaneous colors) requires a 112,000-byte display buffer. Circuitry on the display adapter steps through this memory, reading pixel values and formatting them into the video signal that drives the monitor. (See Figure 2.)

Monochrome Display Adapters

As you would expect, monochrome display adapters produce a black-and-white or monochrome video signal to drive a monochrome monitor. A black-and-white display adapter stores only a single bit for each pixel. A pixel is either on, producing white, or off, producing black. This is the simplest of display adapters, but that doesn't mean it can handle only simple graphics. A standard Apple Macintosh has a display of this type and has very sophisticated graphics capability.

Monochrome display adapters that store more than 1 bit per pixel generally display *gray scale*. A multi-bit pixel is not simply on or off, but can have any one of a number of values. These values are treated as shades of gray, varying from black to white. The number of bits per pixel, called *pixel depth*, determines how many shades of gray are available. For example, 6 bits per pixel allows 64 shades of gray (since each bit can have only one of two values, a 6-bit pixel can have 2^6 values or 64 values). This type of display is seldom used in business, except in electronic publishing, but is used frequently in science and industry. Often, gray-scale displays are used for natural images in applications that don't require color, such as in medical imaging. The most popular pixel depths are 4 or 8 bits per pixel, which allow 16 or 256 levels of gray scale, respectively.

Color Display Adapters

On a color monitor, a particular shade of color is produced by combining various amounts of red, green, and blue. In a color display adapter, the pixel value specifies the amounts of each primary color that will produce the pixel's color. The two ways in which the pixel value determines the pixel color distinguish two types of color displays.

True-color or direct-color display adapters. In this type of display adapter, the pixel value directly specifies the pixel's color. For example, a display adapter might store 3 bits per pixel, with each bit specifying an on or off state for each color primary. In this display system, each pixel could be any one of eight colors ($2^3 = 8$). All 3 bits off would be black; all bits on would be white; red and blue on with green off would produce magenta, and so forth.

Consider a display board that stores 8 bits for each primary, or 24 bits total per pixel. In this board, each primary can have one of 256 levels of brightness, which gives the pixel a range of more than 16.7 million possible colors. This range approaches the total range of colors that can be perceived by the human eye.

Color-mapped or pseudocolor display adapters. Display adapters of this type contain a table called a *color look-up table (C.L.U.T)* or *palette*. A pixel's value specifies a location in this color-mapping table, the contents of which specify the levels of the RGB primaries that define the pixel's color. The number of bits allocated to each palette table location determines the total number of colors that can be displayed, while the number of bits per pixel determines the number of colors that can be displayed simultaneously.

Consider a display adapter that stores 4 bits per pixel and has a palette with 12 bits per entry (4 bits each for red, green, and blue). The 12-bit palette allows 4096 possible colors, but the 4-bit pixels allow only 16 of them to appear on the screen at the same time.

In such a display system, a pixel's value doesn't relate directly to its color. Depending on how the palette table assigns pixel values to colors, pixel value 0 might be black at one time, light blue at another, and orange some other time. You can instantly change the color of all pixels of a particular value simply by changing the value's assignment in the palette table. In fact, limited animation is possible without redrawing a display by simply cycling through colors in the palette table.

Graphics Processors

The computer's drawing speed often limits the level of sophistication an image can have. In computer graphics, faster is always better, and the push for improvement is constant. A graphics processor (GP) is a specialized pixel processor that provides extra hardware support for drawing graphics, thus improving performance. This type of board usually features dedicated screen memory and intelligent graphics microprocessors, which together unburden the host system of the problems of display management.

Until recently, graphics processors cost more than an entry-level desktop computer. Prices now are falling dramatically. A new generation of single-chip graphics controllers is reducing the cost of display drivers while delivering higher graphics performance. Texas Instruments, Intel, Hitachi, NEC (Nippon Electric Corp.), and Motorola are key players in this area.

Single-chip graphics controllers are superior to their multichip predecessors in two important ways. First, they handle computer memory with great efficiency. They can work with conventional memory chips or with a special form of random access memory (RAM) known as *dual-port RAM* or *video RAM*. Dual-port RAM enables the graphics processor to rapidly change the bit-image mapping of the memory without interrupting the stream of data to the display screen or printer. Second, the graphics processors can rapidly create basic image shapes. Working in tandem with specialized on-board firmware and user software, they can create graphics at blazing speeds.

For example, the Intel 82786 contains two independent on-chip processors. Its GP executes commands from the host processor and automatically updates graphics and text in the display's dedicated RAM or the host's memory. Meanwhile, the Intel chip's display processor independently collects bits from display memory and generates the video signal, which displays the graphics and text. The Intel chip and the host computer work independently, but they can share information and bit-mapped images when the application demands it.

Display Software

The CD ROM display system needs both hardware and software to create the graphics environment. The software provides a user interface, reads image data from the CD ROM disc, and displays the images.

Software system designers generally use a layered approach when developing a system. Rather than creating one large program that does everything, they divide the tasks into *modules* with different responsibilities. Each module receives instructions from the level above it and issues instructions to the level below it. By dividing software tasks in this way, the designer can reduce the system's overall complexity (see Figure 3).

In this layered scheme, the lowest level is hardware, not software. Moving up from the hardware, the layers traditionally have been the *device driver* layer, the *operating system* layer, and the *application program* layer.

Figure 3. The modular design of display system software. The data handler and device driver work together to format the data properly for display.

- The *device driver* is responsible for translating instructions from the computer into codes the hardware understands. A display device driver generally performs all tasks associated with the special characteristics of the display hardware. For example, display drivers can initialize the display hardware, read and write individual pixels, and in some cases calculate dimensions and draw characters, lines, and other shapes on the screen.

- The *operating system* usually provides a set of file access services that enable application programs to read and write files to disk. The *application*, sitting on top of all other layers, receives its instructions directly from the user. In carrying out these instructions, the application calls on services from the operating system, which in turn calls on services from the device drivers. The device drivers then manipulate the computer hardware to perform the desired task.

When the software system is layered, the application need not know how the operating system or device drivers carry out their tasks. The applications programmer is assured that, when the program calls for a particular operating system or device driver service, that task will be performed.

Previously, few programs have had to simultaneously process text, graphics, images, and sometimes sound, and certainly not in the tremendous volumes a CD ROM can store. Because of the diverse data types CD ROM applications can use, system developers may soon add yet another layer to the traditional arrangement. This new layer would lie between the applications program and operating system and would deal with the many data types stored on disc. For purposes of this discussion, we will call it the *data handler* layer. The data handlers process and format the data before sending it through the operating system to the device drivers to actually produce the display.

Trade-offs should be considered when deciding where to divide the responsibilities between data handlers and device drivers. On one hand, if the data handler does most of the work, the device driver can be straightforward and easy to design. A simple device driver is easier to modify than a complicated one, and therefore you can adapt it to other hardware configurations with little difficulty. On the other hand, functions based in a device driver tend to execute more quickly than those based in a data handler. The device driver knows the fine points of the hardware and can make optimizations that a data handler can't make. Placing more responsibilities in the device driver makes programming more difficult, but tends to improve system performance. This is true especially in display systems containing a graphics processor. In these systems, as many functions as possible should reside in the device driver to take maximum advantage of the GP's improved performance.

Consider the drawing of a filled polygon. A filled polygon is an area bounded by straight lines that is filled with a color (see Figure 4). Drawing a filled polygon is fairly difficult for a computer, requiring a rather large amount of programming. If the data handler is solely responsible for drawing the object, it must notify the device driver to write each pixel. This process is very slow, because the device driver must be called many times. Additionally, since the device driver doesn't know the display processor is drawing a filled polygon, it can't take advantage of the fact that the pixels being written often will be adjacent, which would enable most display systems to operate more efficiently. If this filled polygon function were in the device driver, the data handler would simply make a single call to the device driver to draw the object, specifying, for example, the position of each coordinate, the color of the boundary line, and the color of the interior. The device driver would know a polygon was being drawn and could use optimization techniques to speed up the operation. If polygon fill routines are in the device driver, a large, complicated program must be rewritten for each new display system. Locating the polygon fill routines in the data handler, however, would mean the fill routine need be written only once, regardless of how many different display systems the application is to run on.

Figure 4. A filled polygon.

Graphics User Interfaces

Graphics user interfaces are relatively new to desktop computer design. From a software developer's perspective, they are the "toolkits" of user interface and graphics display routines that provide application developers with a standard display framework. From the user's perspective, they are standardized user interfaces that give them a uniform way to interact with the application program. Graphics interface systems—such as the Microsoft Windows environment, Digital Research's GEM (Graphics Environment Manager), and the graphics toolbox used in the Apple Macintosh computer—are examples of intelligent graphics interface systems.

Developing applications to run under these graphics interfaces has a number of advantages. The system's manufacturer writes the device drivers for adapting the program to different display adapters. Also, these systems often provide a library of graphics programs and screen formatting features that simplify an application program's design and let users interact with the system in a consistent way. Many of them support a large variety of text fonts and sizes and can mix text and graphics on the screen.

Graphics user interfaces are proving popular with computer operators, but they do exact a price in host system operating speed. Since the programs are "resident" in memory, the host computer's processor must support them while performing calculations and at the same time operating the CD ROM drive. As a result, these interfaces are pioneering the way for hardware-dedicated graphics adapters that unburden the host processor of graphics responsibility.

Presentation Formats

Virtually all CD ROM applications will display text, and many will display graphics. You can use one of several different methods for recording both kinds of information. You can, for example, store a page of text as a string of characters, an indexed list of words or phrases, or a "snapshot" image of the original document. An illustration might be stored as thousands of pixel bits in a *bit-mapped* image, or as a *structured graphics metafile*, a list of codes that display hardware translates into pixels.

In this section we describe the most common image data structures, including bit-mapped images and structured graphics, but excluding character-coded text, which we discuss in Chapter 4.

Bit-Mapped Images

Converting images to *bit-mapped graphics* is the most popular technique for representing graphics. The term *bit-mapped graphics* actually means two slightly different things. In one sense, it refers to a computer display system in which the computer can access each point on the output display device individually and can operate on each point independently of all other points. This definition tells something about the nature of the system's display hardware. In its other sense, bit-mapped graphics refers to a way of storing and manipulating images. The bit-mapped image is represented by a collection of pixel values stored in some orderly fashion. A fixed number of bits represents each pixel value. The display hardware interprets the bits to determine which colors or gray levels to produce on the screen.

Natural Images

Natural images are those the viewer perceives as being scenes from the "real world," such as photographs and television reproduce. Natural images generally are stored in a bit-mapped form, but displaying them presents special problems in computer graphics because of the wide range of shading and color variation necessary to maintain adequate image quality. The care and handling of natural images are important considerations when a publisher specifies image data acquisition equipment, image storage formats on a CD ROM disc, and the display system the customer will use to view them.

Video images are an important source of natural images for use in CD ROM applications. They make up the bulk of the world's electronically stored pictures, portraits, and scenes. The spread of television production technology worldwide has spurred development of mature production equipment, which has been used to record millions of images in one or more of the world's three prevailing video formats—NTSC, PAL, and SECAM. Videotape and video disc libraries can make collecting, selecting, and editing images rapid. For example, CD publication for instruction on space science might use a wealth of NASA video materials. The space agency and private video publishers offer hundreds of thousands of pictures detailing the U.S. space program and solar system exploration.

135

Animating Bit-Mapped Images

Bit-mapped displays are animated by writing a new bit-mapped image into the display several times a second. The time it takes to read the bit map from the CD ROM disc and the time it takes to write the bit map into the display limit how fast images can be displayed. Depending on how large the bit map is, either or both of these limits are important. In fact, in small computers, both of these limits are reached very quickly and special techniques are required to overcome them.

One way around the problem is to redraw only part of the bit map each time. In many animation sequences, large areas of the display don't change from one frame to the next. Rather than redrawing the entire display for each frame, you really need redraw only the areas that change. Point-addressable (bit-mapped) graphic displays allow you to update only a selected area of the display, without changing the display's entire contents. This technique usually is called *frame delta* after the Greek letter *delta,* which in mathematics refers to a change in something. The key is limiting the amount of image data changed in each frame. When large areas of an image change in each frame, generating successive frames can slow you down to the point that the technique no longer helps.

Another technique often used is *sprite animation. Sprites* are objects represented as small bit maps. A sprite is placed in a scene by drawing its bit map at a specified location. Before the sprite is drawn, the background of the area it will fill is saved temporarily. To move the sprite, you erase it from its current location by redrawing the saved area of the background, and then you redraw the sprite in the new location. In using more than one sprite, you assign each a priority, and when two sprites overlap, the sprite with the higher priority appears on top of the other. In this way, one sprite will appear to pass behind the other one, giving the scene an illusion of depth.

In sprite animation, a background bit map, a series of bit maps for the sprites, and a list of all movements each sprite is to perform are stored on disc. The animation sequence can be thought of as a play or movie. The background bit map forms the stage or set, the sprites themselves are the actors, and the sprite movement list is a script that controls the animation sequence. In place of a movement list, you can store a small program that directs the sprites' motions. If the number and size of sprites allow rapid redrawing, animation can be smooth and sophisticated. Some systems even provide hardware support for sprites as part of the display system. On these machines, sprite animation is particularly attractive.

Structured Graphics

Structured graphics refers to a way of describing an image in terms of a set of simple geometric *primitives.* These primitives—such things as lines, arcs, ellipses, or rectangles—are the building blocks that construct the image. For example, an image of a part in a parts catalog would be composed of a number of lines, arcs, ellipses, and other shapes. Rather than storing the image itself, you store a set of instructions for drawing the objects that comprise it. This can save considerable storage space, but processing this type of image requires complex display software, which must contain a module that can interpret the structured graphics instructions and draw the appropriate objects.

Storing images as structured graphics has a number of advantages. As mentioned, savings in storage space on disc can be significant. If the images aren't compressed, all bit-mapped images of a particular size, no matter how complex or simple, always will require the same amount of storage space. With structured graphics, you don't really store the image, but rather instructions for drawing the image. Thus, if the image is simple (composed of few objects), you'll save space because you don't need to store very many instructions. However, more complex images (those composed of many objects) require more instructions, and eventually images can reach a point of complexity at which structured graphics require more storage space than does a bit-mapped image.

More important than possible space savings, though, is the flexibility that storing images as structured graphics provides. Structured graphic images generally have a great deal more hardware independence than do bit-mapped images. Because the image is stored as a set of instructions to draw simple geometric objects, each display system can present those objects to the best of its ability. On a high-resolution display system with lots of colors, the resulting image may look better than it will on a machine with lower resolution, but in either case it will be basically the same image. Although you can degrade a high-resolution bit map for display on a lower-resolution display system in some cases, this task can be computationally intensive and slow, and the results may not be acceptable.

Another important flexibility is the ability to zoom, pan, and rotate images. *Zooming in* enlarges an area of the image so you can examine fine detail; *zooming out* reduces the whole image for an overview. *Rotation* lets the user turn the image around to view it from different directions and orientations, possibly seeing relationships the original orientation hid or obscured. Zooming and rotation of a structured graphic are simple mathematical operations that can make the image significantly more useful.

Again, although you technically can zoom or rotate bit maps, on a small computer this can take hours, and the results usually aren't satisfactory.

You can also layer objects in structured graphics, assigning various parts of a drawing to different layers. The user then can choose which layers to display. For example, a CD ROM publication concerning the assembly of a complex machine might overlay each component according to its proximity to the viewer so the operator could strip off each image layer as needed or pull out the image of a single component hidden deep within the assembled part.

Structured graphics also deal with the aspect ratio problem with relative ease. A coordinate system with a square aspect ratio can display structured graphics designed for a rectangular aspect ratio—that is, of course, if the display's device driver corrects for the differences. This is simple because the primitives are defined in an abstract form that can be manipulated mathematically, and generally only a few points must be adjusted. For example, to draw a line, you need only transform its endpoints from the abstract coordinates to the device pixel coordinates. Transforming each point on the line isn't necessary.

Many CD publishers believe structured images give their CD publications a high degree of freedom from technological obsolescence in the CD playback system. Because the shapes are described, the quality of the CD-retrieved image can vary greatly depending on the sophistication of the customer's hardware. Structured graphics also enable a publisher to store images of complex text and symbols. Thus, structured graphics systems are the direction in which most hardware manufacturers are headed—a direction in which CD ROM publishers should also head when selecting a data-preparation system.

Note: A number of formal and informal structured graphics standards exist. They are described briefly in the glossary. These standards include GKS, IGES, NAPLPS, CGM, PHIGS, and DGIS.

Given all of these advantages, why not store all images as structured graphics? The answer is that not all images can be easily represented in this way. Structured graphics is effective only for images that you can readily break down and store as a collection of simple geometric objects. Such images as those in engineering or architectural drawings, charts, graphs, and other "line art" diagrams lend themselves to this type of representation. Structured graphics also work well for storing three-dimensional images of objects with simple surfaces. They don't represent "real world" images, such as photographs, well. Generally, images having large areas of fine detail that aren't highly repetitive are not appropriate for structured graphics.

Structured Graphics Metafiles

The file that contains the set of drawing instructions for a structured graphics image is called a *metafile*. The exact format of the instructions within the metafile depends on the interpreter software module (display driver) the user's computer system contains. Obviously, if you store the metafile in a different form than the display driver expects, the driver won't be able to display the graphics when it interprets the metafile. For example, Microsoft Windows has a module called GDI (Graphics Device Interface), which is responsible for interpreting a Windows metafile and drawing the graphics it describes. In the Apple Macintosh, a module called QuickDraw does the same thing. Unfortunately, a GDI metafile and a QuickDraw metafile are quite different and not interchangeable. If you want a disc to be usable on both systems, then you have a problem.

One possible solution would be to not try to make discs playable on both systems. Obviously, with this approach you must produce more discs, one for each computer system you intend to support. This is pretty much how software vendors currently deal with the problem of supporting multiple computer systems.

Another solution is to store two copies of each structured graphics image, one in Windows format and one in Macintosh format, on the disc. CD ROMs are large, and storing multiple copies of an image can take advantage of space you otherwise might waste. But what if you want the application to run on more than two systems? You could simply keep adding redundant copies of the image in each targeted format. One problem with this is the expense of creating these images. You can't store an image in several formats unless you've created it in these formats. If the drawing program your artist uses to create the image isn't capable of storing the image in all of the formats you want to use, the artist will have to draw the same image several times.

Rather than storing several copies of an image in system-specific formats, it might be better to store the image in a system-independent format and provide a different data handler for each target system. This data handler need only be written once for each target system to enable the system to display all images.

Animating Structured Graphics

As can bit-mapped animation, structured graphics can be animated by simply redrawing the entire display for each frame of the animation sequence. The delivery system will read a series of structured graphics images from the disc and draw them in rapid sequence. This type of animation suffers from the same slowness of data transfer from the disc and display drawing that limits bit-mapped animation. Again, special techniques can overcome these limits.

The frame delta technique described for animating bit-mapped graphics **139** also works for structured graphics. You can read the first frame of a structured image animation, then erase and redraw objects that move or change through a series of frame delta commands. This reduces the amount of data read from the disc and also the redraw time, since only those shapes that change are redrawn. As with bit-mapped graphics, this technique breaks down when too many changes occur between frames.

Another technique, which we will call *object animation*, is similar to sprite animation. The concepts of stage, actors, and script we discussed earlier apply. The stage is a structured graphics image that defines the background. The actors are a series of objects, each defined by a small list of structured graphic primitives. The script consists of a list of operations to be performed on the objects. Such things as moving, rotating, scaling (which changes the object's size), defining a new object, and deleting an old object can be listed. Animating images in this way can drastically reduce the amount of data read from the disc during animation. The system's drawing speed will still be a limiting factor, however.

Unfortunately, the only way to really overcome drawing speed limitations when dealing with structured graphics is with hardware assistance. The graphics processors described earlier can be a big help in this area.

Choosing a Display Format

To determine which image structure(s) are best for each publication, a publisher must consider a number of issues, including:

- The kind of images. Color photographs, line drawings, animation, charts, and black-and-white documents all have unique characteristics that may require entirely different processes to prepare and deliver them.

- The type of display the user's machine can produce.

- How much power the user's central processor uses and provides.

- How many images you need to store.

- How many different machines you intend to display the images on.

- How much you want the user to be able to manipulate images.

Deciding which type of graphics best suits your needs is perhaps the most important consideration. For example, if you want to show line graphs to compare stock prices, your graphical requirements will be different than if you wish to show photographic-quality pictures of products in a catalog. Displaying line graphs requires fairly simple graphics, and virtually any computer with graphics capability can do this. The display of photographic-quality images requires a much more sophisticated display system because of the high resolution and the range of colors involved. But even if you only want to draw a chart, you might add significant visual impact to that chart by drawing it over a background that is a photographic-quality picture.

Creating Digital Images

In many cases, you will need or wish to create original artwork when developing a CD ROM-based product. The term *artwork* in this case refers to images an artist or draftsperson creates on a computer. In general, any image created on the computer will be a structured graphic image, a bit-mapped graphic image, or possibly some combination of these two. The artist will, of necessity, create an image, using some kind of computer art system. These computer art generation systems come in two general types, depending on the kind of image they create.

Paint Systems

Paint systems are the generic name for computer art systems that produce bit-mapped graphic images. They generally are pixel-oriented, and the artist creates a picture by setting pixels to specific color values. The better paint systems allow a great deal of flexibility in how an artist manipulates the pixels, generally mimicking the more traditional techniques and tools artists use.

Basic features virtually all paint systems offer enable the artist to draw simple geometric shapes such as lines, rectangles, or circles, and also allow freehand drawing by simply tracking the motion of the artist's pointing device. They usually include a choice of brush sizes and shapes and can fill closed shapes such as rectangles and circles with a color. Generally, paint systems provide a palette of standard colors and let the artist also mix special colors and add them to the palette. These systems can also cut, paste, and merge graphics captured in a bit-mapped format. A paint system can edit any image in a bit-mapped data file, whether the artwork originally was a line drawing, block graphic, or digitized natural (video) image.

Advanced systems also may feature airbrushing and frisketing (using a mask with the airbrush), and translucency in colors for watercolor effects. Some systems allow you to extract textured patterns from an image and use them for painting. Some paint systems actually let you paint with polka-dot paint on a textured surface that resembles canvas.

Paint systems' capabilities and prices range widely. Generally, sophisticated systems are a complete package that includes the host computer, display system, and paint software. Many of these professional systems can capture and digitize images using TV cameras and then edit the artwork using the paint software. Recently, reasonably priced high-powered and professional paint systems have been marketed to run on personal computers, but prices for top-of-the-line systems still range from about $50,000 to $250,000.

A variety of pixel-editing, or *paint* programs are designed to let you manipulate captured electronic images. Most of these programs require that you first convert the scene to a bit-mapped format. But certain computer paint programs work only with specific image data file structures. These file structures can vary with the computer manufacturer and may be specific to a single computer (or display driver adapter) manufacturer.

Some data file formats, such as those used on DEC, IBM, and Apple desktop computers, are well defined, and a number of application programs and utilities allow pixel-by-pixel touchups. Other paint programs will work with specified image capture, with digitization, and with video processing boards.

Draw Systems

Draw system is being used here generically to mean a system that can create structured graphics images. Like paint systems, these systems' capabilities can be simple or quite complex. A very simple system might support only two-dimensional line drawings, while a sophisticated system might support three-dimensional modeling of solid objects with surface shading. Drawing systems have much in common with CAD (Computer Aided Design) systems, and in fact you can treat many CAD systems as drawing systems by simply ignoring the features that aren't graphics oriented.

A draw system differs from a paint system in that the artist manipulates distinct objects rather than pixels. The program includes commands for creating these objects, assigning them attributes (such as color), and manipulating them in various ways.

Drawing programs treat structured image elements as objects. Each object is defined by mathematical commands to create dots, lines, boxes, polygon shapes, and fill patterns. Because each element is defined mathematically, its location can be changed easily during editing. This lets a publisher select which elements the user will view as foreground and which as background.

Computer Animation Systems

Just as you need special systems to create still images, you also need special systems to create animation. Animation systems can be either bit-map oriented or object oriented. An animation sequence is composed of a series of frames presented sequentially. Each frame is an image, and must be created using either a paint or drawing program that is part of the animation system.

Animation systems are specially designed to deal with a large number of frames. Animation for television requires 30 frames per second, so a 60-second sequence requires 1800 frames. It is no longer considered economically feasible to have artists draw each frame, so most animation systems use what are called *key frames*. The animator decides which frames are key points in the motion, and these frames are drawn by hand. The computer then interpolates the frames between the key frames, drawing them automatically.

Digitizing Systems

In many cases, when creating a CD ROM product your source material will be on paper, film, or video. This is especially true when your CD ROM product will be based on a previous publication. To proceed, you will have to convert the original image to a machine-readable format that the computer can store and manipulate. This process of converting an image into computer form is called *digitizing* and requires special hardware.

For a bit-mapped system to display an image, the image must be divided into pixels. The process of converting an image into pixels is called *sampling* or *digitizing*. The terms often are used interchangeably although, strictly speaking, *sampling* refers to dividing an image into pixels and *digitizing* refers to the process of converting each sample from an analog, or continuously varying, form to a digital, or binary, form.

Sampling

Converting a picture into a digital image usually requires use of a scanning device, which scans the image, detecting minute variations in the light the image reflects. The scanner converts this reflected light to electrical (analog) signals proportional to the light intensity. It then *samples* this signal at regular intervals, and converts the signal amplitude of each sample to a binary value using an Analog-to-Digital converter (ADC). A display system reads these values and displays them as pixels. The degree to which the resulting image resembles the original picture depends on the number of bits stored for each sample and the number of samples, or pixels, stored for each image.

Information is lost in the sampling process. It is easiest to understand how this happens if you think of a photograph overlaid with a grid of small squares. The grid squares are the samples taken during the digitizing process. Each square represents one pixel of the encoded image. On the photograph, a square covers a fixed area that includes some internal detail. However, only one value is assigned to each square, so each square can represent only a single brightness level or color. Thus, all internal detail is lost in converting a square into a pixel.

The sampling frequency determines the amount of detail in an image, or the *image resolution*. The display device determines how many pixels can be displayed at one time, or the *display resolution*.

Matching image resolution to display resolution involves a number of design trade-offs. For example, an image sampled at 320 by 240 pixels completely fills the screen on a display device with a resolution of 320 by 240 pixels. On a display with a resolution of 640 by 480, it fills only a quarter of the screen. On a display with a resolution of 1280 by 960, this same image occupies only one-sixteenth of the display. In each case, software can enlarge the image to fill the display, but the result will look no better on the higher-resolution display than on the lower-resolution one.

This example teaches a couple of lessons. First, the sampling resolution of an image determines its quality. Secondly, the display resolution and the image sample resolution together determine the screen area an image occupies. If you wish to display the same image on display devices with different resolutions, you must carefully consider how best to store them.

Digitizing Monochrome Images

The number of bits used to encode each pixel, or the *pixel resolution*, is of major importance when encoding monochrome images. Also called *pixel depth*, an image's pixel resolution determines how many levels of brightness or gray scale it can have.

A four-level gray-scale system can generate images that feature white, black, and both light and dark gray. This requires that two bits be stored for each pixel. The following gray scales might be assigned: 00—black, 01—dark gray, 10—light gray, and 11—white.

In deciding how many bits to store for each pixel, you make a trade-off between the storage space an image requires and the quality of the display. Storing too few bits for each pixel can cause an undesirable side-effect known as *contouring*. Contouring happens when too many of the subtle shadings in the original image are compressed into the same gray level. Where previously the brightness changed in small steps, it now changes in big jumps. This makes an image look blotchy and unnatural. The lower right picture in Figure 1 shows a highly contoured image.

For most images, 4 bits per pixel (16 gray levels) will not prevent contouring, 6 bits per pixel (64 gray levels) will adequately represent the image, and more than 8 bits per pixel (256 gray levels) will almost never be required. Actually, 256 gray levels approaches the limit of human perception, and unless the image is being used for some kind of quantitative scientific purpose requiring that you record the precise light intensity of every pixel, 8 bits per pixel is all you would ever want to store.

Digitizing Color Images

To encode a color pixel, you must specify the brightness level for each of the three color primaries that comprise it. You can encode color and brightness information in a variety of ways, each having advantages and disadvantages. Choosing a coding technique is complicated by the varying requirements of different types of imaging and the range of ways that color display adapters work. You must find an image-encoding strategy that takes into account the type of image, the resolution required, and the various display adapters that will display the image.

RGB Encoding. As mentioned, a color monitor generates colors by combining various amounts of the RGB color primaries. The simplest code for color in this kind of system is three numbers, each representing the brightness level of one of the primaries. This, in fact, is how most color computer display systems specify color. Conveniently, the display hardware can use this coding; you don't have to translate it.

When color is stored as simple RGB values, the number of bits stored for each primary determines the range of colors that can be displayed. Storing 1 bit for each primary would allow eight colors; 2 bits per primary would allow 64 colors; and 8 bits per primary would allow about 16.7 million colors. Obviously, the more colors you wish to represent, the more bits you must store for each pixel and the more space each image will occupy on the disc. For natural image displays, storing 4 bits per primary (12 bits total per pixel) allows you to specify 4096 colors, about the minimum pixel depth acceptable for high-quality images. Some expensive computer animation systems used to produce movie and TV special effects store as many as 16 bits per primary (48 bits total), but the color shadings this produces really are beyond the range of human perception. Storing color with this much precision isn't necessary. Eight bits per primary color are about the most you will ever need for a CRT monitor display.

Just as different coordinate systems can specify locations in space (for instance, rectangular, polar, spherical), coordinate systems other than RGB can specify color. We discuss several widely used systems below.

HSV color system. One popular color system is *HSV,* which stands for *Hue, Saturation, and Value.* Think of a color wheel with all possible color hues (or gradations) around its edge, starting with red, then progressing to magenta, then to blue, cyan, green, yellow, orange, and back to red. Along the wheel's circumference the colors are pure. They become more pastel as your eye moves toward the center, at which point all have become white. The *hue value* specifies an angle on this color wheel, which selects a hue of the color being specified. The *saturation* specifies the distance from the center, and thus the purity of the color. The *value* coordinate specifies how bright the color that the hue and saturation coordinates specify will be.

The HSV color system is important for two reasons. First, HSV represents color in a way artists naturally understand. It models colors in the same way that artists think about them and for this reason is used in many computer painting systems. Selecting a hue coordinate, with saturation and value set to 1, is like selecting a pure pigment. Decreasing the saturation has the effect of mixing in white, and to decrease the value is to mix in black. The other reason for the HSV color system's importance is that the Postscript page-layout language incorporated in many computer-based publishing systems uses it.

YUV color system. Another important color system is *YUV* (the letters *Y, U,* and *V* don't stand for anything in particular). Like the RGB color system (and unlike HSV), YUV is a rectangular coordinate system. In it, brightness information and color information are separate. The Y axis represents brightness (or *luminance,* as it is called in television) and the position on the UV plane specifies the color (or *chrominance*), the U axis being in the blue-green direction and the V axis in the red-green direction. This is difficult to visualize, but the important point is that the brightness and color are separate.

One immediate advantage of YUV coding is that it gives you a monochrome image for free, since each pixel's Y value is the brightness value you would store for it in encoding a monochrome image. Another benefit is that YUV takes advantage of the way the human eye responds to color.

146

The eye is less sensitive to fine shadings of color than it is to brightness. Because of this, you can cut back on the information you store, storing color information at a lower resolution than brightness information, without significantly affecting perceived image quality. When you store color information at a reduced resolution, small regions of adjacent pixels all have the same color. For example, a 640 by 480 pixel image stored with 24 bits per pixel requires 921,600 bytes of storage. If, instead, the Y information is stored at full resolution, but the U and V are stored at a resolution of 320 by 240, only 460,800 bytes are needed. In the displayed image, each 2-pixel by 2-pixel cell will have different brightness or Y values but the same color. Nothing is really lost by throwing away the detail in the color information, because the eye can't distinguish it anyway.

One problem with storing an image in a color system other than RGB is that virtually all display systems today work with RGB values. Thus, you must convert it from the form it was stored in on the disc to RGB before the display can process it. Translating images into a new color system takes a lot of computation and perhaps too much time on some small computer systems. A fast computer system, or a slower one with special display hardware that works directly from the color system the image data is stored in, takes better advantage of alternative color-encoding systems.

Digital Scanning Equipment

Converting printed images to a form the computer can manipulate requires that the image be digitized. The equipment that does this includes digitizing tablets and a variety of optical scanning devices.

Digitizing tablets. A *digitizing tablet* is basically a pointing device. The user holds a pen or puck, moving it over the tablet's surface. Embedded in the surface of some tablets is a grid of wires that can be energized with pulses of electric current to produce a magnetic field. A pickup coil in the pen senses this magnetic field, by knowing which grid wires were energized. The field strength it receives determines the pen's location on the tablet. The user presses one or more buttons on the pen to cause the computer to read the pen's position and store the associated value. In this way, you can trace over a paper drawing and build a list of coordinates for points of interest in the drawing. Most drawing programs allow the use of tablets as pointing devices for input.

Flatbed scanners. *Flatbed scanners* use CCD (charge-coupled device) linear arrays to scan a printed document (we will explain CCD devices further in our discussion of video cameras). Most flatbed scanners look like compact photocopiers. An original is placed face down on a glass surface, and the horizontal CCD sensing array moves vertically (back and forth) from underneath. Usually, a fluorescent lamp illuminates the document being scanned and, depending on the light source and photodetector used, some flatbed scanners are blind to certain colors in the original. Scanning resolutions typically vary between 75 and 300 dots per inch (dpi). A few prototype scanner systems can record resolutions of up to 400 dpi.

Most scanners let the host system control the image area being scanned. The system can bring the full resolution of the scanner array to bear on documents ranging from business-card size to 11 by 17 inches. Scanners generally output data in either parallel or serial form in a bit-map image format, not in video. Some scanners allow the host system to capture two- or four-level gray-scale data. Others merely allow the operator to set the threshold level at which the scanner will distinguish white-to-black transitions in images. Yet others are part of a system that captures letters, analyzes their shapes, and converts them to equivalent ASCII code values. These systems are called *optical character recognition* (OCR) devices. We describe them in more detail in Chapter 4.

Color scanners also are available, and work in a fashion similar to monochrome scanners, but most of them must scan the document three times in succession to produce the three-color bit maps that make up the image. The illumination source is three special mercury vapor lamps that have strong emission colors matching the red, green, and blue primary colors.

With a very few exceptions, most flatbed scanner systems cannot handle mixtures of text and graphics on the same page. The few systems that can cost about five times the price of those that perform either OCR or graphics digitizing alone. So generally the publisher must break out the images from the text. Tagging those images with their appropriate text is a problem for CD ROM publishers that currently is being tackled by makers of CD publishing equipment.

Laser image scanners. A new approach for scanning at ultrahigh resolution involves the use of a *laser image scanner.* In this technology, a rotating laser beam scans image elements at resolutions approaching a few ten-millionths of an inch. The low-power laser does not harm the original, and the reflection of the microscopic laser beam spot effectively produces a raster-scanned video signal in a nearby photoreceptor.

The technology is already at work, using three-color laser beams to enlarge rare original photographs. Its use with priceless and fragile documents, microfilm originals, and works of art is being explored.

Drum scanners. *Drum scanners* are practical when you need to get images of very high resolution from a flexible two-dimensional original. The original document is attached to a rotating cylindrical drum. A precision mechanism slowly advances the rotating drum past a light sensor. Very high positional accuracy can be achieved because the optical sensor is mounted in a fixed position, the diameter of the drum is known, the rotational speed is controlled very accurately, and the lead screw that advances the drum is manufactured to very high tolerances.

In addition, some drum scanners can accept original documents that are several feet across. This often is needed to convert engineering drawings and large X-ray originals. Drum scanners are slower than flatbed systems, but offer greater positional accuracy and far higher resolution.

Video digitizers. A video digitizer (also called a *frame grabber*) is basically a TV camera with a special display adapter board. A normal display adapter board contains an image memory and circuitry to step through the memory and send pixels to the monitor. A video digitizer contains the image memory and circuitry to write pixels to memory as the camera sends them. Much of the circuitry for video digitizers is similar to that of display adapters, and most video digitizers can also function as display adapters.

Video digitizers generally are designed to receive input from normal TV cameras and, because of this, they can't achieve very high resolutions. The NTSC television signal is inherently limited to about 480 lines of resolution, so most video digitizers allow resolutions of 640 by 480 pixels or less, with 512 by 400 pixels a common density. Note that the video input to the digitizer need not be a TV camera, but can be any video source that provides a compatible signal, such as video disc players or videotape. So the vast library of existing videotape material can be a source of images for CD ROM products.

A wide variety of video digitizers are available, and you need to consider the following characteristics when deciding which to use:

- Does the digitizer produce monochrome or color images?

- How many bits per pixel does it produce?

- What resolution or resolutions does it provide?

- Which types of video input (NTSC composite video or separate RGB inputs) does the digitizer accept?

- What is the conversion time for a frame?

- Which computer systems will it work with?

- What type of file structure does the digitizer create?

Video cameras. Video cameras can contain many different sensing elements and signal output formats. The majority of camera systems use vidicon tubes as the image-sensing element. A vidicon tube, like the cathode ray tube, contains an electron gun and a screen. In the vidicon tube, however, the screen is a thin photoconductive film rather than a glass plate coated with phosphor.

In a *color vidicon camera,* a special color filter matrix mounted in the vidicon tube enables the tube to distinguish colors. This filter matrix reduces the camera's ultimate resolution to below that of monochrome-only cameras, because the sensing mechanism that actually captures the image light levels must be divided into three areas—one for sensing each primary color. Nevertheless, color vidicon cameras are well suited to many portrait forms of color image capture, and they are a proven technology.

An alternative to using a color vidicon camera is to use a high-resolution (up to 1000 lines horizontal) monochrome camera in conjunction with a rotating color filter assembly. By focusing the camera through successive color filters, you can assemble a high-resolution image. This is the system astronomers and NASA use to compile high-resolution images from space.

A rapidly emerging technology is challenging the vidicon camera's supremacy in image capture. As mentioned, CCD cameras use a solid state image-sensing element called a *charge-coupled device.* Two forms of CCD imagers currently exist. The first uses a high-resolution linear array of sensors (usually between 512 and 2048) to sweep across an image scene. The electronic image is built up line by line as a rotating mirror traverses the image field. While the CCD sensor fixes the resolution width of the image, you can reduce the mirror's vertical scan rate to produce resolutions matching those of the horizontal axis, or, you can speed up the scan for lower pixel densities.

The other style of CCD camera uses a fixed horizontal and vertical array of pixel sensors. This approach freezes the resolution limits of the camera to match the pixel count of the image chip. The CCD camera's silicon array sensors can align each pixel sensor much more accurately than can conventional vidicon image sensors. This positional accuracy reduces geometric distortion. That characteristic can be important to CD publishers who need to reproduce graphic material with great accuracy.

149

Most CCD cameras scan in the range of 256 by 256 pixels to 500 by 400 pixels. Eastman Kodak and Tektronix are developing larger single-chip CCD imaging arrays capable of scanning an entire page at once at resolutions of greater than 150 pixels per scanned inch. Video camera makers should be able to buy these over 1-megapixel sensors by some time in 1987.

Both camera types use conventional optics and accept a variety of filters for specialized applications. Postproduction video processing systems can modify the analog image before it is digitized for CD ROM editing and premastering.

Some video scanners work with color slide transparency originals. These are scanned and converted into NTSC-compatible or RGB video signals which can be digitized using a video digitizer. With some video scanners, the operator can scan, crop, and enlarge selected areas of an image. This can greatly speed the production process, as a publisher can compose images before scanning.

Flying spot scanner. When film transparencies are available for scanning, *flying spot scanners* offer very high resolution. These systems employ a single photoreceptor and a high-resolution CRT display to "scan" a film image from behind.

In a flying spot scanner, the film transparency is placed over the screen of the CRT. A single spot on the CRT is illuminated, and the light from this spot passes through the transparency and falls on the photosensor. The illuminated spot is moved over the screen of the CRT in a raster pattern that covers the entire transparency, and variations in the amplitude of the photoreceptor's output signal correspond to variations in the gray scale of the transparency's image. Color scanning is achieved using red, green, and blue filters, in sequence, over the photoreceptor.

Computing Image Size

The storage space an image requires is a function of the number of pixels in the image and the space required to store coding for each pixel. This can be computed using the following formula:

Size = (Height x Width x Bits) / 8

Where:

Height is the number of pixels displayed vertically.

Width is the number of pixels displayed horizontally.

Bits is the number of bits stored per pixel.

This formula computes the storage space required in bytes to store an image that hasn't been compressed. When the image is compressed, this number is multiplied by the compression factor to get the space required.

When using a scanner to digitize images, the values of height and width can be determined as follows:

Height = Vertical Dimension x Vertical Resolution

Width = Horizontal Dimension x Horizontal Resolution

Where:

Vertical Dimension is the height of the page being scanned (generally measured in inches).

Horizontal Dimension is the width of the page being scanned (generally measured in inches).

Vertical Resolution and *Horizontal Resolution* are the number of pixels per unit length of the scanning device in the two directions (generally given as dots per inch, or dpi). Often these are the same, but not always.

An 8½-by-11-inch page that is scanned at 1 bit per pixel using a page scanner with a horizontal resolution of 300 dpi and a vertical resolution of 100 dpi requires more than 350,000 8-bit bytes when stored as an uncompressed monochrome image.

Height = 11 x 100 = 1100

Width = 8.5 x 300 = 2550

Size = (1100 x 2550 x 1) / 8 = 350,625

Converting Image Formats

In addition to the problems of getting noncomputer images into computer form, a publisher often must convert image data from one computer format to another. The image's form may already be machine-readable, but may not be readable by the targeted display system. The conversion of images from one computer format to another is a broad and nebulous subject because of the multiplicity of formats in which you can store the data. To make this discussion more manageable, we will consider each of three broad areas separately.

Reformatting Images

Sometimes you will need to convert bit-mapped images from one color-coding format to another. For example, if your video digitizer produces RGB output, but you want to store the image on CD ROM in YUV form, you will need a program to convert the data. Similarly, you may need to convert a structured graphics metafile into an equivalent metafile encoded in a different form (such as converting an Apple Macintosh QuickDraw metafile into a Microsoft Windows GDI metafile).

Converting Bit Maps to Structured Graphics

In other cases, you might want to convert a bit-mapped image to a structured graphics image. Understanding the conversion of bit-mapped image data into structured graphics is important because most digitizers or scanners produce a bit map, but you may want to store the images as structured graphics to conserve space. Bit maps can take up a lot of disc space; an 11-by-17-inch document scanned at 300 dpi produces a bit map larger than 2 MB; a structured graphics file of the same image might require only 30 to 40 KB. Structured graphics also allow certain special effects, such as zooming, that are impractical in bit-mapped images—another good reason to convert formats.

Converting bit-mapped images to structured graphics (or *raster-to-vector conversion*, as it is called) is very difficult. A bit-mapped image is simply a large mass of dots, and the problem you face is figuring out which dots belong to which lines. A human being has no trouble spotting the lines, but the task of instructing a computer how to do this is not simple. Fortunately, a number of companies have solved the problem to some degree, and software is available to perform this conversion (see the Resources section, Appendix B).

Converting NonImage Data

This category is somewhat catchall, and publishers probably will have to deal with these conversion problems on a case-by-case basis.

For example, you might want a publication to display bar charts of demographic data. You could have the charts drawn manually using a draw program, but if the tables of numbers were already available on a computer, you could also write a program to automatically produce the charts from the tables. Obviously, you need to weigh the cost of writing the program against the cost of having the charts drawn.

Issues in Image Processing

In its broadest sense, *image processing* is any manipulation of images by computer. Here, though, we will use the term more restrictively to cover the areas of image enhancement, image compression, and dithering.

Image Enhancement

Basically, *image enhancement* is a process of "touching up" an image to improve its appearance or to cause particular features to stand out. This can be done manually using a paint program or algorithmically using techniques we describe later.

To get quality images on a CD ROM, you are better off starting out with a quality original and digitizing it with quality equipment than trying to enhance a poor image using image-processing techniques. These enhancement techniques can be computationally intensive and slow. If a publication is to include a thousand images, you probably won't have time to touch up each one, so any effort you invest in high-quality originals is well spent. Sometimes you'll be forced to use poor-quality originals or inferior digitizing equipment. In these cases, image processing techniques can improve the quality of your CD ROM images.

Contrast Enhancement

Contrast is a measure of the brightness difference between the bright and dim areas of an image. An image is said to have *low contrast* or *high contrast* depending on whether this difference is small or large, respectively. The human eye can't easily distinguish similar levels of brightness, so detail is less discernible in low-contrast images than it is in higher-contrast ones. Using contrast-enhancement techniques, you can adjust an image's contrast range to show the maximum detail. For example, you can compensate for underexposure or overexposure in a photograph. Of course, you can't create detail the original image never had through contrast enhancement, but the technique can bring out existing detail.

Pseudocoloring

Pseudocoloring is another technique for enhancing detail. In this technique, gray levels that are very close together, and thus hard to distinguish among, are assigned different colors that make the difference noticeable. For example, in an X ray of body organs, two types of tissue with similar X-ray absorption characteristics might have similar gray scale values and be hard to distinguish on the film. You could pseudocolor the image, assigning one of the gray levels a red color and the other green, to distinguish the two tissue types. Color assignment is arbitrary and has nothing to do with the objects' true colors; hence the name *pseudocoloring*.

Pseudocoloring can be used to color black-and-white images—a technique now being applied to old movies to the chagrin of many film purists. You can also apply it to color images, substituting one color value for another to arbitrarily change the color. Photographs might show a red sun in a green sky, for instance. This can be done for aesthetic reasons, to highlight detail otherwise unclear, or simply to add variety to images.

Filtering or Smoothing

Filtering or *smoothing* techniques remove certain kinds of noise or distortion from an image. A weak TV picture marred by "snow" is an example of a noisy image. In this case, the noise appears as random tiny white dots that degrade the image's quality. In other cases, the noise might be regular or periodic rather than random, but in any case noise is a disturbance to the image that you can correct. Filtering can also soften the edges of or blur an image.

Edge Enhancement

Edge enhancement is a type of filtering that sharpens a blurred image. Soft edges can be made harder and more distinct. Enhancing edges unfortunately tends to amplify image noise and in excess can produce an unpleasant harshness.

Correcting Geometric Distortion

Some images sources, such as vidicon cameras, introduce geometric distortion in the images they produce. Another source of distortion is aspect ratio mismatch, when the image's aspect ratio differs from that of the monitor. This distortion might cause circles to appear oval or egg-shaped or might make the corner of an image appear stretched or compressed. In some instances the lenses in the optical system cause these distortions, and in other cases imperfections in the scanner's optical sensor or imaging surface cause them. When precise geometry is needed, these distortions should be corrected.

Depending on the type and severity of the distortion, correcting it can be computationally expensive and very time-consuming. Also, you must calibrate the geometric correction to the piece of digitizing or video equipment you are using, and if you change equipment you must recalibrate. Even two cameras of the same model made by the same company can have very different geometric distortion characteristics.

Image Compression

The one type of image processing that will concern almost all CD ROM publishers is *image compression*. Natural images can gobble up huge amounts of CD ROM memory. You can easily fill a CD ROM disc with fewer than 1000 complex images—each requiring hundreds of kilobytes of space. Large image data files can make rapid transfer of data from a CD ROM disc impractical and can severely limit a system's ability to rapidly access or to animate images. If you can send compressed data to the computer, and then expand it in the computer, your system works more efficiently.

A CD ROM drive transfers data at a rate of 150 KB per second. This transfer rate is often referred to as the *bandwidth*. At this bandwidth a 300 KB image file would require at least 2 seconds to be read from the disc—not counting the time it would take to find the image in the first place. Two seconds is a long time in computer terms, and could also be frustrating for the user. Animation, which requires a continual update of 15 to 30 frames per second, would be impossible.

Clearly, if the image file size can be compressed, the transfer time will lessen, reducing the total time required to display the image. The down side to this is that the compressed image file must be decompressed before it can be displayed. Decompression also takes time to perform, and if done in software may take more time than was saved by reducing the transfer time. When rapid display updating is necessary (such as in animation), the display system may require special hardware to perform the decompression.

As with most issues in computer imaging, choosing the best data-compression scheme is quite involved. The method you choose should be the one best suited for the type and number of images you will be storing on a disc, the display hardware your customers will use, and the speed with which the images must be displayed. No one method is best.

Recoverability is a term you often encounter in dealing with image compression. A *recoverable* compression algorithm is one that reproduces the original data when decompressed. A *nonrecoverable* algorithm destroys some of the original data and does not reproduce an exact match when the data is decompressed. Generally, nonrecoverable compression algorithms give higher compression factors, but, of course, they introduce distortion into the resulting image. With some images this is a problem, and with others it isn't, so you must make design trade-offs.

Figure 5. Linear and non-linear delta encoding tables.

Input delta to encode

156

Delta to use when decoding

a. Linear delta encoding range

255

7	14	7
6	13	6
5	12	5
4	11	4
3	10	3
2	9	2
1	8	1
0	7	0
-1	6	-1
-2	5	-2
-3	4	-3
-4	3	-4
-5	2	-5
-6	1	-6
-7	0	-7

-255

b. Non-linear delta encoding range

255

Value	Code	Range
64	14	255
32	13	64 / 63 / 32
16	12	31 / 16
8	11	15 / 8
4	10	7 / 4
2	9	3 / 2
1	8	1
0	7	0
-1	6	-1
-2	5	-2 / -3
-4	4	-4 / -7
-8	3	-8 / -15
-16	2	-16 / -31
-32	1	-32 / -63
-64	0	-64

-255

Run-Length Encoding

Some images, especially in computer-generated graphics, contain large areas of the same color. Several scan lines may have pixels with one color value. In these cases, you need not store the value of each pixel; instead, you store the color and a count of the number of pixels of that color. This coding is known as *run-length encoding.*

Run-length encoding compresses images by storing only the color value and number of pixels in a single-color sequence. For each color change a flag bit signifies whether the new color value will apply to one pixel or several pixels; the color value follows, and then the "run length," which tells how many sequential pixels have that color value. When long stretches of pixels in an image share the same values, run-length encoding can produce worthwhile compression ratios. How much compression you can achieve depends on the number and size of areas of the same color that an image contains.

Run-length encoding tends to work poorly for natural images because of the large areas of subtle shading they contain. A stretch of blue sky might contain dozens of subtle shadings of blue. This would produce very short run lengths, providing little data compression.

Delta Encoding

Natural images tend to have large areas where only slight color variations occur. In these areas, the pixel values along a scan line change very little from one pixel to the next. This is not true for edges the image contains, but it is frequently true over large portions of the image. *Delta encoding* takes advantage of this characteristic to reduce the number of bits required to store the image.

With delta encoding, you don't store the actual value of each pixel along a scan line; instead you store the amount that must be added to the current pixel value to produce the value of the next pixel. You store the true value for the first pixel on each line, but thereafter you store a series of differences, or *deltas,* for each subsequent pixel. This can save storage space, because it takes fewer bits to store a small number than it does to store a large number, and the assumption is that the range of deltas will be small relative to the range of the true pixel values.

When encoding the image for the disc, you can store the actual deltas in the encoded image or, alternatively, you can store code values that represent the deltas. Figure 5a illustrates the code table for a hypothetical delta-encoding system that can be used to encode a series of 8-bit pixels using a 4-bit code.

This illustration shows, for example, when encoding the image, a delta value of -4 produces a code value of 3 to be stored in the encoded image. When decoding, a code value of 3 would indicate that a delta of -4 should be applied to the current pixel value to produce the next pixel value. This table illustrates a *linear encoder*, which means that spacing between adjacent deltas in the system is uniform.

Notice that this system can encode only a fairly small range of deltas. Although pixel-to-pixel differences can range from -255 through $+255$, the encoder can only represent deltas in the range -7 through $+7$. If the image being encoded actually contains deltas outside this range (which is quite likely), then the encoded image will contain errors. These errors produce what is called *slope overload distortion*. This type of distortion occurs whenever the difference between one pixel and the next is too large to be encoded. Places where large pixel differences exist generally correspond to the edges of objects in a picture, and the effect of slope overload distortion is a blurring or softening of edges.

Figure 6 illustrates this effect. A part of this original image shown in 6a contains scan lines that have a series of dark pixels (with a pixel value of 70), followed by a series of lighter pixels (with a pixel value of 120). At the dark-to-light transition, a delta of 50 occurs. However, our encoder is only able to encode a maximum delta of 7. So in this decoded image, rather than making the dark-to-light transition in one leap of 50, the transition is made in smaller steps of 7. The decoded pixels would have values of 77, 84, 91, 98, 115, and 120, requiring 6 steps to make the transition that ideally should occur in a single step. Figure 6b shows the result.

Although linear delta encoding in the example above theoretically would allow 2:1 compression, this could not be achieved in practice. This particular encoder would produce quite severe distortion. Generally, when using linear delta encoding, you can achieve only 1 or 2 bits per pixel of reduction (from an 8-bit original) before slope overload distortion becomes objectionable. This allows compression factors of 1.125:1 to 1.25:1.

One way to reduce the effects of slope overload distortion is to use a *nonlinear encoder*. In a nonlinear encoder, the range of deltas that correspond to different code points isn't uniform. Figure 5b illustrates a hypothetical nonlinear encoder. You can see that a pixel-to-pixel difference of -1 would be encoded as a 6, or that any pixel-to-pixel difference from 8 through 15 would be encoded with the value 11. When decoding the code value 6, a delta of -1 is applied to produce the next pixel, and when decoding 11, the delta used is 8. You can encode a broader range of deltas using this type of encoder, but the coding of many of the deltas will not reflect their exact values.

158

Even with the nonlinear encoder, the exact value of the maximum possible delta cannot be encoded, so slope overload distortion still will occur. In fact, you can encode very few deltas precisely, and deltas that can't be encoded precisely will have slope distortion. Despite this, nonlinear delta encoding still is superior to linear encoding.

The nonlinear encoder can represent a wider range of deltas than can the linear encoder. Because of this, when slope overload distortion occurs, the decoded value approaches the correct value more quickly than with linear encoders, so the distorted area is smaller and less noticeable. Also, when brightness levels change rapidly, the eye is less sensitive to the absolute level than during slower changes. Thus, even though a large delta in the input image necessitates a large delta in the decoded image, the precision of the coding in representing the deltas isn't so important. The distortions occur only in those places where the eye is less sensitive to the error.

Figure 6 illustrates this principle. The transition from 70 to 120 would occur in a step of 32, taking us to 102, and then steps of 16 and 2, taking us to 120. Where the linear encoder requires six steps to make the transition, this nonlinear one requires only two, resulting in much less distortion.

The example is one of many types of nonlinear delta-encoding schemes. Using this type of trick, you can radically compress data without objectionably distorting the images it produces. But you must carefully decide the trade-off between compression and distortion.

a. Original image   b. Delta encoded using   c. Delta encoded using
                              linear encoder   nonlinear encoder

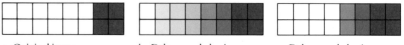

Figure 6. Effects of linear and nonlinear encoding on the displayed image.

Huffman Codes or Optimal Codes

Most encoding systems for storing digital data use *fixed-length codes.* This means the same number of bits are used to encode each code point. ASCII, for example, is a fixed-length code that uses 8 bits to store each character. However, in text, various characters don't occur with the same frequency. The letter *e,* for instance, occurs far more frequently than the letter *z.* To save space when the items you are storing occur at various frequencies, you can use a Huffman code, which assigns frequently occurring items codes with few bits and infrequently occurring items codes with more bits. The code for the letter *e* might use only 3 bits, whereas the code for the letter *z* might use 12 bits.

Most images tend to contain large areas of a single color, so certain color values occur more frequently than others. Because of this, images are candidates for data compression using Huffman codes. Also, as mentioned in the discussion of delta coding, most images not only have large areas of the same color, but they have even more areas in which the differences between adjacent pixels are small. For this reason, Huffman encoding an image composed of deltas achieves even greater compression than converting true pixel values to Huffman code.

Since Huffman demonstrated a way to produce optimum codes, why don't we always use them? Huffman codes have basically two shortcomings. They are variable-length codes, so you can't jump into the middle of a Huffman-encoded image or document and begin decoding it. Huffman-encoded data can be understood only by starting at the beginning. The other disadvantage is that Huffman codes contain no error protection. A bad bit anywhere in a Huffman-encoded image will cause all data following it to be decoded as total garbage. Worse yet, the computer can't even tell that an error occurred and attempt to correct it. In addition to these problems, encoding and decoding using Huffman codes can be pretty time-consuming.

Facsimile Encoding Schemes

For more than 20 years, the most common method of transmitting images has been through facsimile machines (*fax* machines). The CCITT (Consultative Committee on International Telephone and Telegraph) defines international standards for facsimile encoding and transmission. The organization has defined four standards, which it calls *groups.* Groups 1 and 2 define analog devices, and so are not useful for CD ROM. Groups 3 and 4 define digital devices, and the compression standards they set can be very useful for CD ROM.

The transmission component of a facsimile machine is basically a flatbed document scanner that produces a large monochrome bit map with a single bit per pixel. As the machine converts the bit-mapped image, it transmits it over the telephone lines. To speed the transmission, it compresses the image. Compression has been a major concern for the engineers designing fax machines, and the technology they have developed is often applied to bit-map data compression for CD ROM documents.

CCITT Group 3 encoding specifies two ways of compressing a bit map. The first technique is a one-dimensional, modified Huffman-encoding method. Each scan line of the bit map is encoded using run-length encoding. The runs then are further compressed using a Huffman code that the standard specifies. The Huffman-encoded images consume from 10 percent to 20 percent as much space as the original images. The second type of compression is a two-dimensional technique called *READ* (relative element address designate). The first line is encoded using the one-dimensional method just described. Then a number of the following lines will be encoded using an encoding scheme that describes differences from the previous line. The standard encodes and transmits blocks of from two to seven lines in this way. The READ-encoded images usually take from 6 percent to 12 percent as much storage space as the original.

The CCITT Group 4 standard builds on the second Group 3 encoding technique, but does not transmit error correction data; the transmission system handles error correction. With less data to transmit, this method can achieve even greater compression than Group 3 facsimile encoding, using only READ encoding. The Group 4 fax machine assumes that the first line in an image is a row of white pixels. It then encodes each line as a series of changes from the previous line, and the entire image is transmitted as one large block. Compression using the Group 4 standard can reduce an image to from 3 percent to 10 percent of its original size.

Dithering

Many display systems can display only a limited number of gray levels. In fact, a great number display only black and white. When you try to display natural images on such a display system, severe contouring results and the image is almost worthless. A process called *dithering* can help give the illusion of more gray levels, producing a more realistic image.

With print media, *halftones* solve a similar problem. In the halftone process, the image is converted into a large number of tiny dots. Multiple gray levels are achieved by varying the size of the dots; the larger the dots in a region, the darker the gray level produced. This works because the human eye, when confronted with detail too small for it to resolve, simply averages the light intensity over that area. What we see in a halftone is varying levels of gray rather than black dots of varying sizes on a field of white.

In the world of computer imaging, dithering solves the problem. Dithering also trades upon the eye's tendency to blur small regions of black and white into an intermediate level of gray. In dithering, small regions of pixels are treated as a single larger pixel. You can vary the gray level of the composite pixel cell by turning on different numbers of pixels in the cell. Figure 7 shows the patterns a 2-pixel by 2-pixel cell can have, allowing the formation of five pseudo-gray levels. You can create more gray levels by using larger cells that contain more pixels to be turned on in varying combinations. Dithering can also be used on displays that support more than two gray levels. In this case, you can get more gray levels while sacrificing less spatial resolution than is the case with two-level displays.

Loss of spatial resolution is the primary drawback to dithering. Using a 2-pixel by 2-pixel dither cell, for example, cuts the display's effective resolution in each direction in half. For this reason, you need a fairly high-resolution display to get a reasonably large number of gray levels using this kind of dither. This technique works especially well for printing gray levels on laser printers, for which very high resolutions are inherent. It works less well on video displays unless they are very high resolution.

This technique also works for color displays. Since each RGB color plane is treated as if it were a monochrome plane, you can dither them separately. For example, a display with 1 bit per pixel per color plane normally can display only eight colors. By using dithering with 2-pixel by 2-pixel cells, you can produce five gray levels per color plane, which allows 125 different colors on the same display. Of course, again, the main drawback is that spatial resolution is sacrificed.

An *ordered dither* is a variation of the dither technique that reduces spatial resolution loss somewhat at the expense of adding some unnatural texturing to the image. A good deal of research has been conducted into various dithering techniques, and some can produce very good results.

Dithering can be used in reverse to create a continuously toned gray-level image from a bilevel bit map. In this case, the input image is divided into a number of cells. The pixels in each cell are counted, and that number is stored as the gray level that is associated with the cell. Again, some resolution is lost with the technique, but it enables a certain amount of data

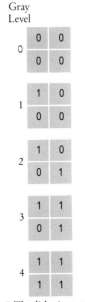

Figure 7. The dithering patterns of a 4-bit pixel, representing five levels of gray.

compression. For example, an 8-pixel by 8-pixel cell is encoded into a single gray level. Storing the original cell of pixels requires 64 bits, while it takes only 8 bits to store the single encoded gray level (8:1 compression). The compression is obtained, of course, at the expense of spatial resolution. The assumption is that the actual arrangement of pixels within the cell is not important; only the number that are turned on is. When the resolution of the input image is sufficiently high to warrant this assumption, reverse dithering becomes a valuable data-compression technique.

What About CD-I?

Thus far in this chapter, we have talked about a lot of areas related to computer graphics and computer imaging, generally in rather abstract terms. CD-I, Compact Disc-Interactive, is a standard being developed jointly by Sony and Philips that incorporates many of these concepts.

CD-I is a specification for a computer system built around a CD ROM device. The specification covers details of the hardware and many aspects of the software involved in providing an interactive CD ROM environment. With respect to imaging, CD-I specifies the hardware for a sophisticated display system capable of displaying bit-mapped graphics and natural images in several modes and resolutions. It provides display hardware to perform some video-like special effects, such as wipes for transitions between screens. It also specifies ways for performing real-time animation and coordinating this animation with audio. In addition, CD-I specifies standard encoding and compression algorithms used to produce image data files for storage on the CD ROM disc and provides hardware assistance for the decompression and display of these image files. Figure 8 summarizes some details of the CD-I specification.

Standards such as CD-I provide numerous advantages. Having a standard allows publishers to aim for a known target when developing an application, knowing it will be compatible with the user's hardware and software. Also, because the target machine's capabilities are rigidly defined, a publisher can take advantage of these known characteristics to improve the application's performance, and can incorporate special effects without worry about incompatibilities.

Nothing ever comes free, though, and the down side of the CD-I specification is that it is not an appropriate environment for every application. CD-I seems to be targeted more toward the consumer and the home-entertainment market than the business market. This is not to say that you

CD-I DISPLAY RESOLUTION		
320 x 210 pixels	Normal-resolution safe area	*Normal resolution* is intended for use with standard televisions.
384 x 280 pixels	Normal-resolution full screen	
640 x 420 pixels	Double-resolution safe area	*Safe area* is the region guaranteed to be visible on all displays.
768 x 560 pixels	Double-resolution full screen	*Double resolution* is for use with high resolution monitors.

CD-I DISPLAY FORMATS		
Delta YUV	Natural images	Delta YUV (DYUV) uses 4-bit, nonlinear encoding. U and V values are stored at half the resolution of Y. The coding scheme achieves 3:1 compression of 24-bit-per-pixel images.
Absolute RGB	High-quality computer graphics	Absolute RGB yields high-quality computer graphics (15 bits per pixel, 32768 colors).
Color lookup table	Computer graphics and animation	Color look-up table (C.L.U.T.) mode uses less storage than RGB mode (4, 7, or 8 bits per pixel), but allows 24-bit color definition (enabling 16.7 million colors), though its display is limited to 16, 128, or 256 colors on the screen at one time.
Run-length encoded	Animation	Run-length encoding combines with C.L.U.T. to provide data compression for animation, allowing 7 to 12 frames per second.

CD-I SPECIAL EFFECTS		
Wipes & Dissolves		Wipes & Dissolves are used for transitions between screens.
Overlays		Overlaying allows simultaneous display of combinations of formats.

Figure 8. Graphics specifications in the CD-I standard.

can't target business and professional applications for CD-I drive machines, just that not all such applications will be a good match for the CD-I hardware's capabilities. For example, CD-I does not deal well with large monochrome bit maps requiring very high-resolution displays. So CD-I probably would not be ideal for document storage and retrieval or for applications such as microfilm replacement. As with all standards, CD-I gives you a solid target to shoot for, but it is up to you to decide whether or not it's a target that interests you.

Conclusion

Computer graphics and imaging raise a world of broad and diverse issues. We have tried to briefly describe those that apply to CD ROM publishing. In summary, we will present some potential CD ROM applications and discuss graphics and imaging processes that might enhance them.

Document Distribution

Many early CD ROM applications will distribute previously published documents. In some cases, the transfer from paper to CD ROM may involve little change in content or function. In other cases, publishers may take advantage of the computer in a CD ROM delivery system and create applications that the user can manipulate (this would involve storing character-based data, which we discuss in Chapter 4).

In most cases, preparing images of document pages is very similar to transmitting the pages by facsimile machines. Most likely you will digitize the pages into a single-bit-per-pixel bit map, compress them using CCITT Group 3 or Group 4 encoding, and then master them to disc. The application program you choose should allow you to index image files. When the user retrieves a particular image, the program displays it on the monitor or prints it using a high-resolution printer.

In this sort of application, you may want to store the page images in a form other than single-bit-per-pixel facsimile form. For example, a museum might wish to record and distribute copies of an ancient manuscript to researchers. In this case, it would be desirable to record exact images of the pages in the document with sufficient resolution and accuracy to enable researchers to get any information from the CD ROM disc they could get by examining the original manuscript (except, of course, such things as the composition of the paper). You would probably need to digitize the image in monochrome with several bits per pixel, or possibly even in color if the colors in the original document are important.

Depending on the nature of the original document, you might use a flatbed scanner or a drum scanner to digitize the data. Fragile or otherwise hard-to-work-with original documents may require developing special digitizing techniques. For example, you might photograph the pages first, then digitize the photographs. To minimize geometric distortion, you'll need to carefully match aspect ratios of the digitizer to those of the displays that will display the images.

To compress the resulting bit maps, you'll want to use a compression algorithm that does not distort the image. However, fully recoverable compression algorithms tend to produce less compact data than do non-recoverable algorithms. Because of these factors, storing these kinds of documents probably will require lots of disc space and so limit the number of images that fit on a disc. However, CD ROMs can distribute the documents to many more people than might otherwise have access to them, making this trade-off acceptable.

Mixed-Text and Graphics Storage

Many documents contain mixtures of text and graphics. Of course, one option for this type of data is to store the pages as bit-mapped images. However, storing simple page images restricts the features you can provide. For example, your customer won't be able to perform word searches on the text. The only way to enable this is to store the text in character-coded form, most likely using ASCII-coded characters. If you also want to display a bit-mapped image on the same screen, you must perform two processes for every page.

In this case, you will want to store the two parts of the page, the text and the graphs, separately. You can separate them after digitizing the page. On one copy of the page image, all graphics are masked out so only text remains. On the other copy, all text is masked out. Using an OCR system, you can process the text into character codes and produce formatting information that describes the text layout. After correcting the newly coded text, you will generate the indexes to enable the user to perform various kinds of searches (for more information on these techniques, refer to Section II of this book).

To process graphics, you mask out the text and extract the graphics. You can leave these graphics as bit maps or run them through raster-to-vector conversion software to produce structured graphics. In either case, the graphical images will also require formatting information that describes where they will appear on the page.

When the user asks to view a particular page, the application program will find the appropriate text for the page and, using the extracted formatting information, will display the text. It will then find the appropriate graphics for the page and place them in the display, again using the formatting information that describes the page layout.

In applications such as this, you probably will store the images as single-bit-per-pixel bit maps. Most scanners generate this form, and it is the one best suited for OCR manipulation of the text areas of pages. You can compress these images using facsimile compression techniques.

Catalog of Images

Another form of CD ROM application that will occasionally be published is the picture-book type of application. The content of this kind of application is primarily graphical or visual rather than textual. For example, a CD ROM might contain a "guided tour" of an art gallery.

The nature of the images to be used is the most important factor in this kind of application. In the case of a tour through an art gallery, images must be recorded with considerable fidelity, so the publisher will need to store them in color with a fairly large number of bits per pixel. Using 15 bits per pixel allows 32,768 colors, which the display can reproduce with high quality. When you store this many bits per pixel, image bit maps are quite large, necessitating compression. You can use nonrecoverable compression algorithms in many cases, especially for images that won't be used in a quantitative way and whose aesthetic qualities will be paramount. Using a nonrecoverable compression algorithm always involves a trade-off between the degree of compression and the severity of image distortion. Images of this kind are good candidates for use of delta encoding.

Maps

Another highly graphical application area of CD ROM is map display. In basing any CD ROM application on map displays, you should consider a number of graphics options.

You must, of course, decide whether to store the map image as a bit map or as structured graphics. For simple map applications, a bit map might suffice. You can digitize a printed map and store the resulting bit map on the disc. This is not very different from storing page images. Most maps differentiate between kinds of information with colors, so you must store color information. But since few colors generally are used, you should be able to store a relatively small number of bits per pixel. Using 4 bits per pixel allows 16 colors.

Storing maps in structured graphics form has several advantages. With structured graphics, you can let the user zoom in to view detail at different scales. Layering might also be desirable. By including different types of features, such as contour lines or textures distinguishing precincts that vote Democratic from GOP precincts, on separate layers, you enable users to view them or not at their discretion. Another possibility is to tag map features with attribute codes. You might tag each road with a code that identifies the type of road it is (such as interstate highway or secondary road). This would let users planning a route specify display of only certain kinds of roads.

One of the biggest problems in publishing maps on CD ROM is getting data into usable form. For storing a bit-mapped image, you can digitize a paper map using a flatbed scanner or drum scanner. For generating a structured graphics map, you would probably use a digitizing tablet, placing the map on the tablet and then tracing its features. This process is much more laborious than using a scanner. Assigning features to particular layers, associating attribute codes with features, and other formatting of data also require a good deal of labor. For these reasons, producing CD ROM map applications may take longer than producing some other types of CD ROM applications.

CD ROM's Multimedia Future

CD ROM's arrival is simultaneous with a number of other technical developments. The coming together of high-performance microprocessors, very-high-density memories, high-resolution monitors, and very-high-performance graphics processors, all at very *low* cost, with the CD ROM medium's tremendous storage capacity will revolutionize the ways people deal with information. Combining the microprocessor's search and retrieval capabilities with information presentation capabilities of high-resolution graphics and imaging, and the further addition of high-fidelity audio, will enable us to present information in ways never before possible. Such science fiction like machines as the *Dynabook* or *Memex*, which people have dreamed about for years, soon will be a reality.

CD ROM's multimedia potential won't be realized for some time. No one yet knows how to do it. Structuring and indexing the text, including images, and cross-linking the images will require new authoring tools and techniques. Some publishers and software houses are trying to work out some of these details, but much work, and many lessons, remain. However, the inexorable drives of competition and user demand will force us all to work out these details and usher in this new age of information.

About the Author

Gene Apperson is a software engineer working in the areas of computer graphics and imaging for CD ROM for Microsoft Corporation. He previously worked for Boeing Computer Services, developing CAD applications programs for electrical systems. He holds a bachelor of science degree in electrical engineering from the University of Washington.

Rick Doherty is president of Kyra Corporation, a Seaford, NY, computer graphics and publishing company. Before forming Kyra Corporation in 1983, Doherty was president and founder of Optronic Labs, Inc. An engineer working with video systems since 1965, he holds several U.S. and foreign patents and has written articles and reports on technology for *Electronic Engineering Times* since 1978.

Resources

Artwick, Bruce A. 1984. *Applied Concepts in Microcomputer Graphics.* New York: Prentice-Hall. Good overall coverage of computer graphics, including discussion of animation.

Castleman, Kenneth R. 1979. *Digital Image Processing.* New York: Prentice-Hall. Good intermediate level text on most aspects of digital image processing.

Computer Graphics World. Pennwell Publishing Company. This is a good magazine that covers the entire computer graphics industry. Generally not too technical, it covers the latest equipment and software and discusses various graphics applications.

Foley, J.D., and A. Van Dam. 1982. *Fundamentals of Interactive Computer Graphics.* Reading, Ma.: Addison-Wesley. Very thorough treatment of computer graphics. One of the best books around on the subject.

IEEE Computer Graphics and Applications. Magazine published by the Institute for Electrical and Electronics Engineers.

Using Audio

In the rush to deliver CD ROM's mass of megabytes to the desktops of the world, we often forget the compact disc's original use: audio. Text, images, and programs have been the main concerns of software developers and electronic publishers. Pictures and words on the screen naturally dominate the media mix in personal computers, leaving the machines merely to beep at us, usually when we make a mistake.

The compact disc can change that balance. High-quality interactive audio adds realism, drama, and fun to the personal computer environment. We can now make these machines talk to us in warm, human voices instead of the artificial "drunken-Scandinavian-trapped-in-an-oil-drum" quality of early synthesized speech. And potential uses for music, sound effects, and well-known voices are virtually endless.

Despite audio's promise for enriching computer programs, few CD ROM products or demonstrations during CD ROM's first two years have incorporated audio. (This chapter's brevity reflects the industry's dearth of experience.) One reason is that hardware to support CD interactive audio is only now becoming commonly available.

This chapter covers two main types of audio delivery systems for CD ROM, the types of applications that audio might enhance, digital audio standards in the industry, and the processes of producing and preparing audio for CD ROM mastering. (For more information on audio applications and design issues associated with CD ROM, see "Compact Disc Interactive Audio" in *CD ROM: The New Papyrus* [Microsoft Press, 1986].)

Audio Delivery Systems for CD ROM

The method you use to deliver audio in a CD ROM system depends on the format in which the audio is stored. The three ways to store audio on a compact disc are: *CD audio,* the high-quality sound used on consumer music CDs as specified in the Compact Disc Digital Audio standard; *CD ROM audio,* in which digitized audio of various levels of quality is stored as data according to the CD ROM standard; and *CD-I audio*, which uses one of the three alternate audio formats as specified in the Compact Disc Interactive (CD-I) standard. Pending the availability of CD-I audio hardware, CD ROM typically delivers audio in one of two types of delivery systems:

A dual-mode CD ROM/CD audio drive. This type of drive accesses both CD ROM data and CD audio tracks stored on the same disc, sending image and text data to the computer for processing and playing back CD audio tracks through an on-board Digital-to-Analog (D-to-A) converter. The D-to-A converter changes the digital audio data into an analog electrical signal that is amplified to drive a set of headphones or speakers in the same way as is done for a CD audio player.

A CD ROM drive with a D-to-A converter board installed in the computer. The converter board plays back audio stored in CD ROM data format. All data is sent to the computer, where the CD ROM audio is routed to the D-to-A board, which converts it to sound.

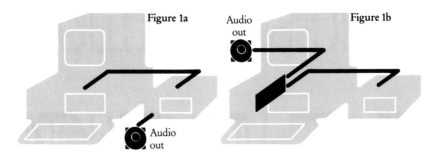

Figure 1a. Dual-mode player configuration (scheduled for commercial availability in 1987).
Figure 1b. D-to-A converter board in computer (available now from some vendors).

These two delivery systems influence the quality and the amount of audio the CD ROM holds. Dual-mode drives are equipped for direct playback of CD audio, the high-quality music standard for commercial music discs. These discs can store a maximum of 74 minutes of stereo sound. On the other hand, you can design systems using a D-to-A converter on an expansion board in the host computer for lower-fidelity CD ROM audio. Lower-fidelity audio requires less disc space, thus allowing longer playing times. This topic is discussed further in the Fidelity *v* Storage section.

Audio Applications for CD ROM

Combining audio with software, text, and images in CD ROM applications can involve three approaches:

- Enhancing existing software, text, and images with audio. For example, you might add interactive audio to a software tutorial.

- Enhancing existing audio material with text and images. Music appreciation and language training courses are likely candidates for this.

- Combining audio, software, text, and images in new ways. This "multimedia" field is wide open.

Although audio's role may be primary only in applications for music, foreign languages, or special sounds, audio can enhance almost any CD ROM program. For example, a useful CD ROM product would be a comprehensive writer's disc that includes a word processor, a semantically linked thesaurus and dictionary, writing-style guides, grammar-checking programs, a training course in writing technique, boilerplate business form letters, and a tutorial/help system for using the application. This system might consume as much as 50 MB, only one-tenth of the space on a compact disc. The rest of the disc could contain audio to support the program's help, training, and error-message functions.

As part of the user interface—to instruct, alert, acknowledge, guide, or reinforce—audio makes any program more inviting, especially to the new user. And audio uniquely can give the user more information without disturbing the screen display. Of course, audio feedback should be optional in a business-oriented application.

In most cases, an audio application alone won't justify buying a CD ROM/CD audio drive. But once dual-mode hardware is on the desktop supporting database applications, additional audio-enhanced products may start appearing. Since including audio capability in CD ROM hardware adds relatively little cost, it may be wise to buy dual-mode hardware even if at first you don't need audio.

Audio-based applications for entertainment, personal enrichment, and reference are likely to follow. Audio on CD ROM will extend beyond the office—for instance, into stores as sales aids and into vehicles as navigation and information systems.

Audio Standards

As mentioned, delivery systems for audio on CD ROM can be designed to play back audio recorded at several levels of quality, or *fidelity,* the highest being the Compact Disc Digital Audio standard of commercial music discs. For some CD ROM applications, this fidelity isn't necessary or desirable.

Fidelity v Storage

Compared with the amount of space ASCII files require, digital audio requires a lot of disc space. A CD ROM's approximately 600 MB of space stores roughly a quarter of a million typewritten pages but only 74 minutes of high-quality CD audio. A 2 KB block of data on a CD can fill a computer screen with text; the same size block storing stereo sound plays only $\frac{1}{75}$ of a second.

The CD audio standard yields high-quality sound reproduction but consumes a great deal of disc space. Lower-quality sound consumes less space. This trade-off between sound fidelity and digital storage is critical in planning audio for a CD ROM disc. Understanding the trade-off requires knowledge of how sound is converted from its original analog form to a digital signal in a process called *digitization.*

An *analog signal* is any electronic signal that is continuously variable, flowing and changing much like an ocean wave or an electric current. Sound, which is the result of vibrations traveling through air, produces an analog signal that is usually measured by the number of pulses per second, or *hertz* (Hz). The average person can hear sounds ranging from 20 to 20,000 hertz (20 kHz).

To store sound on a digital medium such as a compact disc, the analog signal must be converted to a digital signal. A digital signal is composed of discrete *samples* of the analog signal, each of which is converted to a fixed value and stored as a set of binary numbers. When the digital signal is played back, it must be converted back to an amplified analog signal for us to hear it.

Converting an analog signal to digital form requires two processes, *sampling* and *quantization.* The degree to which both processes are invoked determines the fidelity and the amount of space that is required to store it in digital form.

Sampling Rate

To digitize an analog signal, it must be continuously sampled at discrete intervals. For the player electronics to recover the original analog signal when it is played back, the sampling rate must be at least two times the highest frequency the playback system can reproduce. Since compact disc players can play back sound with frequencies of up to 20 kHz, CD audio is *sampled* at a rate of 44.1 kHz, or 44,100 times a second.

Lowering the sampling rate has two effects: It lowers the frequency range, and it reduces the storage required. For example, lowering the sampling rate from 44 to 11 kHz restricts reproduced sounds to 5.5 kHz, but increases the amount you can store by four times.

You can hear the effect of frequency range on audio quality by listening to AM and FM radio. AM radio broadcasts at frequencies of about 5 kHz. This accommodates speech and music but excludes higher tones that improve the timbre of the sound. FM radio broadcasts at frequencies of about 10 kHz, and you can clearly discern the improved timbre. The compact disc's frequency range extends to 20 kHz, providing the best commercially available sound.

Quantization

When the digitizing circuitry captures a discrete sound, it converts the sample into a digital value. This process is known as *quantization*. The number of bits assigned to the quantizer determines the accuracy of the sound conversion. An 8-bit quantizer can store 256 discrete levels of sound, while a 16-bit quantizer (typically used to produce CD audio) can store 65,536 different levels.

Converting a continuous analog value into a discrete digital value always involves some error. Clearly, the more bits assigned to a quantizer, the less error will result. The difference between the actual sample and the assigned digital value is called *quantization error* and is essentially equivalent to noise in an analog system—commonly referred to as the signal-to-noise ratio (SNR).

The 16-bit quantization scheme of CD audio yields a theoretical SNR of about 98 decibels (dB). When you reduce quantization, you save disc space but also decrease the SNR. The higher the SNR, the cleaner the sound. The lower the SNR, the more extraneous system noise you hear. So, for example, if you were to reduce the quantization to 8 bits, you would have an SNR of about 50 dB, which produces noise roughly equivalent to what AM radio might produce.

Data Compression

Sampling rate and quantization directly affect digitized audio's frequency range and signal-to-noise ratio. Adjusting them to save disc space fundamentally affects the quality of the audio recorded and reproduced digitally. So the relationship between fidelity and digital storage requirements is direct: Better sound requires more bits.

However, it is not necessary to suffer fidelity degradation when you reduce the sample size. Several data compression techniques exist that can significantly reduce the number of bits per sample without sacrificing audio quality.

Pulse Code Modulation (PCM) is the most common method of sampling and quantizing sound digitally, as is used in the CD audio standard. This is also called *linear* PCM, because it uses a linear measurement scale and does not involve any data compression. One compression technique, called Differential PCM (DPCM), measures and records only the differences between one sample and the next, and thus can require fewer bits to record a series of signal levels. Adaptive Differential PCM (ADPCM) is an encoding scheme in which the relative scale of measurement changes dynamically; it adapts to large changes in signal characteristics, thereby reducing the data required to represent the sound levels. The industry's proposed specification for CD-I calls for ADPCM encoding for hi-fi music, mid-fi music, and speech audio levels.

Playback Environment

The playback environment inevitably affects the perceived quality of audio on a CD ROM. Quality audio stored on a CD sounds lousy if you play it back on lousy equipment. This could be critical in the acceptance of audio on CD ROM products.

Playback equipment includes headphones or speakers. When using either, you may need to amplify the analog audio output signal. Design your audio CD ROM applications to play on good equipment, and your efforts to record and store high-quality audio will be rewarded.

Audio Formats for CD ROM

As mentioned at the beginning of this chapter, there are three main formats for storing audio on a CD ROM: CD audio (Red Book), CD ROM audio (Yellow Book), and CD-I audio (Green Book). The characteristics of each format affect the design of an audio application on CD ROM.

CD Audio

The CD ROM standard provides for combining the highest quality CD audio tracks and CD ROM data on the same disc. As mentioned, this type of disc is designed for use on a dual-mode CD ROM/CD audio drive. Each data block on a compact disc contains header information that identifies the type of data it contains. The player directs textual, visual, and program data to the computer for processing or display. Audio data is played back as an electrical sound signal through the drive's analog outputs.

Although adding audio to a CD ROM in this way produces high-quality stereo audio of the Red Book standard on all dual-mode drives, several limitations might make it unattractive. It requires a lot of storage space. If you store only audio, you can record a maximum of 74 minutes and 33 seconds of high-quality audio on a disc. To add CD ROM data, you must cut back on audio storage. For example, with 300 MB of CD ROM data you can store only about 30 to 35 minutes of CD audio.

Note: Some dual-mode drives may be able to play back only either the left or right stereo channel under software control. In this environment, you can store twice as much audio—a maximum of 149 minutes—as monophonic sound, but you can play it back only by using this special dual-mode hardware configuration.

CD audio's other major drawback is that playing it back requires exclusive use of the drive's reading and decoding functions. You cannot access CD ROM data tracks while CD audio is playing. You can, however, access small amounts of data stored in the subcode channels of CD audio tracks. This subcode data includes track-timing information and can include other user data stored by the application as well. However, the subcode channels provide only about 5400 bytes of user data per second.

CD ROM Audio

Digitizing audio to standards other than CD audio can alleviate the problems with storage and disc access contention. Usually the sampling rate or quantization value is lowered to reduce the required storage space. For example, audio digitized at a 22 kHz sampling rate (half the CD audio standard) using 8-bit samples (half the CD audio standard) occupies only one-quarter as much space as CD audio. This also permits buffering of CD ROM audio data in memory, so the CD ROM drive can access other data while the D-to-A converter, usually located on an expansion board, plays audio.

Drawbacks of this approach are twofold. The sparser audio values produce lower-fidelity audio (although data compression, discussed above, can lessen this effect). And the industry hasn't established recording and play-back equipment standards for audio digitized at levels lower than that of CD audio.

Several expansion boards on the market enable A-to-D (Analog-to-Digital) recording and D-to-A playback. Formatting requirements for this technology are diverse. Various audio boards use a number of sampling rates and quantization values. If you digitize your audio with one of these boards, the user's playback system must use the same board (or compatible equipment) to convert the digital data to an audible analog signal.

CD-I Audio

The proposed Compact Disc Interactive standard includes three levels of audio in addition to the CD audio specified in the Red Book. The four CD-I audio levels have these characteristics:

Level	Encoding	Freq. Range	Quantization	S/N Ratio	Maximum Playback Time	Fidelity Equivalent
CD Audio	PCM*	20 kHz	16-bit linear	98 dB	74 min stereo	CD audio
Hi-Fi Music	ADPCM†	17 kHz	8-bit compressed	90 dB	2.4 hrs stereo/ 4.8 hrs mono	LP album
Mid-Fi Music	ADPCM	17 kHz	4-bit compressed	60 dB	4.8 hrs stereo/ 9.6 hrs mono	FM radio
Quality Speech	ADPCM	8.5 kHz	4-bit compressed	60 dB	9.6 hrs stereo/ 19.2 hrs mono	AM radio

* Pulse Code Modulation
† Adaptive Delta Pulse Code Modulation

Table 1. CD-I Audio standards.

Three ADPCM levels are available in both stereo and mono, and data storage of each level is twice as efficient as that of the level above it. This standard gives producers a broad range of audio format choices, accommodating from an hour and a quarter of very-high-quality stereo audio to more than 19 hours of good speech-quality mono audio.

Encoding and decoding the ADPCM levels require more processing than does CD audio coding. The CD-I standard specifies the encoding algorithms, and Philips and Sony—originators of the CD-I standard—say CD-I audio real-time decoding chips will be available in the OEM market. By incorporating these chips into the CD ROM controller boards and dedicated audio playback boards of your system, you could play back CD-I audio not only on CD-I players, but also on multimode CD ROM/ CD audio players.

Producing Audio for CD ROM Applications

In many ways, producing audio for CD ROM applications is much like producing audio for any audio-visual production, such as a film or videotape. The process follows audio recording steps of preproduction, production, and postproduction well known in the audio world. Standard recording studios are well equipped to help you produce your master audio tape.

Design and Scripting

In producing audio for an interactive application, you first must design and script it. Scripting interactive audio for CD ROM applications involves special considerations. These include deciding which roles audio characters will play in the user interface; coordinating screen/audio timing; deciding which mix, or *interaction matrix*, of sound, screen display, and user input operations best serves the application; and providing appropriate branching and transitions between audio segments.

Audio Recording

Recording and mixing audio for interactive CD applications involves essentially the same process as any other audio production. If you design and script the audio with the above considerations in mind, the recording process is straightforward.

You need not record your source audio with digital recording equipment. Although digital recording is superior, you may be able to get adequate sound quality for your application using good-quality analog recording equipment in a recording studio. The audio track you produce is digitized later for storage on the compact disc.

Audio Sources

Audio tracks can include three sound sources—voices, music, and sound effects. You can make original recordings of any of these or use prerecorded material. Effective interactive audio productions probably will use combinations of voices, music, and sound effects.

In making any audio recording, you must get legal clearance to use any audio for which ownership rights are established. The recording studio manager should be able to give you some direction on payments and rights. A good reference is *Billboard* magazine's *The Business of Music.*

Voices

You can, of course, use voices that are male, female, young, old, native-language, foreign-language, serious, comic, robotic. You should plan the characters that the voices are to create when you design your script.

Actors' fees will cover their time in recording sessions and their residual rights for sale or performance of the recording. Union rates dictate how much you pay members of AFTRA (American Federation of Television and Radio Artists) for both time and residuals. You can buy residual rights with a lump-sum payment when the recording is made. Fees for nonunion actors are negotiable, but your agreement still should cover both recording time and residuals.

Music
With music, your options include classical, popular, jazz, electronic, short, long, background, foreground, transitional, and so forth. Payments to musicians are structured like actors' fees—you pay for the recording itself and performance rights. If you commission original compositions, you need to agree on who owns the copyright and the publishing rights to the composition. Production music libraries usually have standard agreements for using their prerecorded music.

Sound Effects
Sound effects (*SFX*) can enhance a product when they are coordinated with visual images. You can record your own sound effects or use prerecorded sources from a production library. Producers of sound effects usually license use on a fixed-fee basis.

Mastering Audio on CD ROM Discs

Some basic steps in mastering audio for CD ROM have a counterpart in the process for text and images. But because the audio is merely accessed and played back, premastering for audio is simpler than preparing text for complex search and retrieval operations. Preparing data for the two types of CD ROM delivery systems—CD audio and CD ROM audio—involves different procedures.

Mastering CD ROM Audio

Step 1: Converting information. Collecting information and producing a master audio tape, as discussed earlier, is by far the most important step in mastering any audio format for CD ROM. For CD ROM audio, you must digitize the master audio tape in the A-to-D conversion scheme required by the D-to-A playback equipment in the target delivery system. You can store the digitized audio on any magnetic medium (disk, tape, and so forth) while processing it, but ultimately you must put it on the type of tape used for premastering.

Step 2: Preprocessing. The next step is to arrange the digitized nonstandard audio data in blocks that correspond to the data blocks stored on the CD ROM, grouping data blocks for each audio segment. Then you must convert the segments of audio blocks to the file system format used during the remainder of the mastering cycle. Any compression or encryption takes place at this point.

Step 3: Data indexing and inversion. The blocks that constitute a CD ROM audio segment must be indexed, and each must be assigned a start and stop point. The delivery system's control software uses this audio index to find an audio segment so that it can read the segment into memory for playback through the D-to-A converter on the expansion board.

Step 4: Logical formatting. This step is the same for any CD ROM data: it involves blocking the data to premastering requirements, building a disc image of the audio data, and building a file directory for the file manager that includes the audio files. Also, any interleaving of audio with text or visuals occurs during this step. When you have built the final disc image, you will record all data on a tape ready for premastering.

Step 5: Premastering. As with any CD ROM data, you or the disc manufacturer must calculate the error detection and correction information and record a disc image that includes the CD ROM audio data.

Step 6: Mastering. Mastering CD ROM audio, like mastering any other CD ROM data, involves reading the data into the mastering system. The mastering system produces the glass master, nickel stampers, and eventually the replicated discs.

Mastering CD Audio for CD ROM

Step 1: Converting information. As mentioned above, collecting the sounds on a master audio tape is the most important step in mastering any audio format for CD ROM. Since CD audio is not converted to digital format until premastering, it requires no further processing until that stage. Steps 2, 3, and 4 above are not required for mastering CD audio for CD ROM.

Step 5: Premastering. Premastering CD audio involves two operations. First, you must convert the master audio tape to digital format. This is done as real-time playback of the audio tape through a PCM processor such as the Sony 1610 or Sony 1630. The PCM processor translates the audio into the 16-bit PCM digital data specified by the Red Book. This digitized audio data is recorded in digital format on a ¾-inch videotape, with SMPTE time code on an analog audio track. The SMPTE code denotes time in hours, minutes, seconds, and frames, based on 30 frames per second. The PCM processor also adds the initial level of error correction data to the audio data.

The second step involves annotating the CD audio track timing information using the SMPTE time code on the ¾-inch videotape. To do this, you play back the digitized audio, noting the starting and stopping points indicated by the SMPTE time code. You will later use the codes during mastering to insert timing information, which are called *P-Q subcodes*, in the data stream.

Mastering. Three methods can be used to combine the CD audio data with CD ROM data for input to the mastering system. These vary among CD ROM manufacturers, so it is critical that you ask your manufacturer about the appropriate method. One method involves switching back and forth as required between the CD ROM premaster tape and the PCM audio premaster tape as each tape is synchronized and played in real-time during the mastering process. This method requires creating each premaster tape with blank information during the time that the other tape has valid data. The two tapes are played as a controller switches between the tapes to create a single stream of data for input to the mastering system. The result is a master disc image that combines CD audio PCM data and CD ROM data in a single track/minute/second/frame structure.

The other two methods involve creating a single tape for input to the mastering system: You can add CD audio PCM data to a CD ROM premaster tape, or you can add CD ROM data to a CD audio PCM master tape to create the tape for mastering. The latter method may not be the best approach, since the ¾-inch videotape format for CD audio may not be able to handle the additional level of error detection and correction data provided in CD ROM.

Disc Storage Considerations

The most straightforward method of storing CD audio tracks with CD ROM data on the same disc is to store all the CD audio tracks after the CD ROM data. However, if quick access and playback of the audio are important for the application, you may want to intermix the sequences of CD audio tracks and CD ROM data.

In general, you should store the audio segments close to where the drive's reader head will be when the audio is accessed. If space permits, you may wish to store frequently accessed audio segments in more than one place and include software that determines the fastest access. If you master CD audio tracks with CD ROM data using simultaneous playback of a PCM audio tape and a CD ROM data tape, you may need to allow a gap of a few seconds between the two types of information to accommodate the mechanical switching between the two tape machines.

It is also possible to interleave CD ROM audio with CD ROM data to allow for continuous audiovisual output. Interleaving of the two data types would occur in Step 4, data preparation, when the disc image is built. Any interleaving scheme must be closely coordinated with the software that will control the simultaneous output of audio and visual information.

Conclusion

Audio plays a critical role in the emerging multimedia uses of CD ROM. Its major benefits—emotional impact, characterization, multisensory stimulation, and audiovisual coordination—can powerfully enrich the content and usage of CD ROM products.

The media emphasis of CD ROM products and development systems follows a natural progression. At first, the awesome possibilities of 600 MB of text occupied the attention of developers. As retrieval software and data preparation methods have been developed, attention has shifted to the treatment of images on CD ROM. The third stage will focus on audio. True multimedia authoring systems will be required to fulfill this exciting promise of CD ROM.

About the Author

Bryan Brewer is president of Earth View Inc., a Seattle-based company specializing in interactive Compact Disc software. He is contributing editor for *Digital Audio* magazine, and he wrote two articles for *CD ROM: The New Papyrus* (Microsoft Press, 1986).

Resources

Pohlmann, Ken C. 1985. *Principles of Digital Audio.* Indianapolis: Howard Sams and Company.

Haskell, Barry, and Raymond Stelle. 1981. *Audio and Video Bit Rate Reduction.* Proceedings of the IEEE, 69(2).

DISC PRODUCTION

Disc Origination

Disc origination is the process of arranging your files so that you can find them again after they are mastered on the CD ROM. Unlike many of the steps that precede it, such as text preparation or index building, disc origination is a relatively straightforward process that will be much the same for every product and every publisher. The task can be performed in-house using commercially available *origination systems,* or it can be performed by a service bureau.

Disc origination is a process you can almost take for granted. Even so, you will find a number of options available as you shop for origination software or for a service bureau. Understanding your options requires a general understanding of the entire disc origination process. You need to know what exactly you input for disc origination, what comes back as output, and what processes intervene.

Input for disc origination is simply the files that the publisher wants on the CD ROM. At this point, these files are already in the form that the delivery system will eventually require: Indexes are built, data is properly formatted, digitized images are scanned and compressed, and all control and support files are present. Everything is ready to go.

Output from the origination process is a set of tapes that is sent to the disc-mastering facility. The mastering process simply transfers the files on these tapes to the CD ROM disc. Mastering adds no structure to the files; it merely places what it finds on the disc, byte for byte. We therefore speak of sending a *disc image* on tape to be mastered. The final disc will precisely reflect the structure and content of this disc image.

The origination system performs four functions as it makes output tapes ready for mastering from the input files:

1. Input files are transferred to the appropriate location on the tape.

2. *Volume identification* information is added so the disc can be identified once it is in the CD ROM drive. (A single disc is called a *volume.*)

3. A directory of input files is built and recorded on the output tape. This directory lists the name of each file and tells where to find it on the disc.

4. The disc image is written out in a tape format the mastering facility can handle.

Logical Formatting

The first three steps of this disc-origination process often are called *logical formatting*. This concept uses the term *logical* in a specialized sense that requires some explanation. The counterpoint to logical formatting is not, as one might suspect, *illogical* formatting. It is *physical formatting*, which refers to the way individual bytes of data are written physically onto the disc. Physical formatting involves matters such as the tightness of the spiral in which you record data on the disc, the arrangement of error correction information, the number of bytes a sector contains, and many other specifications that Philips and Sony have required for making CD ROM discs. Physical formatting is not of concern to us in disc origination; it is the concern of the mastering and disc-replication facility. We can take it for granted.

Because CD ROM discs all have the same physical format, we are assured that we can "read" them. That is, we can pull the data bytes out of any sector on the disc. But merely "reading" isn't sufficient. Applications must also know which sectors contain the files we need. That kind of information is what logical formatting provides. It arranges all files on the disc and provides us with a directory that enables us to find them.

Logical formatting implies the use of some conventions that both disc originators and disc users agree to. For example, a location for disc volume identification must be established, along with a convention for locating the disc directory. A structure for that directory must be defined so the delivery system can interpret it and find the files on the disc. This set of conventions is called the disc's *logical format*.

For specialized applications you will sell to a small, narrowly defined group, establishing a logical format that all users' delivery systems will understand can be easy. This logical format need not make any sense to users outside the group; general agreement about the conventions you use isn't necessary. But if you intend to sell your discs to a broad group of people, it is important that they have a standard, widely understood logical format. The High Sierra Format (HSF) for CD ROM discs, and the international standard format being developed from it, involve such broadly agreed upon conventions. The High Sierra Format is described in Chapter 11.

Most publishers will not write their own, specialized software for formatting and reading discs. They will instead use software or services that firms such as Microsoft, Reference Technology, TMS, and VideoTools offer. This software uses the High Sierra Format and eventually will use the emerging international standard format. Publishers using these systems and services are assured that their discs' logical format is a widely used one that enables a broad class of systems and users to find the files on the disc.

Steps in Disc Origination

Disc origination involves a sequence of distinct steps. Some of these steps require assistance from the disc publisher, and others are automatic. Although different vendors' disc origination processes vary widely in detail, the following general steps are common to most systems.

1. Collection. Files to be placed on the CD ROM are collected for input into the origination system.

2. Format specification. The publisher provides disc volume identification information and specifies a directory structure for the files.

3. Assembly and loading. Disc layout is determined, directories are built, and the files are transferred to a hard disk or tape that stores the disc image.

4. Testing. The disc image is tested to ensure it is usable and correct.

5. Copying to tape. The tested disc image is copied to magnetic tape for delivery to the mastering facility.

Because each of these steps often presents the publisher with a number of alternatives, we will discuss each briefly later.

Collection

By the time a publisher has performed text preparation, image capture, and database indexing and otherwise prepared its data, the resulting files may be in a number of different places on a variety of media. To input the files in the origination process, they must be brought back together. The complexity of this collection process will affect your choice of a software system or service bureau for disc origination. For example, if a portion of the files you want to place on CD ROM come from an archival WORM (Write Once Read Many) disc storage system, you must ensure either that the software you license accepts input from WORM discs or that an available service bureau can read your brand of WORM disc.

Format Specification

Once the files are collected, you need to communicate some information about the logical format to the originating software or to the service bureau. This information usually includes:

- *Disc volume identification* information.

- Specifications for the disc's directory structure and for which files will reside in which directories.

- Specifications for the use of special features such as interleaved or hidden files.

We won't discuss special features here. Rather, we'll focus first on the bread-and-butter matters of volume identification and directory structure. Specifying the volume identification information, which includes such things as names of the disc and publisher and the disc's effective date, expiration date, and serial number, is always easy. For some systems, you fill in a form with this information and give it to your service representative. Other systems present questions on a screen. In all cases, this more or less involves simply filling in blanks.

Specifying the directory structure can be more complicated. If you only want 30 or 40 files on your CD ROM disc, scattered across a half-dozen or so subdirectories, matters still are simple. If you are working with a service bureau, you usually can simply give its service representative a diagram of the directory structure showing the names and arrangement of the subdirectories along with the files each directory will contain. Some service bureaus provide a small program for use with personal computers that will allow you to create your directory structure interactively much as you would create directories on a hard disk. This program produces a *specification file,* which can be copied to a floppy disk and then sent to the service bureau.

But suppose you intend to place 10,000 files on the CD ROM, distributed across a directory structure that contains hundreds of subdirectories. How do you communicate this complicated structure to your in-house origination system or to a service bureau? Clearly, you don't want to draw a picture or fill in a form; just as clearly, you don't want to create this directory structure interactively, file by file. If this structure already exists on a magnetic disc, you often can capture the structure by using a system utility program that walks through the entire structure, creating a record of all directories and files in an output file. Some service bureaus can use this file as an input specification for disc origination. In other cases, other

automated methods will be provided for creating the directory specification, such as extracting it from a database. The point is that if you want
your disc to include a large number of files, the question of how to specify
the directory structure is a serious one. It is crucial that you ensure that
the service bureau or the software you will use can meet your needs.

Assembly and Loading

Given a set of files and a specification for how to arrange them, we are
ready to make the disc image. Different systems proceed with this process
in different ways and provide different options. Typically, assembling and
loading the disc image involves the following operations:

- Determine the sizes of the files to be loaded.

- Devise a "layout" for the files, accounting for those that are to be interleaved (discussed later).

- Create directories according to the directory specification that describes
this disc layout.

- Create the blocks of information that describe the entire disc volume.

- Transfer the files into their reserved spaces in the disc image.

If you are shopping for an origination system for in-house use, your principal concerns with regard to these operations will involve speed and con-
venience. You will be moving large amounts of data, so one concern will
be how many times you will have to move the data during this process.
What happens if an input tape contains a bad spot? Can you recover from
the error or must you start the whole process over? What kinds of reports
does the process generate? What happens if the files and directories exceed
the size of a CD ROM? How user-friendly is the system? What if you
mount tapes in the wrong order?

You should also be aware that enormous speed differences exist among
various ways of moving data. Merely changing data transfer procedures
used during loading can extend or reduce processing time. Thus, you
should be able to watch a system load a full disc's worth of data before you
commit yourself to paying for it. You want to buy a fast one.

Clearly, these efficiency issues are less of a concern if you are working
with a service bureau. If a vendor offers you a good price and can deliver
within the time you have allotted, it doesn't matter to you how much
computer time the vendor uses to get the job done. Concerns such as the
firm's reliability, its ability to handle your particular input format, and the
quality of its testing services will be more important to you than its raw
processing efficiency.

Testing

Once the disc image is made, you need to test it. You need to verify the disc image's internal consistency. Does the directory contain all of the specified files? Can all of the files be opened? Are all files in the disc image the same size as they were on the input medium? These kinds of tests usually can be automated and performed relatively quickly.

A more important and difficult question is whether the disc, once mastered, will do what it is supposed to do. Are all of the files that the delivery system will expect actually included in the disc image? Are the files in the correct format for use by the application software? Do the addresses within index files really match up with the data locations? The only really satisfactory way to answer these questions is by actually running the delivery system's application software with the newly constructed disc image. It is important that service bureaus or software that you use in-house provide this emulation capability.

Some origination systems run on the same kinds of equipment as does the delivery system. For example, some use an IBM PC/AT running MS-DOS to create CD ROM disc images. If the disc image is to be used with application software that runs on a PC/AT, creating the disc image and then testing it with the target application is a simple matter.

Other systems create the disc image on a larger computer, such as a VAX, even if the CD ROM is to be used with smaller, personal computers. With these systems, testing the disc image might necessitate downloading it to a PC-based system that is tied to a large magnetic disc. Alternatively, you can connect a PC directly to a VAX, running software on the VAX that allows the PC to access the disc image on the VAX as though it were actually available on the PC. There are other solutions as well. The important thing is to guarantee that you or the service bureau is able to "run" the application software against the disc image, verifying that the disc image contains everything the application needs, and that it is in the right form.

Some system manufacturers advertise the ability to move beyond testing for completeness and usability, toward actually *simulating* the operation of the CD ROM. The idea is that the publisher will want not only to make sure everything works, but also to simulate actual CD ROM performance characteristics. This capability could be very useful for firms developing applications software for CD ROMs that wish to test a number of different file structure approaches without having to make a disc. However, once application software is established and in use, periodic publishing of new discs for use with that application rarely will require simulation. By that time you know the characteristics of your software and file structures; the fact that the testing system responds more slowly or quickly than an actual CD ROM is irrelevant to establishing that the disc image is complete and usable.

Copy to Tape

Once the disc image is complete and tested, it is time to copy it to tape. (Some systems actually create the disc image directly on tape and then load it onto a magnetic disk for testing.) Usually the entire disc image is recorded on the tape as a single enormous file. All user's files, directories, and volume identification information is included in this file.

The tapes must be in a format the mastering facility can handle. This usually means you must label them according to the ANSI (American National Standards Institute) tape label standard (ANSI X3.27 [1978]). If you are using a service bureau for disc origination, you need only tell them where the tapes will be mastered and the bureau will be able to format the tapes appropriately. If you are handling the origination in-house, contact the mastering facility for a description of their input specifications.

Logical Formatting Options

We noted earlier that most publishers will use the proposed High Sierra Format or, ultimately, the emerging international standard format derived from it. At this point, we will briefly discuss some of the more important and interesting formatting options the High Sierra Format makes available to CD ROM publishers.

- High-speed access to files. The HSF proposal provides rapid access to directories through a structure called the *path table*. This fast directory access can translate into fast file access if each individual directory holds no more than about 40 files. You should avoid placing hundreds of files in a single directory; access will be quicker if you break such a large directory into several smaller subdirectories.

- Use of different character sets. The proposed HSF specifies use of the familiar 7-bit ASCII standard character set used for personal computers in the United States. File and directory names are restricted to a subset of these characters consisting of the uppercase letters A through Z, the digits 0 through 9, and the underscore character. Most publishers will work within these restrictions to guarantee maximum interchangeability of their discs. However, the High Sierra Format also contains provisions for using international character sets and larger varieties of characters for file and directory names.

- Multivolume sets. A single CD ROM disc is a *volume*. A *multivolume set* is a set of discs that use a single, common directory structure. Multivolume sets are useful if you are working with very large files that cannot fit on a single disc. In a multivolume set, the entire file system spans across disc boundaries. Note the distinction between a multivolume set, in which all the discs are closely coupled through a shared directory, and a set of related files that are placed on separate volumes. In the latter case, each disc is independent; the group of discs are related only because the application software ties them together. In a multivolume set, the discs are tied together at a more fundamental level: Each disc actually contains information about the files on the other discs. Either option is open to a publisher.

- Extended-attribute records. The High Sierra Format provides a structure called an *extended-attribute record* (XAR), which allows you to place information in a record located before the start of the actual data in a file. The XAR can contain information about dates on which the data in the file becomes effective or expires, about record structures the file uses, or about other matters specific to an application. You may also associate an XAR with a directory file.

- Interleaved files. Usually files on a CD ROM consist of a set of contiguous sectors. In an interleaved file, some sectors that are not used by the file are *interleaved* with the valid sectors in some regular pattern. A file might, for example, contain four sectors of data, then skip two sectors, then have four more data sectors, another skip two more, and so on. Interleaving a file serves two purposes. It slows down data transfer without making the CD ROM drive stop its reading (stopping reading on a CD ROM, and then restarting, can waste time). For example, if our targeted delivery system can accept data at no more than half the CD ROM's usual data transfer rate (150 KB/sec), we can accommodate this limit by interleaving the disc's files, putting data in every other sector. Interleaving alternate files containing data in different formats also can be useful. You might, for example, want to interleave sectors from a file containing sound with sectors from a file of related images.

- "Disc geography" options. The proposed HSF says nothing about the sequence of files on the disc or about where to locate directories. The layout of files on a disc is known as the *disc geography*. On a single-volume disc you can scatter directories across the disc so that they are near the files they reference. You can also store all directories together in a single area. The first of these options is attractive if appplications usually will be opening a single file, reading from it, and closing it. The latter option is more attractive for systems that will open many files at once, leaving them open while the application runs. Although the High Sierra Format specifies no particular method, you probably will find that most origination software ties you to one specific form of disc geography. If the option to control the placement of files and the arrangement of directories is important in designing your CD ROM, you should inquire carefully about these capabilities before committing yourself to a system or vendor.

- Use of nonstandard directory structures. The High Sierra Format specifies a standard directory structure, but it also provides for nonstandard directory structures such as MS-DOS directories or some proprietary structure in an orderly way.

This list of features and options available through the High Sierra Format is not exhaustive. But it should give you a general idea of the kinds of options you will have. The important point to remember is that not all origination systems will offer all of these options; some will offer only a small subset of them. Before you purchase a system or sign a long-term agreement with a vendor, you should be sure the system can deliver the options that are important to you.

About the Author

Bill Zoellick is Director of Technology for the Alexandria Institute, a nonprofit organization dedicated to making CD ROM information retrieval systems more widely available to users through libraries and other resource centers. Before joining the Alexandria Institute, Bill was Manager of Software Research at TMS, Inc., where he designed and implemented information retrieval software and lower level, file system software for CD ROM. He was a key participant in the High Sierra Group, playing an active role in producing the CD ROM logical format proposal. He has written and spoken widely about a broad range of CD ROM publishing issues and is co-author of a major new textbook on file structures.

High Sierra Group Format Description

Since 1985, the CD ROM publishing industry has worked to establish a standard format for placing files and directories on CD ROM discs. At this writing, a proposal for a standard format is working its way through the international standardization process.

The *High Sierra Group Proposal (HSG Proposal),* which emerged from an ad hoc committee of computer vendors, software developers, and CD ROM system integrators, was the first draft of the format description that is under consideration in the standards committees. This initial proposal is important because it is the "common format" that is being used by firms such as Microware (software developers for CD-I), Microsoft, Reference Technology, and TMS until an official standard emerges.

This chapter was written by two members of the High Sierra Group who contributed substantially to the design of the proposed format. It describes the format, looks at the current state of the art, and previews the functionality that will be embodied in the final, international CD ROM logical format standard.

We have tried to ensure that the information presented here does not contradict the actual proposal. If inconsistencies occur, the proposal governs. Readers interested in more detail than we present will find it useful to study the proposal. We simplify this task by including bracketed references (for example, [13.1.3]) to section numbers in the HSG Proposal. When we reference specific *byte positions* inside structures described in the HSG Proposal, we use the abbreviation *BP* (for example, BP 12). If you need a copy of the HSG Proposal, you can get one from:

> Pat Harris
> NISO
> National Bureau of Standards
> Administration 101, Library ED106
> Gaithersburg, MD 20899

Content of a Logical Format

You can simplify the design of a logical format for the CD ROM by dividing the task into two steps: (1) designing a set of structures that provides information about the whole disc, or *volume*, and (2) designing structures that describe and locate the files on the volume.

This is the approach the HSG Proposal takes. The proposal's formal title is *Working Paper for Information Processing — Volume and File Structure of Compact Read-Only Optical Discs for Information Interchange.*

In the sections that follow, we describe the most important features of the structure the HSG Proposal defines. We proceed in bottom-up fashion, beginning with *logical sectors* and *logical blocks*, then discussing *files*, and eventually working our way up to the structures that describe the entire disc volume.

Separating Physical and Logical Views

When the HSG began discussing the logical format of a disc, we concluded that the design should avoid specific references to physical characteristics of the CD ROM disc. We did this because the Yellow Book on which all discs made today are based is not in the public domain and thus not controlled by any standards body. Changes to the Yellow Book could outdate the HSG's work if the logical format were coupled too tightly with the disc's physical format. The HSG therefore framed its proposal in terms of *logical sectors* and *logical blocks*.

Logical Sectors [6.1.2]

Currently, the capacity of a physical sector on a CD ROM disc is 2336 bytes, not counting the bytes devoted to header information. For most applications, part of the sector (288 bytes) is used for error correction. The remaining 2048 bytes, or 2 KB, can contain user data. As CD ROM technology stands, this 2 KB data field is what the HSG Proposal considers a logical sector. If the physical size of a sector is enlarged in future versions of the Yellow Book, the HSG Proposal can accommodate these changes by allowing for larger logical sector sizes.

A unique *logical sector number* (LSN) identifies each logical sector. The first sector available for user data on a CD ROM is at the physical address 00:02:00 and is regarded as LSN 0.

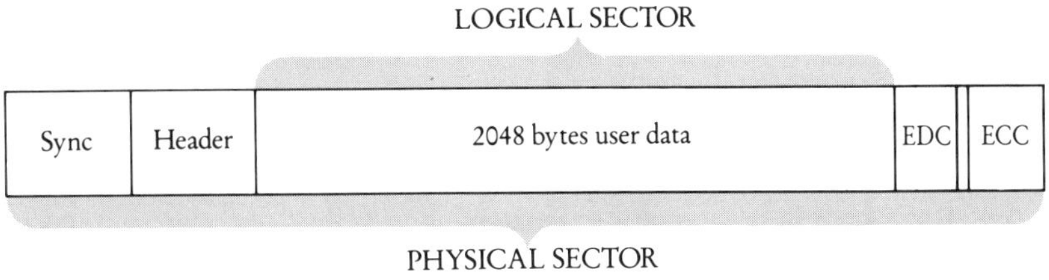

LOGICAL SECTOR

| Sync | Header | 2048 bytes user data | EDC | ECC |

PHYSICAL SECTOR

Figure 1. A logical sector is the 2048-byte user data area of a physical sector. It can be divided into one or more logical blocks.

Logical Blocks [6.2.1]

A logical sector can be divided into one or more logical blocks to provide more *fine-grained* addressability. This is useful, for example, if you put several hundred thousand very small files on the disc. Different CD ROMs can have different logical block sizes. Given the current logical sector size of 2048 bytes, a logical block can be 512, 1024, or 2048 bytes. A logical block can never be larger than a logical sector.

Each logical block is assigned a *logical block number* (LBN). The first logical block (LBN 0) is the first block within the first logical sector (LSN 0). Successive logical blocks are numbered 1, 2, 3, and so forth. The HSG proposed that all files and other important entities on the disc be addressed in terms of LBNs.

Files

The HSG Proposal provides rules for naming files and a number of mechanisms for finding files, but does not specify what a file can contain [7.5]. Files can contain ASCII text data, index structures, digitized video images, compressed speech data, or anything else you might want an application to store.

Structure of the File Space—Extents [7–7.3]

A file is associated with a file space, which is a collection of logical blocks. Usually these logical blocks are sequential and form a single *extent,* or sequence of contiguous logical blocks. The HSG Proposal, however, also permits files made of a number of separate extents. This happens, for example, if a large file spans two CD ROMs. Then, one extent exists on one disc, and a second extent, containing the rest of the file, exists on the second disc. In the HSG format, a file can also be broken into a number of extents on a single disc. Not all operating systems, however, will support multiple extents on CD ROM.

File Identifiers [10.5]

A *file identifier* can consist of a filename, followed by a filename extension, followed in turn by a file version number. All three components are optional, although a file identifier must contain either a filename or a filename extension.

The HSG Proposal allows CD ROMs to use both a *standard* character set and alternative character sets, referred to as *coded character sets*. When a program uses a coded character set, the file identifier can contain any of the characters in that set. The disadvantage of using special character sets, of course, is that delivery systems may be unable to interpret the characters properly. So, for most CD ROM applications that will be used on many different machines, publishers would be wise to restrict file identifiers to the *standard* character set specified in ISO 646. This is the familiar 7-bit ASCII character set.

Because certain popular operating systems also limit the type of characters allowed in a filename, the HSG Proposal actually restricts the set of characters used in a file identifier (in the standard file structure) to only part of the 7-bit ASCII character set. File identifiers may contain:

- Digits 0–9

- Capital letters A–Z

- The underscore character (_)

The file identifier may also contain a single Full Stop character (period) between the filename and its extension, and a single semicolon may separate the filename or file extension from the file version number. Examples of legal and illegal filenames are in Table 1.

Legal Filenames
FILE.DAT
FILE.DAT;1
DATA_FILE_FOR_INTERCHANGE.DATA
FILENAME_WITHOUT_AN EXTENSION
.NO_FILENAME_JUST_AN EXTENSION
Illegal Filenames
file.dat
ONLY.ONE.PERIOD.ALLOWED
NO-HYPHENS-OR-$-SIGNS
THIS_FILENAME_IS_LONGER_THAN 31 CHARACTERS

Table 1. Legal and illegal forms of file identifiers.

The length limits of legal filenames and file identifiers vary at different levels of the HSG Proposal. At the lowest level, the proposal restricts filenames to eight characters and filename extensions to three characters, guaranteeing the names on the CD ROM can be used by CP/M, MS-DOS, and other operating systems with restrictive naming conventions. At higher levels, the HSG Proposal limits the entire file identifier (not just the filename) to 31 characters, including any period or semicolon.

Directories [8.1]

The HSG Proposal allows files to be placed on the disc in subdirectories descending from a root directory. Subdirectories may be arranged hierarchically, with subdirectories descending from other subdirectories, as in the file systems of operating systems such as VMS, UNIX, and MS-DOS. To conform to the limitations of some popular operating systems, the HSG Proposal limits a directory hierarchy to eight levels.

Structure of a Directory File [8 and 13]

A directory is similar to a normal user file. Unlike a user file, however, the directory file structure is specifically defined in the HSG Proposal [8.3.1, 8.3.2]. Directory files contain variable length directory records, which include fields for the file identifier, the file length in bytes, the LBN of the first logical block in the extent, and other information required to open and use the file [13.1]. Each file extent—not just the file—has a separate directory record. When a file consists of multiple extents, the order of the directory records in the subdirectory follows the logical order of the data in the file. In other words, the first directory entry is for the first extent, which contains the beginning part of the file; the last directory entry is for the file's last extent, which contains data at the end of the file [7.3]. Figure 2 (on the next page) illustrates this arrangement.

Additional information about a file can be stored in something called an *extended attribute record* (XAR). We will look more closely at the contents of XARs later. For now, note that the XAR is located immediately before the file on the disc [8.4.1]. The LBN stored in the directory for the file location actually points to the beginning of the XAR. Since the directory record also contains an XAR length, a system can easily jump over the XAR to the start of the data in the file.

Like other files, directories are located using a record entry in the parent directory. Therefore, the HSG proposal doesn't dictate the directories' physical location on the disc and may be placed anywhere that best serves the specific application's needs. For example, placing a directory amidst the most frequently accessed files can minimize access time.

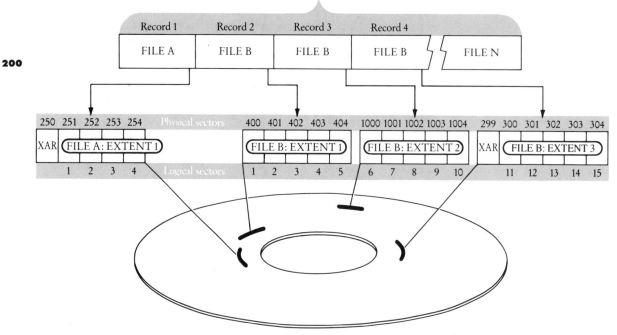

Figure 2. The logical order of the file determines the order of the extents within the directory.

Lengths of directory records vary [13.1], but they may not span logical sector boundaries [8.3.1]. In other words, directory records are blocked into units that correspond to the logical sectors on the disc. Complete sectors are convenient *natural* quantities of data to read into and keep in system buffers. By blocking the directory records into sectors, the HSG Proposal ensures that each buffer holding part of a directory will contain only complete directory records, never fragments.

The Path Table [8.2 and 12.1]

One problem with hierarchical directory structures of this type is that they can require a lot of seeking to open files deeply nested in the directory hierarchy. If opening a file in a subdirectory of a subdirectory of a subdirectory involves finding and opening each of the parent directory files, the process can take a long time. The HSG Proposal provides a shortcut. This shortcut uses a *Path Table*, a kind of index to all directories. The proposal specifies that the Path Table contain the LBN of each subdirectory, providing direct access to any subdirectory through the Path Table. Thus, if the complete Path Table is kept in RAM, a single seek can access any subdirectory on the disc.

Performance Considerations for Directories

The Path Table only guarantees access to a directory's first sector. A very large directory containing thousands of files spread over many sectors of the disc may require substantial reading and searching for the system to find the file within the directory. For this reason, users should try to distribute their files among many directories, limiting subdirectories to about 40 files. The directory records for 40 files with names of average length will fit in a single sector. If all directories are limited to a single sector of records, the Path Table index provides direct access to the directory record for any file.

Stated another way, the Path Table is an index to the entire directory structure, treating it as one big, flat file. But the Path Table does not reach below the subdirectory level. By limiting the number of files in a subdirectory to 40, a system's file-opening performance can be quite good even with a large number of files on the disc; following the Path Table to the subdirectory immediately reveals the file's location. If, however, the disc publisher places thousands of files in the root directory or in a few very large directories, the Path Table's indexing function is not being used to its best advantage. In other words, it may be necessary to read many sectors from the disc before finding the desired file reference.

Extended Attribute Records

Extended attribute records allow you to store additional information about individual files. The information stored in the XAR extends and supplements the directory record. By placing this extra information in the XAR, rather than keeping it all in the directory record, you significantly improve performance. If directory records are small, more can fit into a *block* of the directory structure, giving you information about more files with a single seek and read from the disc. The HSG Proposal keeps the directory records small by storing only the most frequently used information about each file. All other information goes in the XAR.

The operating system or application can use the XAR to hold such things as the record structure associated with a file; the creation, modification, expiration, and effective dates of the file; or special application-specific information. Use of XARs is optional [8.4]. A field (BP 2) in the directory record for each file extent indicates whether the XAR is present [13.1.2]. If an application does not need any of the information in the XAR, the record simply is omitted, and BP 2 is set to zero.

If a file has multiple extents, each extent can have its own XAR. Information in these XARs can conflict, which can cause problems. To prevent

202

this difficulty, the HSG Proposal specifies that the last extent of a file (the last in logical sequence) must contain valid XAR data for the entire file [8.4.1]. If the XAR of the last extent differs from those of earlier extents, the other XARs are ignored. If the last extent has no XAR, the whole file is regarded as having no XAR attributes even if the earlier extents had XARs associated with them. This feature is particularly useful when a file is updated in a multivolume CD ROM set. You can change the permissions (see below) for the entire file, for example, by providing a new XAR with different permission settings for the last extent.

Placement

When an application uses extended attribute records, they are placed at the beginning of the file. The value of the Extended Attribute Record Length field (BP 2) in the directory record tells how many logical blocks the XAR consumes. Actual data of the file begins at the logical block following the XAR [8.4.1].

Directories, because they are simply files, can also have XARs. When directories have XARs, the Path Table field labeled Extended Attribute Record Length (BP 5) indicates how many logical blocks the XAR occupies and thus where the directory records begin [12.1.1.2].

Standard Contents of XARs [13.2]

The XAR stores information on file-level access control, file dates, and record structures within files, and has a reserved field for system use, a complete directory record, and a field reserved for application use. These fields can be used both by operating systems and by applications that require such information.

File-Level Access Control [13.2.1–13.2.3]
The first three fields in the XAR to provide information on file-level access control are as follows:

Owner Identification Code. This code identifies the file's owner. It is a 16-bit number that, when used in conjunction with the permissions field, enables an operating system such as UNIX or VMS to determine whether the user who is trying to access the file has the appropriate permissions to do so.

Group Identification Code. This specifies the group ID of the user group to which the file owner belongs. The operating system again checks for appropriate permissions and grants or denies access to members of other groups.

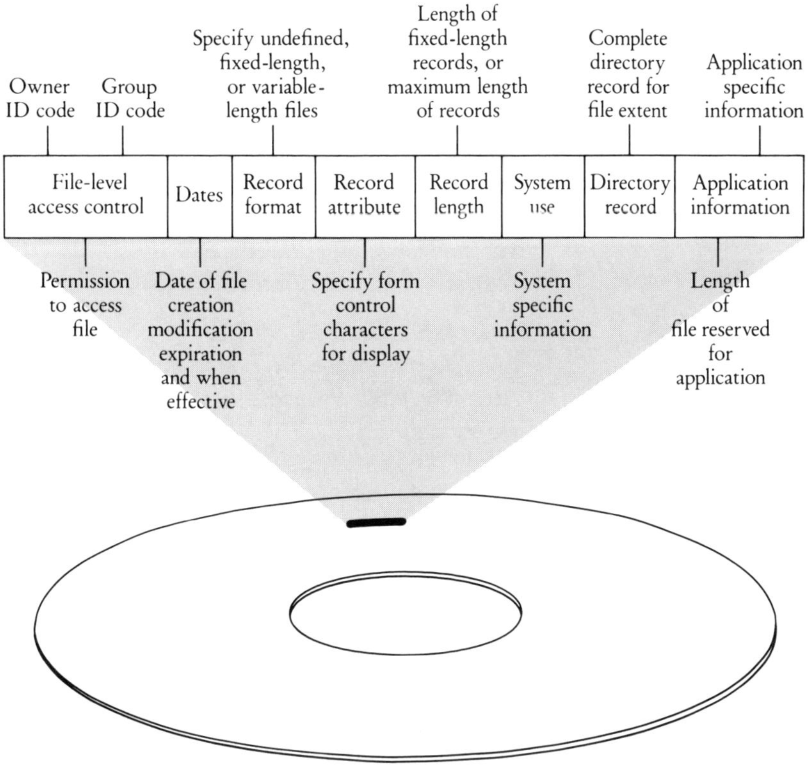

Figure 3. The fields of an extended attribute record (XAR).

Permissions. This field specifies the conditions under which users (system, owner, group, and world) will be allowed access to a file. These permissions are replicated from magnetic media specifications and therefore contain some bits that are always set (including the write and delete bits). When permissions are restricted, the operating system and/or file manager checks the owner or group identification to determine whether the user attempting access has authorization.

The format of discs made to specifications of the HSG Proposal is widely known and probably will be implemented across a wide variety of hardware and operating systems, some with no file-level access control. If the system has no access control, permissions will be useful only if you can physically control the discs. If the system has no built-in access control, it will read all files regardless of how the permissions bytes are set. For example, a user denied access by a VMS system can carry the disc to a PC and read it under MS-DOS.

File Dates [13.2.4–13.2.7]

The XAR also allows you to record when the file was created or modified, when it will expire, and when it will become effective. Many operating systems and applications use these dates to provide information about a file's currency or status. For example, if the application contains time-critical data (for instance, new tax laws) that becomes effective only on a future date, the application might inform the user that the data is not accurate until the date specified in the effective date field. You can use the other date fields for similar purposes.

Records [9 and 13.2.8–13.2.10]

The next part of the XAR stores information on a file's record structures. The HSG Proposal supports two record formats: fixed-length and variable-length. The Record Format (BP 75) field indicates whether the record structure is undefined, fixed-length, or variable-length. Values of 2 and 3 in this field indicate the use of variable-length records, but distinguish between two possible byte orders for the Record Length field (*record control word*) associated with each variable-length record in the file. If the value of Record Format is 2, then the value stored in the record control word is written with the *Least Significant Byte* (LSB) first. If the value in BP 75 is 3, then the value stored in the record control word is written *Most Significant Byte* (MSB) first [9.4]. Unless informed otherwise, the application will record all files as a stream of bytes with no implied record structure.

The Record Attribute field (BP 76) specifies which form-control characters will be used to display a file's records. *Display* can mean any output, such as a screen or a printed page, that ultimately shows the file. A value of 0 (zero) in this field indicates that a linefeed will precede each record in the file and a carriage return character will follow each record as it is displayed. A value of 1 indicates the first byte will be interpreted as the FORTRAN carriage-control character specified in ISO 1539. Finally, a value of 2 specifies that the application knows the form-control characters in the record and will process them accordingly.

The final field in the records portion of an XAR is Record Length (BP 77–80). This field contains a 16-bit binary number that is interpreted based on the value in the Record Format (BP 75) field. When the value in BP 75 is zero, the value in BP 77–80 must also be zero. This indicates the file doesn't have a record structure specified in the HSG Proposal. A value of 1 in this field means the value in Record Length specifies the length of fixed-length records. A value of 2 or 3 in BP 75 means the value found in BP 77–80 is the maximum length of any record in the file.

System Use [13.2.11, 13.2.12]

A third use of the XAR is to record system-specific information. The System Identifier (BP 81–112) field contains the name of the system using the following field, Reserved for System Use (BP 113–176). The 64 bytes in Reserved for System Use can store any system-specific information. The HSG Proposal doesn't specify the field's contents. You should use this field only for information that an operating system or a CD ROM delivery system requires. You should not use it for data that is application specific. Application-specific data should go in the Reserved for Application Use field, which we will discuss later.

Directory Record [13.2.17]

A complete directory record for the file extent associated with this XAR is duplicated in the XAR. This duplicate information is provided to ensure that the XAR is the one place where a system can find all information about a file. Some delivery systems may use this extra directory record to facilitate file access. The parent directory number (as used in the Path Table) is also provided to enable a system to locate a parent directory within the Path Table.

Application Information [13.2.18]

The last field in the XAR is for application-specific information. The HSG Proposal doesn't specify the size of this field, but it can't be more than 65,536 bytes [13.2.16]. The field in BP 247–250, Length of Reserved for Application Use, indicates how large an area the application will use. This is the HSG's only specification for the application use area; the application determines its contents. Consequently, this field generally is ignored unless an application predetermines its use. For example, for a file containing text extracted from a book, a library application might record the ISBN number of the book in this part of the file's XAR.

The Disc Volume

The area of a disc where information can be recorded is known as its *Volume Space* [6.2]. The Volume Space is all available sectors for which the Philips/Sony Yellow Book doesn't define a use.

Overall Structure

The Volume Space starts with logical sector 0 (LSN 0 is physical sector 00:02:00, as explained earlier) and extends to the end of the recorded area on the disc.

Two areas, a System Area and a Data Area [6.3], make up the Volume Space. The System Area is the first 16 logical sectors (LSN 0–LSN 15). The HSG Proposal doesn't define its content. Disc designers can use it as they see fit. For example, the area can store volume access information, special code required to boot a disc, encryption keys, or other kinds of system data. If you use these first 16 sectors, be sure that your targeted delivery system has the intelligence necessary to interpret and act on what you write there. The Data Area occupies all remaining recorded sectors of the disc and contains all other information written on the disc. The HSG Proposal is concerned primarily with organizing its contents.

Volume Descriptors

A CD ROM disc is called a *volume*. At the beginning of each volume's Data Area (LSN 16) is a structure that contains the *Volume Descriptors* [6.3.1]. Volume Descriptors describe the entire disc's contents. They provide information about the disc's logical organization; the location of the root directory for the standard file system structure; the number and location of any unspecified structure; partitions on the disc; the authors, data preparers, and time and dates of creation; and much more. The Volume Descriptors sequence is the only part of the data area for which the HSG Proposal specifies a location. The system can find the locations of other important structures on the disc by reading the Volume Descriptors.

Arrangement of Volume Descriptors [6.3.1]
Volume Descriptors are 2048-byte, fixed-length records. They must all be recorded sequentially, starting at LSN 16. The sequence of Volume Descriptors can be as long as necessary to describe all structures on the disc. A special Volume Descriptor, the *Volume Descriptor Sequence Terminator,* indicates the end of the Volume Descriptor sequence.

Five types of Volume Descriptors are defined in the HSG Proposal. They are summarized in Figure 4. The sequence of Volume Descriptors may contain many types of Volume Descriptors in many combinations. However, two constraints are placed on sequence organization:

1. Each disc must contain at least one Standard Volume Descriptor. An HSG-formatted disc must have the Standard File Structure and needs a Standard Volume Descriptor to locate this File Structure. However, a disc can have only one Standard File Structure. Consequently, if the disc author wishes to place more than one Standard Volume Descriptor in the sequence of Volume Descriptors (for redundancy in case of a disc error), each one must refer to the same Standard File Structure.

2. At least one Volume Descriptor Sequence Terminator must be placed after all other Volume Descriptors.

Figure 4 shows three examples of Volume Descriptor sequences.

Standard volume descriptor	Volume sequence terminator

Example 1

Boot record #1	Standard volume descriptor	Boot record #2	Standard volume descriptor	Volume sequence terminator

Example 2

Coded character set #1	Boot record	Standard volume descriptor	Unspecified volume descriptor	Coded character set #2	Volume sequence terminator

Example 3

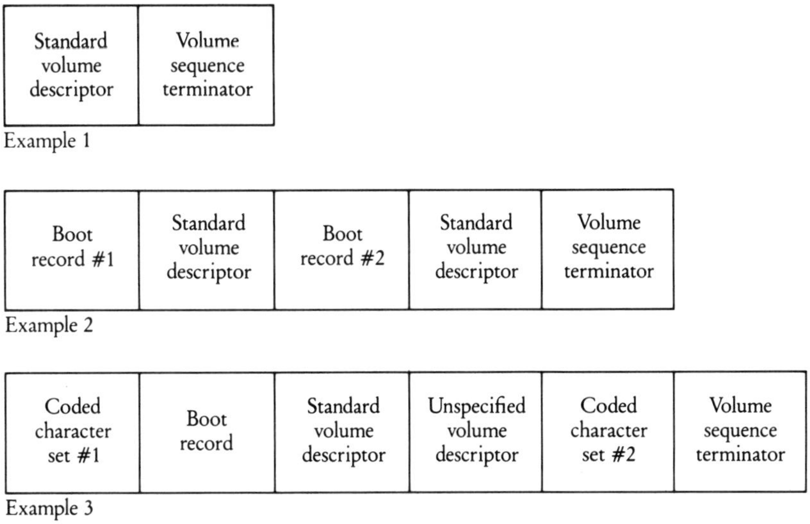

Figure 4. Examples of Volume Descriptor sequences. Any combination of Volume Descriptors can constitute a sequence, but the sequence must end in a Volume Sequence Terminator, and it can include only one Standard Volume Descriptor.

The Standard File Structure Volume Descriptor [6.3.2 and 11.4]
The HSG Proposal requires that each disc contain a Standard File Structure. This is simply the hierarchical directory system and the Path Table that were described earlier. The Standard File Structure Volume Descriptor provides essential information about this fundamental part of the disc format.

To ensure that discs are interchangeable, fields in the Standard File Structure Volume Descriptor that contain character string identifiers use the standard ISO 646 character set.

The fields of the Standard File Structure Volume Descriptor show the HSG Proposal's flexibility.

System Identifier. This field provides a means to identify the system using the disc's System Area (LSN 0–LSN 15 [9.1]). If an implementation recognizes an identifier in this location, it can proceed to process the data in the System Area.

Application Identifier. An application can use these 128 bytes to tell how the data on the disc will be interpreted. In fact, this is how discs made in the CD-I format will be identified by CD-I "Green Machines." The Green Book will designate a specific sequence of characters which, when found in this location, indicate the disc is a CD-I *green disc.*

Volume Set Identifier. We will return to this field when we discuss multivolume sets, but its primary use is to name a set of discs. This field is used in conjunction with the Volume Set Sequence Number to construct multivolume disc sets.

Directory Record for Root Directory. You must know the location of the root directory before you can traverse the directory structure. This 34-byte record points to the root and is one way to locate the root directory. A second way is to read the Path Table, which points to the root directory's location. The root directory contains a copy of the root directory record.

Copyright File Identifier. Authors of discs can name a file to store copyright information and store the filename in this field. This file resides in the root directory. The filename can have no more than eight characters, and its extension is limited to three. Reserved names aren't used, to prevent conflicts with reserved names associated with other systems and applications.

Abstract File Identifier. This field is used and restricted in the same ways as the copyright field. The abstract file may contain any information the authors wish. Both this file and the copyright file are, however, intended to be text files that are easily displayed and read.

Coded Character Set Volume Descriptor [6.3.3 and 11.5]
As mentioned, the HSG Proposal limits file and directory names in the Standard File Structure to a subset of the ISO 646 characters to ensure that discs are interchangeable. The proposal also recognizes, however, that different character sets often are desirable for filenames and directory names. Consequently, the HSG Proposal allows disc authors to build directory structures using coded character sets in place of the standard ISO 646 character set.

These alternate directory structures are physically separate from the Standard File Structure and use different directory files and a different root directory. However, the structures are isomorphic, having the same form of Path Table, directory records, and so forth. A delivery system that can read the Standard File Structure can also read the directory structures associated with coded character sets with only minor additions to the program code.

A variety of relationships are possible between the Standard File Structure and file structures associated with coded character sets. At one extreme, the directory and file references can be identical except for their character sets and names. That is, the structures can actually reference the same files and provide the same hierarchical view of these files. At the other extreme, the directory and file systems can refer to wholly separate sets of files. Of course, an enormous array of combinations is possible between these extremes, allowing directory systems to provide different *views* (different directory hierarchies) of the same set of files. For instance, they can provide common access to certain files but separate, unique access to others. Just as the Standard File Structure Volume Descriptor provides essential information about the Standard File Structure, the *Coded Character Set Volume Descriptor* provides essential information about each coded character set file system. This descriptor contains two significant additions to the Standard File System Volume Descriptor:

1. The Coded Character Set for Descriptor Identifier field specifies the escape sequences used to interpret descriptor fields in the Volume Descriptor and directory records for the coded character set file system.

2. The Volume Flag Byte (BP 16) indicates whether the Coded Character Set Identifier field has one or more escape sequences that aren't registered according to ISO 2375.

Unspecified Structure Volume Descriptor [6.3.4 and 11.6]

The *Unspecified Structure Volume Descriptor* describes a partition of the disc in which a disc author can record data that does not conform to the HSG Standard File Structure. Because this area's contents aren't specified, a creative author may use this partition for a number of purposes. These might include recording digital audio or placing alternative file systems on a disc. This partition is part of the Volume Space described in the Standard File Structure Volume Descriptor, so you can reference data within it from the Standard File system.

Boot Records [6.3.5]

The final type of Volume Descriptor the HSG Proposal describes is the *Boot Record*. Systems or specific applications use this descriptor to bring the computer system to a desired state. For example, a Boot Record might load an operating system, or it might load an application program associated with the mounted disc. A disc can have an unlimited number of boot records, but the combination of the Boot System Identifier (BP 16–47) and Boot Identifier (BP 48–79) fields should be unique to guarantee that the host system or application can properly identify the Boot Record.

Multivolume Sets [6.4]

Although the capacity of a CD ROM is tremendous, data sets can easily fill more than one disc. Consequently, the HSG Proposal provides for combining discs into multivolume sets.

The Standard File Structure Volume Descriptor lets the disc author specify the name of the set and the number of volumes in it. In general, two situations prompt the creation of a multivolume set. In the first, the disc author has a data set of a known size that exceeds the capacity of a disc. The number of discs required for the data set is known before the volume set is mastered.

The second situation occurs when publishers handle data sets that grow over time and they must periodically add discs to an existing volume set.

"All at Once" Multivolume Sets

We begin with the first scenario. For a multivolume set of known size, a publisher must set three fields in the Standard Volume Descriptor to appropriate values.

Volume Set Identifier (BP 215–342). The first field names the volume set. All discs in the set must have the same name in this field. This is how a system knows whether all the discs mounted belong to a set.

Volume Set Size (BP 129–132). The second field of interest stores a number that specifies how many discs a set contains. Numbering starts at 1; thus, 2 is the minimum value this field may contain for a multivolume set. The HSG Proposal allows a maximum of 65,535 volumes in a set.

Volume Set Sequence Number (BP 133–136). The third field of interest specifies multivolume sets. Each disc in the set has a different number in this field. Numbering starts at 1 and continues sequentially to the value specified in the Volume Set Size field.

There is one further consideration when making a multivolume set under this scenario. The HSG Proposal specifies that each disc in an "All at Once" set contain a Path Table and directory structure that are valid for every volume of the set. (That is, any disc in the set may be read for a Path Table, and the directory structure found on any disc works for all discs in the set.) This necessitates locating directory files in the same place on all discs of the set. The duplicated directory structure enables a one-player system to read a multivolume set, since a user can find any file in the set without mounting each disc. Of course, actually reading the file may require a disc change, but the user will have to mount at most one disc to access the file.

Updated Multivolume Sets

The second scenario is a bit more complex, but lets a publisher add volumes to a set after the initial disc(s) are mastered. Suppose that we create a two-volume set and subsequently add a volume. The values for the Volume Set Identifier, Volume Set Size, and other relevant fields from the Standard File Structure Volume Descriptor for the discs are shown in Table 2.

Set	Volume ID	Volume Set ID	Volume Set Size	Volume Set Sequence No.
Disc 1, initial set	SAMPLE_1	SAMPLE_SET	2	1
Disc 2, initial set	SAMPLE_2	SAMPLE_SET	2	2
Disc 3, added later	ADDED_DISC	SAMPLE_SET	3	3

Table 2. Adding an extension to an existing multivolume set.

The Volume Identifier, as you can see, varies from disc to disc. The Volume Set Identifier, however, must be the same for all volumes in a set.

For the initial volume set, the Volume Set Size is 2. Each volume in the original set has a *Volume Set Sequence Number* (VSSN) that tells its position in the set. When we add the new volume, its Volume Set Size field reflects this. Its VSSN also indicates that the volume is the last in the set. We cannot, of course, change the Volume Set Size fields of earlier volumes.

It should be clear that only the new volume can reflect the updated status of the volume set. This is why, as noted, the HSG Proposal specifies that the disc with the highest value in the Volume Set Size field contain the version of the Path Table and directory structure valid for the set [6.4]. In our example, the last disc, with a Volume Set Size of 3, is the one that must be mounted as the system is brought up. The directory on the higher-numbered disc makes the directory structures on any lower-numbered discs obsolete. This new directory is the only one that can provide information about all files in the volume set.

This feature is very powerful. With this updating scheme, you can logically delete or replace files on lower-numbered discs. You can omit files you wish to delete from the directory on the higher-numbered discs. This mechanism can also replace files. The new directory simply references a replacement file on the update disc and ignores the earlier version of the file. Obviously, these files are not actually erased from the other discs. If a lower-numbered disc is mounted first, in place of the updated disc, the *deleted* file suddenly becomes available again.

Other Format Options

The HSG Proposal provides a rich set of optional features that authors may implement. Since the HSG Proposal is a leveled proposal, not all features are available at all levels. We highlight some of the more interesting features below.

Interleaved Files [13.1.8, 13.1.9]

Many real-time applications require a specific rate of data transfer from the disc. The rate for reading all sectors sequentially is fixed at 150 KB/sec. If this transfer rate is too high, data can overload the application unless it stops reading. Careful study of CD ROM technology reveals that once an application stops reading from the CD ROM disc, the average time before the next read begins is about two revolutions of the disc. For many applications this lag is too long. Therefore, a real-time application is either faced with receiving data too quickly or stopping the data stream and waiting. Neither alternative is attractive.

The HSG Proposal circumvents this difficulty by providing an interleaving mechanism. Rather than recording the file as a continuous sequence of sectors, you leave blank sectors at carefully calculated intervals between recorded sectors. Thus, the drive can continue to a file sequentially while higher-level software or hardware throws away the unwanted blank sectors. Figure 5 shows how a file (File A) can be expanded in this way to slow down the data transfer rate. Each box represents a sequential sector of the disc. Those sectors labeled *A* contain data from File A. Unlabeled sectors contain no data.

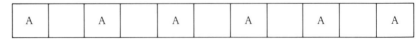

Figure 5. An interleaving technique that slows the data transfer rate by inserting blank sectors between file sectors.

Figure 6 illustrates a different use of interleaving. In some applications, alternating between the data from one file and that from a second may be useful. In Figure 6 we read 3 sectors from File B, then read 2 sectors from File C, and then return to File B, streaming data sequentially all the while.

212

B	B	B	C	C	B	B	B	C	C	B

Figure 6. An interleaving technique that reads data from two files at nearly the same time.

Two fields in the directory record specify interleaved files [13.1]. The first **213** of these is labeled Interleave Size (BP 27) and the second Interleave Skip Factor (BP 29–32). The Interleave Size defines the number of consecutive logical blocks recorded in a file. The Interleave Skip Factor tells the system how many logical blocks to skip before reading the next part of the file. The Interleave Size and Skip Factor must be such that each part of the file begins at a sector boundary.

Associated Files [13.1.6]

In some operating environments, having two or more files with the same file identifier is advantageous. The relationship between these files is more intimate than it would be if the two files were given the same name and different extensions. For example, one file might contain the text of a document and the other might contain fonts and formatting information. In this situation, the Associated File bit (bit position 2) of the directory record's File Flags field is set to 1. The application software or the delivery system software must correctly interpret this flag and act accordingly.

Hidden Files [13.1.6]

The Directory Record File Flag byte (BP 25) also contains a bit (bit position 0) that allows files to be *hidden*. That is, when a user issues certain commands (to display the files in a directory, for instance), the delivery system does not acknowledge the file's existence. The hidden files attribute is delivery-system-dependent. Consequently, prospective users should be sure the delivery system's treatment of hidden files is compatible before using this feature.

Levels of Interchange

The High Sierra proposal provides three levels of implementation for software and system developers. Called the *levels of data interchange* in the May 28 proposal, these implementation stages give authors the choice of making discs that incorporate a few of the proposed features, or all of them, depending on the author's needs.

Level One: Level 1, the lowest level of interchange, incorporates a minimum number of features. Most of the proposal's more sophisticated features are excluded. Any CD ROM system (CD ROM player, host computer, operating system, and retrieval software) that can read data formatted according to the HSG Proposal will be able to read this format. Level 1 entails the following restrictions:

- Only single-disc volume sets are allowed; no support for multivolume sets is provided.

- Hidden files are not allowed.

- Associated files are prohibited. This means the Level 1 system will be unable to find two files sharing the same name in the same subdirectory.

- XAR fields associated with record structures may be ignored by Level 1 software.

- Protection fields in the XAR also may be ignored.

- Multiextent files are not allowed. In other words, all files must be stored as a continuous stream of bytes.

- Interleaving of files is not allowed.

- Directory names and filenames may be no more than eight characters.

- File extensions may not exceed three characters.

- File version numbers are not allowed.

Level Two: Level 2 provides additional features that most developers, especially those working with the CD-I standard format, will need. It differs from Level 1 only in allowing interleaving of files and directory names and filenames as long as 31 characters. All other Level 1 restrictions apply. Level 2 delivery systems will read Level 1 and 2 discs, but they will not read Level 3 discs properly.

The HSG Proposal suggests that you can make text on CD ROM discs CD-I compatible by using Level 1 or Level 2 format specifications in conjunction with ISO 646 character codes. The VTOC and directory structures of CD-I and CD ROM are completely compatible. The format of CD-I, however, is simpler because it is designed to work with one operating system. For this reason, CD-I does not act on the contents of XARs.

Level Three: All features and capabilities of the HSG Proposal are provided at Level 3. Fully implementing Level 3 discs requires an operating system that can handle features such as file extents, multivolume sets, and interleaving. If a system merely ignores these special attributes, it may read the data incorrectly, rendering the data unusable. Level 3 delivery systems should be able to read Level 1 and 2 discs without trouble.

The three levels of interchange are meant to give system developers the option to provide downward compatibility, so all delivery systems designed to read Level 3 or Level 2 discs can also read Level 1 discs. However, the opposite is not true. A delivery system designed to read a Level 1 disc will not necessarily correctly read a disc mastered to Level 2 or Level 3 specifications. The NISO version of the draft proposal will specify how a delivery system should react when it cannot read a disc.

For most publishers, the question is not how to detect disc formats but rather how to determine which features of the specification a particular publication will require. After determining which features they need, they will have to find a system that accommodates those features.

Many software and hardware companies have announced they will support the High Sierra proposal, but the levels of implementation they will support are likely to vary. The High Sierra proposal represents several companies' efforts to develop a standard file format that takes into account some of the special features the more popular operating systems provide. Among these features are hidden files, record structure attributes, and associated files.

Since many operating systems are not designed to use all of the proposed features, few system manufacturers are likely to implement the entire Level 3 specification initially. Instead, they may adopt subsets of the specification and develop methods to deal with unimplemented features. Microsoft's first version of MS-DOS Extensions, for example, is an early implementation that reads Level 1 formats, but not those of Levels 2 and 3. As demand for CD ROM grows, Microsoft and other software development companies probably will add features.

Conclusion

The High Sierra proposal was formulated to give companies wishing to develop applications a standard format that a number of delivery systems can handle. It has moved through the standardization process—which can take as long as five years—at an unprecedented speed. The two standardization committees currently reviewing the draft are expected to complete the final document in 1987—less than two years after it was conceived. Many CD ROM developers have joined forces to support the May 28 draft of the HSG Proposal now, even though they expect minor changes in the final document. Publishers, in using the proposed High Sierra Format, should feel assured that its strong industry support will continue.

216

About the Authors

John Einberger, vice president for software development for Reference Technology, Inc., in Boulder, Colorado, is responsible for developing software products optimized for use with read-only optical data systems. He was instrumental in forming and chairing the High Sierra Group, which has proposed a logical format standard for CD ROM discs. Einberger has worked in the computer industry for more than 18 years, has taught at the university level, holds many patents, and is the author of many publications. He holds degrees in electrical engineering, computer science, and business.

Bill Zoellick is Director of Technology for the Alexandria Institute, a nonprofit organization dedicated to making CD ROM information retrieval systems more widely available to users through libraries and other resource centers. Before joining the Alexandria Institute, Bill was Manager of Software Research at TMS, Inc., where he designed and implemented information retrieval software and lower level, file system software for CD ROM. He was a key participant in the High Sierra Group, playing an active role in producing the CD ROM logical format proposal. He has written and spoken widely about a broad range of CD ROM publishing issues and is co-author of a major new textbook on file structures.

Resources

Schwerin, Julie B. 1986. *CD-ROM Standards: The Book.* Pittsfield, VT: InfoTech and Learned Information, Inc. Describes the technical results of the High Sierra Group work as analyzed by four industry experts. Available from InfoTech, P.O. Box 633, Pittsfield, VT 05762.

Premastering and Mastering

Many information providers and publishers devote substantial time and energy to designing a product for CD ROM and then treat the actual manufacturing process almost as an afterthought.

With CD ROM, as with traditional print publishing, manufacturing choices can directly affect the product's success, the quality of workmanship, the price, and the timeliness of delivery. Understanding the CD ROM manufacturing process can help publishers make intelligent choices.

The final production process involves three basic procedures: *premastering, mastering,* and *replication.*

Premastering

If your tape format conforms to the submission standards of the mastering facility and is organized in the proper 2048-byte data blocks, it is ready to be premastered. Premastering is the process in which the error correction and error detection bytes, defined in the CD ROM specification, are calculated and added to each 2048-byte block. Also added are 12 sync bytes, 3 address bytes, and 1 mode byte specified in the CD ROM standard. (See Chapter 3 for an explanation of the CD ROM format.)

Mastering facilities do not check logical consistency, disc layout, data structures, or disc directories. These tasks are the responsibility of the information provider or the data preparation service. The mastering facility may, however, require that the first data file of the tape master contain the total number of data blocks, a volume set identification number, subcode data, and so forth. This information is not transferred to the final disc, and requirements may differ from one facility to another.

Disc manufacturers normally scan tapes when they first arrive to be sure the tapes are readable. If the tape format is incompatible with the premastering equipment, the tape must be reformatted to meet the facility's

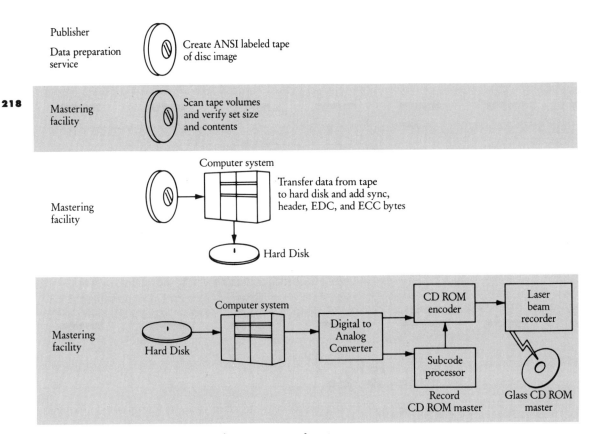

Figure 1. The CD ROM manufacturing process.

specifications. Most data preparation services handle the tape exchange and rescheduling as part of their minimum service. However, if you are planning to work directly with the manufacturer, you may want to send a test tape to the facility several weeks before you send the final data tapes. This will help ensure that your tapes are compatible with the facility's equipment before you reach your production deadline.

Mastering

Mastering, as its name implies, is the process of creating the disc from which all others are produced. The first step in the manufacturing process is to create a master that can be used for replication. A laser burns the pits and lands containing the data into a photoresist surface—beginning at the center track and moving outward in a spiral pattern.

After checking the glass master for accuracy, the replication machinery makes a *stamper*. Different replication processes require slightly different stampers, but the function remains the same—embossing the data pattern on the mass-production disc. Through an injection molding process, a series of intermediate impressions are made that provide a generation of negative stampers that produce positive disc images. The family-tree-like structure of this part of the production cycle has given rise to names such as *mother*, *father*, and *sons* or *daughters* for the various disc generations.

Replication

Compact discs are made from a polycarbonate plastic, which is a material that is less vulnerable to water absorption and heat than the polymethyl-methacrylate (PMMA) used in laminated videodiscs. Because videodiscs are two slices of substrate sandwiched together, they are more rigid than CDs. So manufacturers must take extra precautions to prevent heat or water absorption from warping them. Most manufacturing facilities today replicate discs using some type of injection molding. The polycarbonate resin is heated and poured into molds that shape the discs. The stamper impresses the data patterns into the cooling plastic, and the disc is then put in a vacuum chamber, where a reflective layer of aluminum is added. Finally, the reflective layer is coated with protective lacquer. Labels are silk-screened or printed on the lacquer side.

Injection Molding

Injection molding has a number of advantages. Plants worldwide use the technique, and its characteristics are well known. Yields typically are low when a plant opens, and they increase substantially as technicians gain experience. Critics claim injection molding is messy and expensive, requiring large capital investments in equipment and clean rooms. In addition, they say that during molding, polycarbonate distortions that impair or deflect the laser light can appear in the plastic. Despite its shortcomings, the majority of plants operating today use this process.

Photo-Polymerization

The 3M plant in Menomonie, WI, uses a photo-polymerization (2P) process in which precut polycarbonate resin is inserted between the master and a base plate and then embossed. This polycarbonate *sandwich filling* is then cured with ultraviolet light. One major advantage of this method of replication is its speed, gained partially by avoiding heating and cooling the plastic during production. Critics of the 2P process say yields remain low because improper curing or warpage causes many discs to be rejected.

Continuous Embossing

DOCData of Venlo, The Netherlands, and COMDisc of Los Angeles use two quite different methods that attempt to produce the same result—fast, low-cost replication of compact discs by a continuous printing or embossing technique. Both systems have worked in a laboratory setting, but neither is currently available commercially. Although the techniques show promise and have attracted a great deal of attention, no major company has yet committed itself financially to either process. If and when a manufacturer makes either process available, publishers should expect the new techniques to dramatically affect both prices and turnaround times.

Selecting a Manufacturing Facility

At this writing, most CD ROM discs that are on the market or that have been formally demonstrated come from one of three sources—Philips/PolyGram in West Germany, 3M in Wisconsin, or Hitachi in Japan. LaserVideo's California plant also has made small quantities of CD ROMs. In mid-1986, Sony's Digital Audio Disc Corp. shifted from manufacturing audio-only discs to making CD ROMs.

Although each plant produces compact discs that meet the Yellow Book standard and will play on most drives, all have slightly different manufacturing processes. Even punching the center hole occurs at different stages. The Philips/Sony standard only specifies performance for the final product; it does not dictate how to achieve that performance.

Choosing a plant appears to be getting more difficult, rather than easier. Nearly 30 new compact disc manufacturing facilities have been announced worldwide. Although most organizations plan to emphasize audio discs because of the pent-up consumer demand and large anticipated runs, a hefty percentage say they will also produce CD ROM discs. In addition, at least two companies are developing the continuous sheet replication method mentioned earlier.

Compelling reasons exist for choosing any of the plants now producing CD ROM discs. Price, location, and quality of service are usually good measures for selecting a vendor, but so is experience. When selecting a manufacturer, find one with substantial experience in CD ROM.

Move cautiously in sending data to plants just beginning to operate. Experience has shown that the learning curve is long and that a new plant's yields can be quite low. Because music discs require a lower level of error correction than do CD ROMs, some experts believe the compact disc industry would be best served if new facilities started with music discs and moved to data discs only when they were more experienced.

If you feel overwhelmed by the options, you can get help from a data preparation service.

What to Expect from Service Bureaus

Publishers who enlist the help of service bureaus to prepare their ANSI-labeled tapes usually have the same companies arrange for premastering, mastering, and replication of discs. These firms generally assist in project management, providing such services as monitoring disc progress, dealing with customs if the plant is outside the United States, controlling quality, and arranging fast turnaround or volume-preferential pricing.

Many service bureaus have special arrangements with certain disc manufacturers that you may want to know about in advance. For example, Digital Equipment Corp.'s (DEC) disc-publishing service has been handling production through the Philips/PolyGram European plant since mid-1985. In recent months, Reference Technology has announced a cooperative agreement with 3M, and KnowledgeSet has begun a joint venture with Sony that includes special service at Sony's Terre Haute plant.

Labeling

Most plants apply some form of label art, which the publisher supplies. A simple black-on-silver silk screen is adequate for some purposes. Sony's Terre Haute plant will do four-color silk screen if requested. Reports that silk-screened art wears away with frequent touching have led some manufacturers to study other ways to apply labels. 3M, for example, uses a process called *pad printing*, which employs a special ink developed specifically for compact discs.

No standard currently exists for labeling or identifying CD ROMs. DEC considered its subscription products a form of periodical and has applied for an International Standard Serial Number (ISSN) for each title. The National Information Standards Organization is expected to address the question of external labeling as it considers the technical file format standards that the High Sierra Group proposed.

Packaging

The packaging of choice for CD ROM is a plastic jewel box. Although the compact audio industry has been looking at cardboard sleeves and other alternatives, the CD ROM section of the business seems firmly committed to jewel boxes. DEC even printed disc titles on the spines of the cases so they can be treated like books on a bookshelf. If Philips and Sony add a plastic caddy or cartridge to their standard as expected, the size may force a change in packaging material.

Quality Control

Manufacturers and service bureau executives say more mistakes creep into discs from incorrect data on publishers' tapes than from the production process. Both urge publishers to check and recheck data. In fact, Digital Equipment Corp. asks for two identical tapes—which they then compare, often finding they do not match exactly.

All manufacturers perform extensive quality control in the plant, but mistakes do slip through. Most service bureaus perform additional data integrity checks on discs they receive from the manufacturers before sending them to the publishers. They physically inspect discs for scratches, warping, and flaws in the surface and in addition check for readability and the amount of error correction invoked.

Reference Technology has been performing a 100 percent scan of every disc, but expects to move to sampling soon. The company tests each disc for the raw error rate—or the number of errors that invoke the first level of correction. Even if corrected, a disc with a raw error rate that exceeds RTI's specification is rejected. If a low-level error correction is used very often, the company says, the disc probably will not meet the corrected bit error rate standard of 10^{-13}.

Disclosure, which publishes its financial database on CD ROM, examines every disc it receives. The data processing department has written a program to check the discs, and every byte of data on the disc is read. Office staff perform the read test, which takes about 45 minutes to an hour. After the disc is approved, it is put in a jewel box and sealed with an inspection sticker.

Drive Performance Variations

Differences in the scan velocity and other specifications of the CD ROM drives also can affect disc performance. Although the Yellow Book specification defines drive performance, it gives the hardware manufacturer considerable leeway in some areas. A drive can be within standard but so different from a drive of another vendor that one drive may have difficulty reading a disc manufactured to the specifications of the second. In its start-up phase, 3M discovered that discs made for Philips drives played poorly on Hitachi drives. Adjustments in the mastering process can correct this problem, but many analysts advise publishers to be aware that discs from most plants play better on some drives than on others.

Publishers and service bureaus report many different reject rates for discs, ranging from 1 percent to more than 10 percent. However, without exception, they recommend that publishers perform some quality control check after the discs leave the manufacturing facility.

Guidelines

The CD ROM manufacturing process offers many an opportunity for delay—many of them starting with the publishers. Here are a few pointers that should help you minimize delay and the resulting frustration (courtesy of 3M).

- Prepare your data properly. If you are not sure about the data submission requirements, call the disc mastering plant or a data preparation service.

- If you are changing mastering facilities, check to see whether the new company has different submission requirements. Procedures and formats for receiving data vary among companies.

- Be sure to label your tape and send the correct one.

- Make two copies of the original tape. Save one as a backup, and send the other to the disc mastering facility.

- Fill out the forms the mastering facility or the service bureau gives you. The information they contain is very important to the technicians responsible for mastering your data.

- Schedule as far in advance as you can. Many plants promise production turnaround of three days or less, but only if you can schedule it.

- Artwork for labels often must be submitted before the tapes.

- Be sure the art is readable and properly sized for the disc. Inappropriate designs can delay and possibly spoil the looks of an otherwise perfect product.

- A disc label often must include copyright notices and manufacturers' credit lines. Find out what is required before you approve the label design.

Manufacturing CD ROMs is an unforgiving job—the smallest mistakes can make a disc unreadable or destroy data. From a publisher's perspective, time and resources spent on production may seem unimportant, but they can make or break the product.

About the Author

Anne Armstrong is managing editor of *CD Data Report,* a monthly newsletter that covers CD ROM and related optical storage technology. A journalist by profession, she has been writing about computers and information storage since 1979. She has edited three publications in the field *(Information World, Bulletin of the American Society for Information Science,* and *MicroSoftware Today)* and has been a regular columnist for *Digital Design* and *Abacus.* In addition, her articles have appeared in publications such as *Computerworld* and *Datamation.*

DATA PROTECTION AND UPDATING

Data Protection

In the United States both data collection and data protection involve laws, called intellectual property laws, that are imposed and enforced by the federal government to protect the work of authors and inventors.

The first part of this chapter deals with today's intellectual property laws as they concern CD ROM publishing. It focuses on proprietary rights and copyright law, but includes discussions of patent, trademark, and state trade secret laws. The second part of the chapter discusses other data-protection options available to publishers, including contractual and technological restrictions on use.

In reading the section on intellectual property laws, keep in mind that this subject is complex. The discussion and comments are not meant to be legal advice. No book or article can substitute for the advice and counsel of an experienced lawyer who specializes in these issues.

Data Collection

A CD ROM publication may consist of original materials created expressly for CD ROM. But it is more likely to be based on an existing work, such as a book, a collection of periodicals, or a database.

Using data or information that belongs to someone else obviously requires permission. But what if a publisher wants to use one of its own publications as the basis of a new CD ROM publication? Do the permissions granted in the original work extend to the CD ROM version? The answer is: It depends.

For example, an encyclopedia contains articles by authors who, for the most part, were contractors creating works especially for the encyclopedia. In legal terms and by virtue of a written agreement, they are "works made for hire," and the copyright belongs to the publisher. But what if an article on German literature, for example, contains a lengthy excerpt from a piece of contemporary German fiction? The publisher had to obtain permission to use the quotation in the printed version of the encyclopedia. Does this permission extend to a CD ROM version of the encyclopedia?

It is the publisher's responsibility to closely examine the language in the original contract to determine who holds the copyright. If it assigns "all worldwide copyright rights . . . including, without limitation, the right to . . . use, sell, or license the work in other media presently or subsequently existing," then clearly the publisher may use the work. If, however, the language is ambiguous or permission is limited to print media, the cautious publisher will seek clarification.

The situation has become even more difficult since the passage of the Copyright Act of 1976. This act gives authors exclusive rights that can be assigned to another party only in writing.

Consider the hypothetical case of an author's article that appeared in a trade magazine called *Honey Farming Weekly*. Does the trade magazine have the right to include the article in a CD ROM retrospective collection of *The Best of Honey Farming Weekly*? Or, can the publisher give anyone else the right to include that article in a CD ROM collection?

Many legal experts would say that the article, if unsolicited, can be published only in the magazine and that the publisher cannot assign rights. A cautious publisher would contact the author for a written assignment of rights before proceeding.

Getting permission for pictures (or sound) to be reproduced on CD ROM or CD-I can be even more complex. In our hypothetical case the cautious publisher contacts the author, pays the requested fee, and then receives an assignment of all rights. In assigning the rights, the author assures the publisher that he or she owns the photographs and graphics in the article. But in fact, the publisher discovers that the article contains a market-share chart that was created by an economist specializing in original honey-production forecasts. The economist owns the copyright on the chart, but gave the author permission for onetime use in a product presentation. To use the chart in a CD ROM publication, the publisher must acquire the economist's permission.

Negotiating and acquiring rights to published information can be tricky and difficult. But the laws are designed to protect the rights of the creators—and eventually the publishers.

Proprietary Rights: Inducement to Creativity

Just as the basic First Amendment freedoms are meant to encourage free speech, copyright law and other forms of legal protection for intellectual property are meant to encourage the creativity of authors and inventors. The U.S. Constitution provides a basis for copyright protection (and free speech) for the good of the population as a whole, not for the benefit of any single person. The people who wrote the Constitution believed that our country would be better off if authors and inventors could protect their ideas from being used without compensation. They felt this protection would encourage dissemination of ideas and use of inventions. Section 8 of the Constitution provides for the enactment of legislation "to promote the progress of science and useful arts, by securing for limited times to authors and inventors the exclusive right to their respective writings and discoveries."

Special Issues for CD ROM Developers

The federal scheme of intellectual property protection is under continuing and, in the eyes of some, growing pressure. Technology is responsible for much of this pressure, because it has made copying and transferring information easier. More people can now afford copy machines, telecommunications systems, and software. As a result, people and organizations can copy articles, gain access to machine-readable databases, download data, or copy computer programs. In doing so, they compete with the creator of an intellectual property, even if this is not their intention. For example, photocopying may hurt an author's commercial success, since it makes it unnecessary to purchase additional copies of a book or magazine.

The inconvenience of copying large amounts of information has been a fairly effective deterrent to wholesale copying. Although the photocopy machine makes it easier to copy pages of print, and technological progress has made photocopiers cheaper and faster, it still is impractical to make multiple copies of a 500-page book. In addition, although it is easy to download machine-readable databases through telecommunications networks, high connect-hour charges, telecommunications costs, and output charges make downloading large databases unfeasible.

Some publishers, however, are more concerned about CD ROM. With CD ROM you can own gigabytes of data on a collection of discs, read the data with a microcomputer, download it at a leisurely pace, and print it on a laser printer—producing, at relatively low cost, something closely resembling commercially typeset, camera-ready copy. It's no wonder publishers are nervous.

230

An April 1986 report from the Office of Technology Assessment includes this comment:

> Together, improvements in the cost, speed, and capabilities of information technologies are making traditional proprietor-initiated (civil) enforcement largely ineffective in securing reasonable control over public distribution of intellectual works. The effect of this might be to make investors reluctant to fund the creation of intellectual works.
>
> More likely, proprietors of intellectual property will be more hesitant to distribute their works in forms over which they have little physical control.*

This specter may, in the minds of some, loom over CD ROM (or videodisc) publishing. But although there is cause for concern, CD ROM publishers may in fact be able to control and protect distribution of valuable properties in new ways.

What Are Proprietary Rights?

The rights of an individual to protect his or her creative work are often called *proprietary rights*. Proprietary rights are a complex product of federal and state laws and of the court decisions that interpret those laws. The following overview reviews the U.S. laws currently in place to protect these rights.

Copyright law. Copyright law gives the creator of an original work certain exclusive rights. These rights, however, are granted only for the expression of the idea, not the idea itself, and the protection is subject to certain limitations, such as "fair use," which will be discussed later.

Patent law. Patent law protects devices or processes judged to be truly new (nonobvious and novel) and useful. In general, computer programs are not patented, but patent law can protect them if they are an intrinsic part of a patentable machine or system or part of an improved technique.

Trademark law. Trademark law protects a logo used with a product or service. A trademark (or servicemark) is a word, name, symbol, or device that somehow indicates the source of the product or service.

---

*U.S. Congress, Office of Technology Assessment, *Intellectual Property Rights in an Age of Electronics and Information*, OTA-CIT-302 (Washington, D.C.: U.S. Government Printing Office, April 1986).

Trade secret law. The laws governing trade secrets are state laws. The definition and procedural requirements of federal copyright and patent laws do not apply to trade secret laws. Trade secret protection theoretically is available for an idea or its expression in writing or for the idea's expression as a process or machine, including a computer program. Establishing and maintaining secrecy can be a problem, however, particularly for a widely sold product.

Chip protection. A relatively new form of federal legislation, the Semiconductor Chip Protection Act (1984), creates a unique protection scheme for so-called "mask works" encoded on semiconductor chips.

Effects on CD ROM

How do these intellectual property laws affect the development of CD ROM products and systems? Starting at the ground level, the design of the disc might be protected by patent law, as might the process for encoding data on the disc. Once data, whether text or graphics, is encoded on the disc, it may be eligible for copyright. The commercial name or logo imprinted on the disc or used in connection with its sale may be protected under trademark law. In addition, the software used to search, manipulate, and display the data on the disc could be protected as a trade secret, by patent, or by copyright law. Many software developers try to structure distribution to make both forms of protection available.

Copyright and Other Types of Protection

Copyright law is the primary source of protection for information products. The Copyright Act of 1976 grants the creator of an "original work of authorship" exclusive rights, such as the right to reproduce copies of the work, to prepare derivative works based on the original, to distribute the work to the public, to perform the work in public, and to display or show a copy of the work directly or on film or television.

"Original work of authorship" is broadly defined. It applies to most information products that are described in the Act as "original works of authorship fixed in any tangible medium of expression, now known or later developed, from which they can be perceived, reproduced, or otherwise communicated, whether directly or with the aid of a machine or device" (17 USC 102(a)). This broad definition is a significant contribution of the 1976 Act because it allows the law to cover new information-based products as they evolve. CD ROM is an ideal example.

Despite the broad definition and the specific rights enumerated in the copyright law, an author's rights are limited. One limitation is the doctrine of *fair use*. Another is the *first sale* doctrine. Furthermore, certain activities, such as qualifying library photocopying, are exempt from the defined rights.

It is impossible to discuss the concepts of fair use and first sale fully in this chapter. Because of their importance to CD ROM publishing, however, a brief discussion of each is appropriate.

Fair Use

The doctrine of fair use provides that under certain circumstances someone other than the copyright holder can use copyrighted material in a way that might appear to be an infringement without written permission.

Often the "fair use" of a copyrighted work is allowed for a noncommercial purpose if the copyright holder's stake in the work is not unreasonably threatened or limited. For example, a student can legitimately copy a magazine article if the copy is made for personal use while doing research for a term paper.

It is virtually impossible to define fair use precisely. It is not clearly defined in any legislation. The Copyright Act of 1976 "endorses the purpose and general scope of the judicial doctrine of fair use." This statement only provides guidance as to what fair use is and when it applies. Although the doctrine is far-reaching, advancing technology often is constrained by the interpretations of past court decisions that are only indirectly related to current issues.

The 1984 Sony Betamax case (*Sony Corporation of America* v *Universal City Studios, Inc.*) illustrates the significance of the doctrine for CD ROM publishers. The U.S. Supreme Court decided that the sale of video recorders did not constitute contributory infringement of the copyright law. It reasoned that video recorders are capable of many noninfringing uses, such as taping programs for later, noncommercial use, which the Court classifies as fair use.

Does this mean that a subscriber to a CD ROM publication could download data to a floppy disk? Probably not. The Sony case involved broadcast programs that were displayed at a specific time and then lost to the viewer.

A CD ROM publication differs from a videotape recording is several significant ways:

- The data is fixed on the disc (already recorded) for viewing at any time; hence, no "time shifting" is needed.

- The recording in the Sony case was for private use. Most early CD ROM publications are for business and professional markets. Their use would be construed primarily as commercial.

- The Sony decision was expressly limited to broadcast media. A site license or shrink-wrap license (discussed later) for CD ROM publications might limit the user's right to claim fair use.

The controversy surrounding the Sony case exemplifies the uncertainty concerning the fair use doctrine. Publishers need to consider the fair use doctrine carefully in planning CD ROM publications.

First Sale

British copyright statutes, the forerunners of U.S. copyright law, at one time allowed a publisher to control a book's disposition after it was sold. According to American copyright law, however, when a copy of a work is sold, the new owner can dispose of it in any manner whatsoever. The owner can sell, lease, or even destroy that particular copy.

Two important limitations are placed on this right of disposition:

- It applies to an outright sale only, not a lease.

- The new owner can display a particular copy (right of display is a copyright owner's exclusive right) only as long as viewers are "present at the place where the copy is located . . . either directly or by the projection of no more than one image at a time" (17 USC 109(b)). (See the discussion of performance versus display on pages 236-37.)

The first sale doctrine is important to CD ROM publishers offering subscriptions to CD ROM databases that are updated each month. These subscriptions may cost $5000 to $10,000. Since each new issue will include the entire database, publishers are worried that a secondary market for slightly outdated discs might develop.

To combat this, several CD ROM publishers require subscribers to return their old discs. The best way to ensure this might be to make the subscription card or agreement a license clearly stating the scope of the rights of the subscriber.

Two other factors affect the status of a copyright: *registration* and *notice*.

Registration

Although the broadened definition of what can be copyrighted has helped electronic publishers, registration has been a problem for many online database publishers. A work is fully protected from the moment it is fixed in some tangible form, but it may be wise to register it as well, for several reasons:

- Registration, if feasible, makes good basic business sense because it states who owns the work and provides legal notice of that ownership.

- You must register a work before you can sue for infringement. Fortunately, you can register any time, even long after publication.

- If you wait until infringement occurs before registering the work, however, you may lose some valuable benefits. The 1976 Copyright Act provides that you may recover attorneys' fees and statutory damages. The court will award you up to $10,000 (or up to $50,000 if the infringement is willful), provided your work is registered within three months of first publication. You lose this benefit if the work is registered thereafter.

- If registration occurs within five years of publication, a court is required to accept the certificate of registration as evidence of a valid copyright. The publisher is not required to prove its validity in initiating an infringement suit.

If a database is updated frequently, registration can be a problem. Even if registration is feasible, the expense may outweigh the benefits. Technically, for every new registration, a publisher must file, must pay a fee, and must include a printout of the first 25 and the last 25 "pages" of the machine-readable material or a printout of 50 records of a database.

The Register of Copyrights has authority to grant special relief under some circumstances. The Copyright Office has proposed new, less demanding regulations for machine-readable material. In addition, both the Information Industry Association (IIA) and the Association of American Publishers (AAP) have proposed methods to simplify registration, including group registration and a change in identifying materials that must be deposited. For now, however, CD ROM, CD-I, and videodisc publications probably will be considered machine-readable databases. This means their publishers must comply with the existing registration regulations.

In lieu of registering their products, many online database publishers rely heavily on contractual relationships with users to establish and enforce their proprietary rights. The telecommunications link between users and the computers that store the databases can be a good monitoring and detecting device. Although the validity of the agreements online subscribers sign has not been seriously tested, the contractual provisions have been used to terminate online privileges or otherwise affect users' searching practices by discontinuing their passwords. Database publishers generally believe the contractual relationship is more reliable than copyright law.

Although establishing a contractual relationship with the purchaser of a CD ROM publication may be difficult, CD ROM publishers need to consider this precedent set by online publishers. Many CD ROM publishers whose products are based on existing online databases already utilize contracts.

Notice

Another formality required under U.S. copyright law is *notice*. This is a message that indicates a claim of copyright, "affixed to the copies in such manner and location as to give reasonable notice of the claim of copyright" (17 USC 401(c)).

In the United States, the notice includes the symbol © or the word *Copyright,* the year of first publication, and the name of the copyright's owner. For example, these four notices all are acceptable:

© 1987 Microsoft Press

Copyright 1987 Microsoft Press

© Copyright 1987 Microsoft Press

Copyright © 1987 Microsoft Press

The Register of Copyright regulations include examples of acceptable placement, but other placement also may be acceptable. CD ROM publishers seem to have several options:

- Affix a notice on the disc itself or on a permanent label that is attached to the disc.

- Include a sign-on message to be displayed when the disc boots up (this could be important for providing adequate notice to a user whose only access to the CD ROM is through a network).

- Include a notice with the display or printout of any record or display unit.

These options, and others, may need to be used in combination. In any event, the requirement is to "give reasonable notice." Seeking professional advice may also be a good idea.

CD ROM technology, particularly CD-I, presents an interesting issue regarding notice. Sound recordings (often referred to as *phonorecords*) require a special copyright notice, ℗. The regulations for sound recording were adopted to prevent confusion between claims to copyright in the sound recording and in the musical or literary work embodied in it and to distinguish between claims concerning the sound recording and those concerning the text and artwork on the record label or album cover. The ℗ symbol has been adopted as an international symbol for the protection of sound recordings.

But is a CD ROM that incorporates music a phonorecord? CD ROM audio publishers are using the ℗ symbol. If the disc is a multimedia publication, are both the © and the ℗ required? Publishers should consider the formalities of notice as they develop CD ROM publications.

Another issue for CD ROM publishers is the publication year used in the notice. Confusion may arise because many CD ROM "works" will be based on previously copyrighted material. In compilations or derivative works that incorporate published material, the year of first publication of the compilation or derivative work is sufficient.

Role of Copyright Protection

What is the practical role of copyright law? Copyrights may well be helpful in protecting against blatant commercial reuse if a vendor-user contract proves unenforceable or if the infringer is not, either directly or indirectly, a party to the contract.

Copyright law may also protect data as its form changes with technological developments. For example, copyright law protects both display and performance elements that may be present in a CD-I or CD ROM publication.

Right of Display

The Copyright Act defines *display* as a copy of the work that is shown directly or by means of a device such as a slide projector or a computer. By virtue of the first sale doctrine, a person who buys the work has the right to display that copy publicly. As mentioned earlier, the law limits this right to display for "viewers present at the place where the copy is located" and, further, to direct display or the projection of no more than one image at a time.

A problem arises if you apply this clause to software and databases on a local area network (LAN) or multiuser system. In a networked environment, an image can be displayed on several PCs (in a LAN) or terminals (in a multiuser system) in more than one place at the same time. If a CD ROM product is marketed for use in a networked environment, this apparent infringement is not important. However, displaying a CD ROM publication intended for a single user in a networked environment technically would seem to be beyond the scope of the display rights granted to a buyer by the first sale doctrine.

Right of Performance

The copyright holder also retains the right of *performance*—the right to publicly render (act, dance, recite, or play) the work directly or by means of a device or process. With a motion picture or other audiovisual work, the copyright holder also retains the right to display the images in any sequence and to make audible the sounds that accompany them. A database and its accompanying software may be "rendered" when the software is executed. Therefore, the visual output of the command screens and data could constitute a "performance."

To take this a step further, if digitally encoded data on a compact disc is played to produce music, it is considered a performance just as playing a record is a performance. It could be that "playing" a database is a performance (if the requisite creativity in the output is present). It might also be argued that the software program itself is "performed."

According to the right of performance clause, a copyright holder can claim infringement if the performance is "publicly rendered" without permission. In the sense that Congress intended, an office environment is public. Legislative history suggests the home is not public because of a historic reluctance to invade the privacy of the home and because of the noncommercial nature of private, in-home use.

Although display and performance issues may seem somewhat esoteric when applied to CD ROM technology, they may prove important to some publishers. If nothing more, they expose the ambiguity of current copyright law and point to some potential trouble spots.

Contract Considerations

Contracts with vendors, suppliers, and distributors necessarily must deal with copyright protection issues.

Third-party contracts. If materials used in a CD ROM publication are not works made for hire, the publisher needs to get a written assignment of copyright or a license. If all copyrights are not assigned to the publisher, the contract must explicitly describe the nature and extent of copyright ownership. All parties involved also should consider allocating enforcement responsibilities, agreeing to share information that will help detect infringement and cooperating in litigation.

Third-party licenses. If a publisher is licensing data from a third party (this includes using information with permission but without compensation), the licensor (the third party) should be required to make a written declaration of copyright ownership. The publisher also should try to get indemnification from liability should that declaration turn out to be untrue. The indemnification should cover claims based on errors or omissions in the information. Getting indemnification can be difficult if the licensor is receiving little or no compensation.

Third-party service bureaus and distributors. If the publisher is using a third party for premastering, mastering, marketing, or distribution, the parties' respective responsibilities for the following should be clearly defined:

- Errors or omissions in the production process.

- Liability for copyright infringement claims or any other claims based on the "product" (product liability law may apply).

- Liability for representations made in the course of the distributor's sales and marketing efforts.

- Customer training (if necessary) and ongoing customer service.

- Equipment maintenance.

Trademark Law

Federal law defines trademarks and servicemarks, though both federal and state laws protect them. A trademark is a "word, name, symbol or device, or any combination thereof adopted and used by a manufacturer or a merchant to identify his goods and distinguish them from the goods of others" (Section 45, Lanham Act, 1946).

A servicemark is a "word, name, symbol or device, or any combination thereof, adopted and used in the sale or advertising of services to identify the services and distinguish them from the services of others" (Section 45, Lanham Act, 1946).

The basic principle is that the first party to use a trademark or servicemark in a geographic area is entitled to priority over later users in that area if use of the mark by the second party is likely to cause public confusion about the source of the goods.

If goods or services are used or sold in interstate commerce, federal registration of trademarks and servicemarks is required. Although trademarks can be registered at both the state and federal levels, some states do not allow the registration of servicemarks.

Generally, state registration is fast and easy, but federal registration can take more than a year. A trademark and a trademark that has acquired a true secondary meaning become incontestable after five years unless they are abandoned, they are found to be generic, or registration was obtained by fraud. The federal registration is then good for 20 years, with renewals available for 20-year periods as long as the trademark is used. In general, the less distinctive the mark, the less protection it receives.

You can use the symbol ™ or ℠ (for trademark or servicemark) to give notice that you are using the mark and declaring rights to it. The ® may be used only for registered marks.

Many CD ROM publications may be licensed to third parties for production or distribution. Ownership of the trademark must be preserved in the name of the licensor when the right to use the mark is granted a third party. Therefore, it is important that CD ROM publishers properly license the trademark when assigning rights to use it.

When trademarked data or software is licensed to a third party, the license agreement should carefully restrict that party's rights to use the mark. Some common restrictions are:

- Advertisements using the trademark must be approved by the licensor.

- Materials bearing the trademark after the license agreement is terminated must be destroyed or returned.

- The licensee may be required to monitor all customers for unauthorized use of the trademark.

- Discs with labels bearing a trademark may not be distributed without the label.

Trade Secret Law

Trade secret laws are not part of federal protection for intellectual property. Each state's laws and related judicial decisions define the scope of trade secret protection. In general, a trade secret is defined as qualifying subject matter (a product plan, an invention, a valuable list of customers, or other information used in a business) that is treated as a secret, both inside and outside the company; that has genuine economic value; and that is not generally known in the trade.

240

The presence and importance of these elements vary from state to state. So though a company is dealing with information that clearly qualifies as a trade secret and is able to adequately protect it, the company still may have to deal with separate and differing rules in each state in which the product is distributed. Also, if the trade secret is or can be disclosed legally, protection is lost. Thus, if a product is to be distributed to a large number of customers, it may be difficult to claim it is a "secret."

CD ROM publishers face three serious problems with trade secret protection:

- It is expensive. Material must be protected from disclosure throughout the product development and distribution cycle. Nondisclosure agreements must be obtained from employees, vendors, and customers.

- Given the nature of CD ROM products and their distribution, the number of customers usually would be large enough to make secrecy impractical. In addition, effective use of the data stored on the disc often might require disclosure of "secrets" to others.

- Many CD ROM products include data and software that have been published and publicly distributed, so elements of the data or software may have been disclosed in the copyright registration.

Is trade secret protection necessary in CD ROM publishing? It may be. Trade secret laws may protect a CD ROM product during development. This protection could be valuable if a product involves several types of property: hardware, software, text and numeric information, and new or unique marketing ideas. A publisher might wish to maintain secrecy while the product is being developed and then rely on other forms of protection. For example, a publisher would want copyright protection while publicly distributing a product. Many legal experts believe copyright and trade secret protection need not be mutually exclusive.

Contractual Restrictions on Use

I mentioned earlier that electronic publishers who distribute their works through online vendors rely heavily on contracts for protection from unauthorized use or duplication. To what extent can CD ROM publishers use this relatively comfortable alternative? The answer depends largely on the method of distribution, which of course depends on the market. An encyclopedia mass marketed for a few hundred dollars needs a different kind of protection than does a large business database bundled with sophisticated retrieval software, which might sell for $10,000 or $20,000.

For a high-priced product, the answer is fairly easy. It probably is sold by a field sales force. During the face-to-face contact when the sale is made, the subscription agreement or license can be explained and accepted. The agreement can incorporate basic elements of the traditional online agreement and terms from some not-so-traditional software agreements, known as *site licenses* (to be discussed later).

For mass-marketed products and publications, the answer is less simple. Because there usually is no personal contact between publisher and consumer, publishers may turn to a technique used by software publishers— the *shrink-wrap license.*

In an attempt to create a contractual relationship between the software publisher and the retail customer, many companies create implied acceptance of contractual restrictions and limitations by "shrink-wrapping" into the package a bold-face message stating the terms of a license agreement. The idea is that when you break the shrink-wrap, you consent to the terms of the agreement. Often, trying to provide a practical alternative (that one hopes would impress a judge), the message says that if you don't agree to the terms, you can return the unopened package for a refund. Whether or not such shrink-wrap licenses can be enforced is open to question. As of this writing, two states, Illinois and Louisiana, have passed laws recognizing their validity.

Basic License Agreements

The CD ROM publication license, shrink-wrap or not, is a lot like the traditional software license, only it may incorporate restrictions for both information and software. A software license might include:

- The scope of the license (it is a license for use, not for resale).

- Limitations on the scope of use (for example, limited for use on a single, designated CPU).

- Restrictions on backing up and copying.

- Acknowledgment of the licensor's proprietary rights.

- Promise of cooperation in identifying unauthorized use.

- Warranties and disclaimers.

- Limitations on liability.

License agreements protect intellectual property, but they can also serve as pricing mechanisms. For example, restricting use to one CPU, a stipulation derived from the mainframe computer environment, enabled software publishers to develop today's simple onetime pricing for microcomputer software. Local area networks and multiuser PC systems may make single CPU restrictions for CD publications unrealistic. When licensing agreements for multiuser environments are firmly established, perhaps publishers can develop pricing structures to fit the new environment.

CD ROM publishers and vendors have three major concerns in deciding how to license their products.

First, a publisher must accommodate the customer who has many single-user systems. Software publishers are adapting to the proliferation of PCs in the corporate environment by offering volume discounts for single-user machines. This widely accepted sales strategy would work well for CD ROM publications. A shrink-wrap license might be adequate for this sort of distribution.

Second, publishers must devise a way to license CD ROM products to customers in a multiuser, networked environment. Although LAN products have been on the market for almost 10 years, announcements of the PC Network by IBM and STARLAN by AT&T have increased pressure for site licensing to provide flexibility in dealing with multiple users who share software without owning a physical copy.

Third, publishers must find a way to protect their software and data from unauthorized copying and downloading.

Site Licenses

A true microcomputer software site license is best described as a license to make an unlimited number of copies of a software product. In reality, site licenses vary from one vendor to another and often restrict the number of copies allowed.

A site license is one way to accommodate large business customers who have many users. It allows the customer to buy and copy a single product rather than buying one product for each user. Network licenses, an extension of the site license, let a customer copy the product to a network server, giving a specified number of users access. Some vendors charge a *bump-up* fee for giving additional users access to the software.

At present, site licenses typically restrict use to a site or sites and specify how copying will be monitored. Some licenses require that copies be made at a central location or by a designated group. Others require that a label provided by the publisher be affixed to each copy. This practice is analogous to the warning stamp some publishers require when their copyrighted material is photocopied.

Software publishers have two concerns about licensed copying. First, they want a copyright notice (or warning, as described above) incorporated to inform anyone who gets the copy. Second, if the name or logo on sold copies is a registered trademark, the publisher may want to be sure no copy (except a legal backup copy) is distributed without that trademark. The publisher theoretically should know how many copies each site licensee circulates by the number of labels provided.

A publisher also might require that original printed user documentation accompany each copy. The number of copies of documentation in circulation tells the publisher how many copies of the software are circulating.

Finally, a software site license may also contain audit privileges to assure compliance with its terms. For CD ROM publishers, the microcomputer site license probably is less relevant than the concepts of volume discounts and network licenses. However, a precedent exists for site licenses as a means to protect against unauthorized data distribution.

For many years database publishers, whose primary mode of distribution has been online vendors, have offered direct licenses to large customers. These agreements allow a customer to receive the same magnetic tape the database vendor receives. Customers have the right to read the tape into their minicomputer or mainframe and search the database directly. In the early days these searches were really batch sorts of the database by subject. The results of the searches were printed and circulated. As computer costs came down, however, customers could buy online retrieval software (BASIS, STAIRS, TEXT MASTER, and others) that let them devise their own search strategies and perform the searches in real time.

License fees for online software packages cost as much as $100,000. Database publishers generally charged $5000 to $20,000 for their annual license fees, which meant enough dollars were at stake to justify negotiating individual licenses. The software licensor restricted use of the software to one CPU and access to a specified number of terminals. Even when large customers opened the systems to telecommunications access, dumb terminals (with no downloading capability) were used and few users were involved.

As PC access became widespread and the number of users grew, database publishers usually raised the flat license fee or based the fee on the proportionate growth of the user base. A few imposed output charges in an attempt to approximate the value of information supplied to multiple users. These output charges, when coupled with a prohibition on downloading, were reasonably effective. As provisions were added, these agreements began to resemble site licenses. They controlled multiuser access to the software by restricting its use to a single site or user group.

Licensing CD ROMs

Monitoring CD ROM data distribution will be complex. The information can be copied, downloaded, and shared on a locally distributed network without the electronic monitoring capabilities of an online system. Each of these capabilities concerns publishers to varying degrees. Some publishers seem more concerned about copying and downloading; others worry more about local area networks.

Copying data. Although CD ROM data can be copied to another medium, large-scale copying is no trivial task. Since the data is structured for the search and retrieval software that comes with it, a highly skilled programmer would be needed to reorganize the data to make it usable on another system.

Downloading. The dividing line between legitimate use of a database, including display or printing of data, and illegitimate downloading of data is unclear. Many believe that downloading output produced by a search to a floppy disk, particularly if the data is not put to commercial or competitive use, should be considered fair use. Others believe that anything beyond printing one copy of search output or temporarily displaying it on a CRT is a new form of photocopying and clearly an infringement of copyright laws.

For many years, text database publishers and vendors have tried to prevent or restrict downloading. But some distributors of online systems that primarily carry numeric data have encouraged downloading and have even provided the customer with software to manipulate and display the data. (Of course, they have charged a fee for this service.) Other distributors of online systems, such as the European Space Agency-Information Retrieval System (ESA-IRS), have made available a display mode, for which they charge a higher fee, giving the customer the right to download and reuse the information. (ESA-IRS provides this feature only if the licensor-publisher agrees to enable the ESA-IRS download format.)

Several CD ROM database publishers provide the user the capability to download data from CD ROM to a floppy disk. Apparently, this feature is built into their prices. Although database producers may be accustomed to variable and ongoing revenues that depend on use, they seem willing to charge a fixed price for a CD ROM database.

The downloading issue is more complex if unrelated parties own portions of software and information on the CD ROM. It may be necessary that the site license include a pricing mechanism that accommodates users who need to download data but requires them to pay a downloading fee in addition to the standard access fee for multiple users. The downloading argument no doubt will continue and may one day be resolved by a court.

Sharing data. Sharing the disc on a single-user system is not viewed as a serious problem because a one-to-one ratio of disc to CPU is maintained. A more likely threat is the distributed use of a single CD ROM publication through a local area network. Use of a CD ROM through a LAN, a multiuser PC, or even a telecommunications network limits the potential market for CD ROM publishers, because a customer can buy one disc and distribute it to everyone in the network. However, the long seek time and moderate transfer rate of CD ROM drives may discourage this tactic.

Thus, the publishers of high-end business or scientific and technical CD ROM products seem to expect multiple users. This is reflected in the high prices of their products. The limitations they seek in site licenses seem to be aimed at controlling use on multiuser systems or LANs to prevent direct competition with existing online databases. Software publishers and database publishers then split the revenues, or the software publisher is paid on a traditional onetime basis with additional revenues coming from the site-licensing arrangements.

The site-licensing mechanism is not perfect for CD ROM applications. However, tape leasing practices have shown it is one way to control multiple user access and downloading. It may prove to be effective in capturing revenues otherwise lost to pirates. Regardless of the form of the license agreements, remember that they must meet the needs of the customer as well as the publisher. In the words of one company executive:

> People in control of a new technology often seem to believe they can ignore the market and dictate the terms under which the technology will be made available. We think that if there is a strong need expressed by the market, and it is ignored, then the product will fail. It will fail either because the market will not accept restrictions on use and, in violating the restrictions, will wreck the pricing structure, or it will fail because a competitor will emerge to meet the need.

Technological Restrictions on Use

Publishers who serve a market too large for using individual written licenses and yet are unwilling to rely solely on shrink-wrap licenses are evaluating technological restrictions on use. Technology may offer solutions to the intellectual property law problems that technology itself has caused.

246

Advances in online access—most notably, terminal emulation through a personal computer—created the widespread downloading problem. Earlier, numeric timesharing vendors had designed downloading capability into their systems. Often, however, it was necessary to download data to your own private file space for manipulation and storage, and vendors would charge high front-end subscription costs. The timesharing vendor charged for the software users needed to manipulate the data, for CPU time used to manipulate data, and for storage if the file was saved.

Any producer of databases that are licensed to public online retrieval systems available today is aware that users can download data despite contractual prohibitions in subscription agreements. Only systems such as LEXIS, made by Mead Data Central, which insists that Mead software be used for PC telecommunications access, can inhibit illegal downloading. The substantial market presence of Hayes's Smartcom and other PC access software may make even this kind of mandatory use of certain software as a technological "solution" penny-wise and market-foolish.

In any event, CD ROM publishers are in charge of control, design, and pricing. The problem is that many technological restrictions on use, even if they work, may be expensive and cumbersome from a systems standpoint. Before implementing high-tech solutions, publishers would be wise to examine some low-tech solutions.

Low-Tech Solutions

Low-tech solutions are simple restrictions that make it inconvenient to violate a publisher's proprietary rights and that sometimes call attention to the violation.

CD ROM product development pioneers are using several low-tech solutions, including:

- Requiring that the disc be secured at the licensee's site, perhaps by using a checkout system.

- Requiring the subscriber who wants an updated disc to return the old one. If in addition the software restricts downloading to hard disk, this ploy is effective.

- Selling a bundled system configuration in a sealed environment. This may make it difficult for the user to connect with other systems or LANs.

- Limiting the number of records that may be displayed with any single command and displaying a warning message if any display command is repeated more than a specified number of times.

High-Tech Solutions

Downloading, however, concerns many publishers sufficiently that they are trying to fashion more sophisticated technological solutions. These solutions include:

- Building a system accessed only through passwords and identification codes. The system user is bound by contract to administer the passwords properly. If users can create a password and give it to anyone in their organization, however, passwords become no greater security than an on/off switch. In addition, administering passwords is expensive for the publisher and can be bypassed with clever programming.

- Designing a system that requires both personal and technological passwords for access. The technological password is embedded on a floppy disk that must be in a PC drive when the CD ROM database is in use. The floppy disk is copy protected.

- Designing retrieval software that lets the user send data to a screen or a printer, but makes it difficult to transfer or intercept data and copy it to disk.

- Incorporating data-encryption software that makes reading out the contents of an entire database difficult. Decryption is required (and built into the software) to display or print data.

- Incorporating data-encryption methods that depend on a variable encoded on a ROM chip. The publisher then can sell a card that must be installed in an expansion slot.

A premise of most protection systems is that no method is perfect, so a relatively simple, changeable combination of hardware and software will be most effective.

One company, Effective Security Systems, has developed a technique its president calls *Field Software Management*. Security is managed by a microprocessor that can be part of a computer, a modem, or an independent black box ported to a CPU or file server (in a LAN).

An area of great concern for software and data publishers is the multiterminal or LAN environment, in which many users can access the same disc at the same time. The Software Safe prevents access-control problems in this environment with a microprocessor and an EPROM (erasable programmable read-only memory) cartridge. The cartridge can control a maximum of 500 packages of software for several different publishers. A software publisher can deliver 100 software programs or modules and use the EPROM to allow access only to those packages paid for by the customer. If the customer wants access to more packages, the publisher can dial up the EPROM through a modem and change the authorization code or mail the customer an EPROM with a new configuration (the cartridges are very small).

Using this approach you can control access to data in some unique ways. CD ROM technology lets you compress data to save space. You can incorporate some level of encryption into the compression technique. Four or five slightly different techniques could be used at relatively low cost. Each time a new disc was delivered, the publisher or an onsite system operator would select the appropriate variable, which would already be in the EPROM. A willful thief might need only a few days to break one decryption-decompression code, but with each new disc the technique would be different and the thief would have to start over. The key is to make violations difficult and burdensome.

An EPROM also can record elapsed-time use, store a record of which software modules or databases were used, remember how many terminals/ PCs are authorized for concurrent usage, and record minor violations. These capabilities allow flexible administration of usage-based pricing strategies. When major violations occur, the EPROM can force a message out to the terminal, send a message to a designated person in the licensee organization, or disable the system.

Of course, such approaches may add $800 to $1000 to the cost of a product. An EPROM is therefore appropriate only for LAN or multiuser environments in which multiple software or database products are used so that the value of a single package or database justifies the added cost.

Some computer industry analysts believe that manufacturers should build encryption and software protection into hardware systems. If this were the case, the costs would be lower. When asked why manufacturers are not doing this, Mike Dunham, who is the president of Effective Security Systems, said:

> In the past, the worldwide market was dominated by a relatively small number of manufacturers, and profit margins were based on equipment manufacturing. The proliferation of easily accessible software helped to sell even more hardware. But, as the hardware market becomes more competitive and commodity-like, the major manufacturers will find an increasing share of their profits coming from software and services. They will then have a new incentive to optimize the profits by offering more flexible pricing strategies and data protection.

Emerging high-tech solutions will cost less and be more convenient than those in use today. Hardware manufacturers might incorporate some of the techniques mentioned above in their designs at a cost per user of a few hundred dollars or less. Meanwhile, CD ROM technology may itself improve protection.

In a traditional online environment, a user can pay a variable price (say, $100 for one hour), download data, and use it again and again. Worse yet, a user can download data and sell or distribute multiple copies of it in machine-readable form.

CD ROM publishers might solve the downloading problem by selling the publication for a flat price and granting the licensee unlimited use. The further problem of the downloading and selling or distributing of multiple copies of data may not be solved technologically. Finding a solution may force us to re-examine our legal system of protecting intellectual property and the underlying relationship (known as the *public policy bargain*) between public and private interests.

Public v Private Rights

Let's review that relationship. Private parties who produce a novel and useful invention or an original work of authorship are granted legal protection because public dissemination or application of their ideas is deemed to be in the interest of all citizens. This legal protection lets them capitalize on their creativity and is an incentive for them to disseminate their ideas and apply their inventions.

The primary means of assuring intellectual property rights is the creator's power to bring a private action for damages. This type of lawsuit always has required a specific description of the work and of the nature of the infringement. With new technology, however—the photocopying machine, the computer, and the laser printer, for example—detecting violations can be difficult. Many of these machines are inexpensive, and with them an individual can commit serious violations in relative privacy.

If the nature of intellectual property rights is to remain the same, the mechanism for enforcing such rights must be improved. In some ways the mechanism is changing without legislation. Well-publicized lawsuits initiated by groups of publishers in the United States are attempts to tell American businesses that illegal copying to forward their commercial interests will be monitored and prosecuted.

Legislation that eases the burden of legal procedures is an option. The dilemmas for CD ROM publishers, and publishers in general, are as follows:

- Registration of a copyright is not a legal condition to copyright protection.

- Registration, however, must occur before an infringement suit is initiated.

- The relative privacy afforded by technology may make it difficult to know precisely which work has been infringed before a suit is initiated and the process of pretrial discovery takes place.

Under current law it is not clear whether a case can be initiated that states unknown covert copyright infringement of a number of works.

Many legal experts believe that instead of having to prove copyright infringement occurred, copyright owners should be able to prove they have reasonable grounds *to believe* an infringement occurred. After proving this, a copyright owner could proceed with a suit, establishing the specifics of the infringement through pretrial discovery.

Some acts of copyright infringement do not individually cause substantial economic damage. But, if these infringements are widespread, the aggregate damage can be serious, and pursuing the individual violations can be difficult and expensive.

When copyright law was being revised, the House Judiciary Committee said that the provision dealing with the recovery of actual damages, profits, and so-called statutory damages is "a cornerstone . . . of the bill as a whole." The provision, enacted as part of the Copyright Act of 1976, lets the court award damages of up to $10,000 instead of actual damages or lost profits. The court also can award attorneys' fees to the plaintiff. In the case of willful (knowing and intentional) infringement, the court can award statutory damages as high as $50,000.

From the publisher's point of view, these provisions make relying on private enforcement more practical. Some legal experts argue that this "cornerstone" has been dislodged and that the building is in danger of falling, because elsewhere in the Copyright Act Congress made recovery of statutory damages and attorneys' fees dependent on registration within three months of first publication.

This three-month limitation presumably is an incentive to register works. Perhaps incentives to register are necessary, but the three-month requirement seems unduly burdensome in light of the greatly increased monitoring and detection problems technological advances have caused. These advances benefit society, but caution should be exercised to keep technology from disturbing the balance of the public versus private relationship.

Certainly, exceptions could be made, as they are under the current law, for infringements that are private (within the home) or are committed in a nonprofit educational or library environment. Imposing statutory damages and awarding attorneys' fees, however, should be more important weapons in pursuing commercial infringers.

251

Distribution Schemes

Disclosure, Inc., and the American Society for Hospital Pharmacists (ASHP) have released some new disc-based products. Their protection schemes illustrate how protection methods may differ depending on the target market.

Disclosure, Inc.

Disclosure produces a database, Disclosure II, that contains information from filings with the Securities and Exchange Commission. The database is licensed to almost a dozen online systems, including DIALOG, Mead Data Central, and ADP Network Services. The data is alphanumeric and taken verbatim from the SEC filings. Disclosure II does not include all of the documents, such as an annual report, but they are available from Disclosure on microfilm.

The company has developed a CD ROM version of the online database. An annual subscription to the online product, Compact Disclosure, initially costs corporate subscribers $4500, including quarterly updates. Academic and public libraries can subscribe for $3200 a year. The subscription price includes the software and the CD ROM drive. The system requires a minimum of 256 KB memory and runs on an IBM PC, XT, or AT.

The retrieval software emulates the commands of a major online vendor. The disc can be used with Philips, Sony, and Digital Equipment Corporation disc drives. Compact Disclosure is designed to allow downloading. The next release of the software will include a feature that lets you transfer data directly to IBM PC applications software.

Disclosure believed downloading was essential to product offering. Only employees or patrons of the subscriber can use the product at a single site, and resale of data is prohibited. If subscribers wish to use the information for resale, they pay an additional fee. Disclosure also requires that subscribers return old discs when they receive updated discs.

Although Disclosure incorporates user restrictions in a subscription agreement, it relies on the goodwill and honesty of its customers. Disclosure is selling to large corporations or institutions which, they assume, are willing to abide by reasonable restrictions. Company officers said, however, that they are learning through this initial offering and will adjust the product, its features, and the restrictions on its use in future releases.

American Society of Hospital Pharmacists

The American Society of Hospital Pharmacists produces three databases—International Pharmaceutical Abstracts (IPA), Drug Information Fulltext (DIF), and Consumer Drug Information (CDI)—and dozens of journals and monographs. ASHP is pursuing "local online" publishing in two steps: a PC floppy disk publication and a CD ROM publication. Its protection scheme may be appropriate for a mass-market product.

The floppy disk version of CDI is produced in cooperation with Knowledge Access (KA) of Mountain View, CA. Knowledge Access's KAware software is part of an integrated subscription product that includes CDI and KA's retrieval software. The software is easy to use; with it you can search, retrieve, and display by making menu choices. ASHP is calling the floppy disk product Consumer Drug Information on Disk (CDID). The database describes more than 250 top generic drugs (50,000 brand name drugs) marketed in the United States. These drugs account for more than 95 percent of prescriptions written in the United States.

CDI and CDID both are based on a print product, *The Consumer Drug Digest*, which is a lay guide for everyday use of the most commonly prescribed drugs.

CDID is on two disks. Subscribers also get a third disk—the retrieval software. The package runs on DOS 2.00 and on any IBM PC or compatible. It requires two disk drives for double-sided, double-density hardware or one drive and a hard disk, and at least 256 KB of memory. The subscription price is $150 per year.

ASHP's approach to data protection is more sophisticated than that of Disclosure, because it is selling a low-cost mass-market product. The two data disks contain KAware's proprietary encryption. The user can decrypt the information to print it, but cannot transfer data to a disk. The user can copy the disk, but the data would be encrypted and make no sense. The third disk, which contains the software for search, retrieval decryption, and display, is copy-protected. A side benefit of KAware's encryption process is that it uses data compression techniques that greatly reduce storage requirements.

ASHP also is considering a CD ROM product based on *International Pharmaceutical Abstracts,* an index and abstract print publication also available on several online systems, such as Dialog and Mead Data Central. ASHP is using CDID to learn more about features, pricing, and restrictions for future CD ROM offerings.

The CD ROM product will be sold at a relatively high price. Subscribers will sign an agreement that incorporates significant restrictions on use beyond a single site or use outside the licensee's organization. No restrictions on multiple users or local area networks at the specified site (usually a hospital) are anticipated. ASHP believes the user's potential liability in distributing outdated information will minimize downloading.

Conclusion

A CD ROM publisher must consider three basic issues in designing protection methods:

The nature of the material. If the material changes with each remastering, and previous data becomes outdated and ceases to be useful, data protection may be no problem. A doctor or lawyer will not use outdated data for fear of malpractice suits. Also, if the database is very large, users will be less likely to copy it.

The market for the product. In a high-end market where the product is sold face to face, a written site license easily can incorporate necessary restrictions. If the product is sold to a mass market, the publisher should consider the shrink-wrap license as well as the use of technological obstacles.

The cost of protection. All forms of protection for intellectual property have a cost. Auditing site licenses is expensive. Creating sophisticated software or hardware schemes to restrict access or output also is expensive. The cost of protection must be evaluated in light of the economic harm a determined minority of hackers and pirates could cause.

If you find the current scheme of legal protection inadequate, you might try participating in trade association activities or even personal lobbying. Informed, constructive arguments can have an effect.

Despite the legal challenges, CD ROM publications offer substantial opportunities. As new products are introduced and new standards and software are developed, the issues of data protection will probably become more important to the publisher and more controversial to the user. Resolving these issues will no doubt require tolerance and understanding from both sides.

About the Author

Joe Bremner is president of Database Development of Milwaukee, WI. The firm provides strategic planning, product development, and marketing services to the information industry.

Bremner has more than ten years of product and marketing planning in the investment and information industries, and formerly served as operating officer of Management Contents, a leading producer of online databases and information products. Mr. Bremner is a member of the Proprietary Rights Committee of the Information Industry Association (IIA) and was one of the original members of the association's Database Publishing Committee. He has written and spoken on a variety of industry issues throughout the United States and in Western Europe. He holds a law degree, with honors, from Loyola University, Chicago.

Updating CD ROM Databases

Publishers' options for updating the information stored on CD ROM are many, and they proliferate as the technology matures. They can be as easy as delivering a completely new, updated disc to a customer. Or they can involve telecommunications technologies, transmitting up-to-the-minute updates to the customer, while invisibly combining them with the existing palette of CD ROM data.

In this chapter, we discuss why databases need updating, outline criteria for selecting an updating method, describe technical options for updating, and survey market conditions and current experimental approaches.

Why Update?

CD ROM is a read-only publishing medium ideally suited for electronically distributing large bodies of relatively stable archival and reference materials. So why update? A few reasons are obvious, and several are less apparent.

Augmenting, deleting, and refreshing information in a database are the most obvious reasons. These activities may take several forms:

Adding information to essentially stable data. A publisher might want to describe a new biological discovery more completely, expand analyses of a legal decision, or add the most recent quarter's financial data to a database of public companies.

Deleting obsolete or incorrect information. A publisher might delete books no longer published in an updated database of current books in print, just as it might delete ads for companies no longer in business in an updated electronic "Yellow Pages."

Refreshing or replacing outdated information. Catalog prices or demographic data become outdated quickly and are good examples of this type of information.

Three other reasons for updating CD ROMs are less apparent. These are to:

- Control access to a database by updating a password or other security scheme.

- Enhance the software programs that retrieve, display, and manipulate data.

- Limit product liability by correcting errors in the data.

These reasons for updating address a publisher's need to control commercial information products, particularly database security, software integrity, and legal liability.

Basic Media Options

A publisher can choose from three basic approaches to updating, each employing a different distribution medium and associated hardware. These include: tangible media, one-way broadcast media, and two-way interactive media.

Tangible media. Simply stated, you can see and touch this type of update; the data always has a physical form. The familiar array of magnetic options—floppy disks, nine-track tapes, removable Winchester disks, and removable cartridges—as well as CD ROM discs are in this category.

The publisher physically delivers the new information to customers. This is an attractive option for updating large quantities of information when timeliness is not an overriding issue. (See Table 1.)

	Tape	Floppy	Cartridge	CD ROM
Quantity of information	160 MB	1 MB	20 MB	550 MB
Permanent copy/record	Yes	Yes	Yes	Yes
Geographic scope	Awkward to mail	Easy to mail	Easy to mail	Easy to mail
Hardware requirements	Need tape drive	Universal (no limit)	Need disk drive	Need CD ROM drive
Number of simultaneous users	One-by-one copying	One-by-one copying	One-by-one copying	Can be mass-replicated
Security/data protection	Poor	Fair	Poor	Good
Technical complexity	Low	Low	Low	High
Customer's ease of use	Low	High	Medium	High
Fixed costs of operation	Medium	Low	Low	High
Variable costs of operation	Medium	Low	High	Low

Table 1. Tangible media.

One-way broadcast media. A *point-to-multipoint* method, this type of update involves transmitting data from a central location (the origination point) to many passive receiving locations (the multipoints). Customers can take as much or as little as they need from this *stream* of broadcast information. The user can display and discard the information (as with a current stock quote, which requires no permanent record) or add it to an update file (desirable for information such as financial statements of a newly listed company). The customer can store this update file temporarily on a floppy disk, hard disk, or similar medium until the publisher incorporates it permanently on the next edition of a CD ROM. Ku band satellite, cable TV, radio sideband, and television vertical blanking interval (VBI) broadcasts are one-way media used for updating. These updating methods are not likely to become widely used with CD ROM, but they are suitable for distributing small amounts of highly volatile real-time information to many simultaneous users. (See Table 2.)

	Radio	TV VBI	Cable TV	Satellite
Data transfer rate	19.2 KB/sec	128 KB/sec	1.544 MB/sec	56 KB/sec
Permanent copy/record	Not provided	Not provided	Not provided	Not provided
Geographic scope	Reception areas*	Reception areas*	Service areas	National coverage
Hardware required	Receiver	Decoder	Decoder	Sight dish/line
Number of simultaneous users	No limit	No limit	No limit	No limit
Security/data protection	Poor	Fair	Good	Fair
Technical complexity	High	High	Medium	High
Customer's ease of use	High	Medium	Medium	Medium
Fixed costs of operation	Low	Medium	Medium	High
Variable costs of operation	Low	Low	Low	Low

*Reception can be poor in urban business areas.

Table 2. One-way broadcast media.

Two-way interactive media. These point-to-point update methods move a piece of electronic information from one point to any other point in a network. This lets customers request specific information. Dial-up phone lines that access packet-switched (Tymnet and Telenet) or circuit-switched (AT&T's ISDN) networks use this method. Two-way interactive media give customers convenient access to large databases when the information's currency is important. (See Table 3.)

	Std Phone	Packet Switch	Circuit Switch
Data transfer rate	19.2 KB/sec	56 KB/sec	1.544 MB/sec
Permanent copy/record	Not provided	Not provided	Not provided
Geographic scope	Universal	Most urban areas	Major urban areas
Hardware required	Modem	Modem/DTE*	DTE*
Number of simultaneous users	Limited by computer	Limited by computer	Limited by computer
Security/data protection	Good	Good	Good
Technical complexity	Low	Medium	Medium
Customer's ease of use	Low	Low	Medium
Fixed costs of operation	Low	Medium	High
Variable costs of operation	High	Medium	Low

*Data termination equipment

Table 3. Two-way interactive media.

Because applications differ widely, determining the exact cost of any up-dating method is difficult. The cost depends on the number of customers, the complexity of the database and associated software, how much information is transmitted, the perceived value of the information, and how often it is distributed.

Evaluating the Options

When selecting an updating method, the nature of the CD ROM application will determine which options are most important. Every application will have different requirements; although one method might be ideal for one application, it might be inappropriate for another. Consider these issues when selecting an appropriate updating method:

1. **Quantity of information being updated.** Some applications require that nearly all information in a database be updated regularly (for instance, new census information every 10 years). With others (price changes in a parts catalog, for example), a publisher must occasionally update only a small amount of critical information.

2. **User's need for historical copies.** Some applications require no historical or reference copy of the update (for instance, a revised inflation forecast). Others, such as company credit histories, require a clear audit trail of old and new data.

3. **The range and extent of distribution.** Applications' distribution requirements differ dramatically. Some databases are intended for use in a single office; others are distributed worldwide. Some updating methods are more economical and more appropriate for wide distribution.

4. **Hardware requirements.** The update method must be compatible with the user's hardware. This hardware may include a Winchester drive, removable cartridge, modem, satellite dish, radio antenna, or specialized data termination equipment (DTE).

5. **Number of simultaneous users.** This differs significantly by application and affects the range of technical options available.

6. **Security or data-protection needs.** Applications can involve highly sensitive data (such as defense information or internal company documents), or they can use public domain data. Some updating methods offer no security whatsoever, while others are safer and more reliable.

7. **Technical complexity.** Some updating methods are straightforward, such as sending out a floppy disk containing new data to add to the database.

Others use more advanced techniques that demand complicated preparation. For example, when you add and remove documents from a text database, you must build a new index reflecting the changes. This requires sophisticated indexing software and programming expertise.

8. **Ease of use.** You should always consider the technical expertise of the customer when selecting an updating method. Some methods involve complex software and hardware installation procedures that require a high level of technical competence. For example, updating files by copying the information from magnetic tape to a local storage medium can be difficult for the untrained user. Likewise, operating modems and related telecommunications equipment requires an understanding of the telecommunications process and may elicit demands for special training.

9. **Fixed costs.** Underlying cost structures of updating methods differ. For example, the price of a removable cartridge disk drive adds to the overall cost of a CD ROM system. This type of one-time cost can affect the potential market for your product. As the cost and complexity of your system increases, the market size typically decreases.

10. **Variable costs of operation.** These are the marginal or variable costs of an updating method. Some may vary with the distribution range (standard phone rates increase with distance), number of customers (each might require a separate CD ROM disc), number of simultaneous users (online access to mainframes), or some mix of the above (for hybrid systems that employ a variety of delivery methods).

Software Considerations

The updating hardware and distribution methods are only two facets to an updating scheme. You must also decide to what degree you want to integrate the old data with the new.

At the very least, the retrieval software you originally packaged with the product must be able to read the new data. If the update's data structure has changed to such a degree that the retrieval software no longer can retrieve it, then you may have to provide software updates. The design of the original database—its file structure and indexing system—and the extent of the update determine whether updating involves software changes.

Even more desirable when integrating old and new data is that it be viewed by the user as a single database. This means that the retrieval software must be able to compare the indexes of the old and new data and extract all new information without requiring input from the user. These features should be part of the initial retrieval software design, because they are very costly to add later.

How Is the Database Indexed?

A database is a repository for data. In many ways it is organized like an electronic library. Information records (books) are stored separately from the indexes (card catalog). Users, aided by computer software, consult the indexes to locate particular records. One or more indexes will detail locations of the records, what they contain, and how they relate. When a library adds a new book or loses an old one, the librarian modifies the card catalog to reflect the change. This involves changing the book-title, subject, and author indexes in the card catalog. If the librarian doesn't update these indexes, patrons don't find the books they want and the book collection's value diminishes.

Most CD ROM applications are also centered around an index, through which the retrieval software accesses the database. Updating any kind of information requires that you change the indexes first. This task can be complex for CD ROM publishers because the databases are large and contain many indexes.

Update Models

As with media choices for updating, the publisher can choose among several update models. Their effectiveness depends on whether you are adding, deleting, or replacing data. Generally, adding data to a database is relatively easy; deleting or replacing data can present more problems.

Wholesale Replacement

Perhaps the easiest way to update a database is to reprocess, remaster, and replicate a brand-new version, replacing the original disc. This approach is most appropriate for large, widely distributed databases that fit nicely on one disc and are updated, at most, once a month.

Simplicity is the great merit of wholesale replacement. The data, indexes, and software all are updated simultaneously at a central location without involving the user. This method is most appropriate for applications that require regular updating. Remastering costs may make it impractical for applications that are not widely distributed.

Create a New Database and Indexes

Another dependable updating method, when you are only adding material to an existing database, is to create a new database and indexes and send them to the customer. This update may take the form of a second CD ROM, or it may be some type of magnetic media such as a floppy or cartridge disk.

Old and new databases and indexes are not linked, although they are both designed to work with the same retrieval software. Some retrieval packages require the customer to search the original database and the new database separately, combining results by hand. Others automatically search both databases and combine the lists of all relevant documents.

Although this first method is cumbersome for most applications, it might be appropriate for databases that are time-based. For example, if your database update contains only the most recent financial statements of companies newly listed on the New York Stock Exchange, searching it separately from the main database may not be a problem. However, if you want to compare a company's financial statements over the past five years and perform calculations on that data, you may find it awkward to search one database, then another, and then combine the data manually to perform your calculations. In this case, you should select a software package that can search multiple databases without the user's awareness.

Link Database and Retrieval Software

When you add, delete, or replace information, you need a retrieval program that can link the old and new databases and their indexes.

The search engine must know there are updated indexes and be able to search old and new indexes to find the data. Some retrieval programs allow up to 32 indexes to be added to the original index. The retrieval program searches each one sequentially to find references to the query. A special feature in the retrieval software keeps track of the occurrences in all indexes and lists them for final display. When a product has used up all 32 indexes, a new disc is mastered, and index and new data are merged to form another disc.

Again, like all other updating methods, this method is best suited for database additions and becomes far more complicated with deletions or replacements. If an old index contains a listing for data that has been replaced or deleted from the database, the new index must be able to flag the data so the retrieval software won't retrieve it.

Rebuild Index for Entire Product

Perhaps the most effective update method is to provide updated material and indexes for the entire database. The reprocessed index will contain all references to old and new information and will only index the valid information. If a record is replaced, the new index will point to the replacement—not to the original; if a record is deleted, the index will not contain a reference to it.

Since a database index can require a great deal of space, your update media should be able to accommodate it. Some publishers find the removable cartridge adequate, with its 10 to 20 MB of storage capacity. Others produce a separate index disc that also contains the new data. The latter method, although adequate, can result in some disc swapping as the user searches the index disc to find references to information on other discs—unless the application has a multidrive system. As multidisc jukeboxes become available, this method may become more practical.

Regardless of the type or structure of your data, the frequency and size of the updates are most important in selecting an appropriate update model.

Current Practices and Future Directions

Most early CD ROM applications contain relatively static archival and reference databases, generally replaced by another CD ROM disc. This simple, straightforward approach is well suited to the narrow class of information that has a predictable and predetermined update cycle.

Most personal computer users today get current electronic information from one of two sources, either an internal mainframe link or an external online database. Increasingly, a CD ROM complements these sources.

A number of hybrid systems are currently under development or have been announced that incorporate some of the updating methods mentioned earlier. These systems are designed to combine a historical database published on CD ROM with current information supplied through an online link or a live microwave transmission coming over a satellite link, cable feed, or similar broadcast system. Such systems are closely related, both conceptually and in proposed commercial uses, with the more common hybrid systems combining CD ROMs with magnetic media. They are also related in that they raise similar architectural issues. Looking at an example of such an application may be the best way to discuss the issues.

Imagine a complete historical database stored on CD ROM that contains annual financial data for all companies publicly traded during the past 20 years, including quarterly data for the last 5 years. This product is updated on a quarterly cycle, and monthly updates are provided on a magnetic cartridge. To ensure that the most current data is available to the user, the publisher also provides an online link for such information as the latest stock, bond, or commodity prices.

To use this system, the user would look for specific data, comparing the incoming data with the historical data stored on the CD ROM and update cartridges. The cartridges could serve two purposes by also providing a working space for the application as it analyzes the data, and storage space for the ongoing data capture, as interesting data appears.

By today's standards, this is a rather sophisticated example of a hybrid system, but similar systems actually exist and are sure to proliferate as technicians resolve some of the integration issues to knit the various hardware and software components together. For example:

- McGraw-Hill is experimenting with CD ROM delivery of financial information from Compustat and related textual information from various Standard & Poor's databases. It is updating the database with removable cartridges.

- Lotus Information Services is distributing stock price and commodity quotes to customers via one-way FM radio sideband broadcasts. It has announced plans to integrate its Signal service with archival and reference databases distributed on tangible media by ISYS, a group within Lotus.

- Datext and Dow Jones News/Retrieval offer a hybrid information service that combines reference databases on CD ROM with real-time news and stock quotes they deliver online. This service, called CD/NewsLine, seamlessly integrates access to large local and remote online databases.

The system's architect and the project manager face a complex problem when attempting to build a system that integrates many different update schemes into one user friendly product. One way to successfully integrate such a system is to design all elements into the application program. For example, a financial package that offers a CD ROM-based historical stock price database, which is updated quarterly, might include software that monitors an online system for daily price fluctuations. The application could use one program to monitor the online activity and a different program to retrieve information from the CD ROM database.

With this *modular* approach, each routine accesses the appropriate databases according to the search criteria. A carefully designed database management system can access data from different media, filter it according to specified criteria, and deliver the required information to the application program without that program knowing the source. This allows a query such as: "For any stock having a certain price/earnings ratio, check past financial records against the following pattern, and report any matches."

266

Current database management software is more limited in scope. With existing systems, it is possible to integrate a magnetic device and a CD ROM drive into one *virtual* device—a device that is accessed by the controlling software as though it were a single device. This integration represents an expensive product development challenge, but its potential may be valuable to developers and users.

The challenge—and opportunity—for publishers is to develop these pioneering steps and provide value-added software that makes their product more useful. By necessity, publishers will distribute the bulk of the information in their databases on CD ROM. As the industry matures, this data will be augmented, complemented, updated, and replaced using other distribution methods.

About the Author

David Roux is founder and Chief Executive Officer of Datext, Inc., a CD ROM publisher specializing in financial databases. Datext is a majority-owned, operating subsidiary of Cox Enterprises, Inc., based in Atlanta, GA. Cox is a leading communications and publishing company with business interests worldwide. It is one of the largest privately owned corporations in the United States.

CASE STUDIES

The First CD ROM Publication

In January 1985, The Library Corporation introduced the first commercial CD ROM publication, the BiblioFile Catalog Production System. Because it was the first CD ROM publication, there were no precedents to follow and no off-the-shelf components to use in its development. Consequently, nearly every part of the publication had to be developed from scratch. This case study covers all aspects of BiblioFile's development: its origin, definition, design, and production, and how it changed the nature of one publisher's business.

The Origin of BiblioFile

Like most of the first CD ROM publications, BiblioFile was created by transferring a publication from another medium to CD ROM. The publication was MARCFICHE, and the medium was microfiche. You can best appreciate our motivation for switching to CD ROM by looking at the MARCFICHE publication—what is in it, who uses it, and how they use it.

MARCFICHE contains bibliographic information on publications in the Library of Congress. The MARCFICHE database contains more than 2 gigabytes of unique data. Librarians use this information to create catalogs of their library's holdings. To create a catalog card from MARCFICHE, a librarian goes through the following five steps:

1. Obtain a "key" from the publication to be cataloged. A key can be a title, an author, a Library of Congress call number (LCCN), an international standard book number (ISBN), or an international standard serial number (ISSN).

2. Select the fiche stack for the chosen key. There are five fiche stacks. Each fiche stack contains the bibliographic database arranged according to one of the five keys.

3. Find the fiche that contains the desired key value. The key range for each fiche is printed at the top of the fiche.

4. Put the selected fiche in a fiche reader and search for the key within the bibliographic data.

5. Type the fiche data on several cards—one card for each catalog heading (title, author, and subjects). Include on each card the local call numbers, holdings codes, and any other "local" information.

This method of cataloging consumes a substantial amount of a highly skilled librarian's time. As a result, many libraries find it cost-effective to pay premium prices for access to the same data in electronic form through online subscription services. Using these services, librarians can quickly search and print the catalog entries, dramatically increasing productivity and efficiency.

An online bibliographic database can be several orders of magnitude more expensive than the same product in print or microfiche form. Nevertheless, the success of online bibliographic data publishers demonstrates the advantages of electronic media over print media for finding and retrieving this sort of data. In fact, the primary reason that a market still exists for printed bibliographic information is the huge price difference between the least expensive print medium and the least expensive electronic medium. This price difference substantially diminished with the introduction of CD ROM.

Note: Throughout this chapter, "electronic" media are compared with "print" media. An electronic medium stores information in digital form and users must access this information with an electronic delivery system. Examples are remote, online databases and local CD ROM systems. A print medium is hard copy material such as microfiche and paper.

In evaluating CD ROM as a new publishing medium, we compared our knowledge and expectations of CD ROM with our experience in dealing with an existing bibliographic publishing medium (microfiche). We explored three areas:

1. Publishing cost

2. Product price

3. Product utility

Publishing cost comprised two components: 1) cost of data acquisition and formatting ("data-dependent" costs), and 2) cost of manufacturing and distribution ("media-dependent" costs).

The data-dependent costs vary with respect to the type and quantity of data published, but not with respect to the publication medium. For example, the cost of acquiring 600 MB of bibliographic data in machine-readable form can range from less than $1000 (for public-domain data on tape) to well more than $100,000 a year (for the maintenance of a unique, proprietary database). The cost of formatting high-quality bibliographic data for output to a particular medium is $5000 to $10,000 for the initial development of the formatting programs and $500 to $2000 in processing costs each time the programs are run. Naturally, it is far more expensive to work with low-quality (error-filled) data.

The media-dependent costs vary with respect to the type and quantity of the publishing medium used. A summary of these costs is shown in Table 1. The media types are microfiche and CD ROM. The relevant quantities are:

○ Database size—approximately 2 gigabytes.

○ Publication periodicity—monthly.

○ New data per period—10 to 20 MB.

○ Copies per period—1000.

Cost Item	Microfiche	CD ROM
Media Masters	35 fiche	1 CD ROM disc
Master Cost	$250	$5000
Media Copies	35,000	1000
Copies Cost	$2500	$4000
Distribution Cost	$1000	$1000
Total	$3750	$10,000

Table 1. Media costs associated with microfiche and CD ROM publishing.

Note that the database is accumulated rather than reissued in its entirety each month. For microfiche, this requires fabricating about 35 fiche-pages of data and supplemental indexes. For CD ROM, this requires refabricating the last disc of a four-disc set, which contains new data and new cumulative indexes. The CD ROM update method yields a higher-quality publication than does the microfiche update method, because it produces a cumulative publication; the fiche update stands separate from the rest of the fiche database.

Product price, the cost of the product to the customer, is composed of onetime costs (hardware) and recurring costs (subscription and usage).

The costs for setup and for a year's use of microfiche and CD ROM publications are listed in Table 2 (usage costs are discussed under product utility).

Microfiche	Cost	CD ROM	Cost
Fiche Reader	$800	Computer (PC)	$2000
Typewriter	$300	CD ROM	$700
		Printer	$300
1 yr. subscription	$500	1 yr. subscription	$1400
Total	$1600	Total	$4400

Table 2. Equipment costs and annual fee for microfiche and CD ROM publications.

Product utility, a measure of how helpful a product is to its users, is quantified by combining the product-usage costs mentioned above. For example, the bibliographic publications discussed here are used to produce catalogs. A typical catalog item (book, film, record) requires about five catalog cards—one for its title, two for authors, and two for subjects. If a library catalogs 100 items a month (a small library), then it produces about 6000 cards a year. If a librarian searches for the card data items on microfiche and then types the cards, he or she can produce 10 to 15 cards an hour. However, if a librarian searches on CD ROM, edits the data on a computer, and prints it out, he or she can produce 150 to 250 cards an hour. CD ROM offers the advantages of an electronic medium: 1) It is always faster to search the CD ROM database than the microfiche database, and 2) the searched data is immediately available for electronic editing, and the edited data is automatically formatted into an entire card set.

If the librarian in this example earns $12 an hour, then the library's cost to produce the catalog is $4000 to $6000 a year with microfiche and $240 to $400 a year with CD ROM. Compare these usage costs to the product prices (Table 2), and you can see that a library (even a small one) can cost-justify switching to CD ROM from microfiche.

Using an online publication, a librarian can produce the catalog in about the same amount of time as using CD ROM. However, the cost of simply getting hooked up for online service is about the same as that of a year's CD ROM service. Online services carry additional long-distance phone charges and transaction fees for searching and for record access. These online costs range from two to eight dollars a transaction (printed card set). Online services provide more recent data than can be made available on CD ROM, since an online database can be updated more frequently than can the CD ROM database. Large libraries may have CD ROM and sub-scribe to an online service for access to very recent bibliographic data. If the data is not on CD ROM, then the librarian tries the online database.

Designing BiblioFile

After considering the merits of CD ROM, we began designing BiblioFile. Our goal was to move the MARCFICHE database to CD ROM.

The design stage was divided into three sections:

1. Designing the CD ROM database

2. Selecting delivery system hardware

3. Designing delivery system software

Associated with each task were numerous constraints. Table 3 shows some of these.

The constraints outlined in Table 3 helped us make a number of major de-sign decisions.

Database Development

When we began developing the BiblioFile product, The Library Corpora-tion consisted of a handful of people who managed the fiche-publishing business. Because the data-processing requirements of CD ROM database development were so similar to those of microfiche database development (and because the driving force behind the CD ROM product was the de-veloper of the fiche product), we developed the CD ROM version on the same mainframe computer and in the same environment (COBOL) as the fiche products. Consequently, we used skills and tangible assets already present within the corporation.

The first problem in database design was to define the types of indexes. We indexed the data in categories similar to those used in online databases. This allowed us to design access methods familiar to users of online data-bases—a group we considered prospective customers. Furthermore, we designed the indexes so that any search key could be accessed in a single seek. We did this by using index hash tables.

The second database design problem concerned the size of the BiblioFile bibliographic data file, which was retained in an ANSI standard format for bibliographic data called MARC. This format contains a great deal of

Task	Constraint	Resulting Design
Database Design	Database too large to fit on a single disc.	Put the database on four discs with all indexes and monthly updates on the last disc. Thus, the user can search and access the most recent data without swapping discs. And the user must replace only one disc to update the database.
	ANSI standard format for bibliographic data contains much redundant data.	Store the database in a proprietary, nonredundant format that contains all information required to generate the ANSI format. This assures data compatibility with other bibliographic data-processing systems.
	No DOS CD ROM driver existed at the time that could address the entire BiblioFile database as a single entity.	Store the database as unformatted data—no reason to carry the useless overhead of a DOS disk file system.
	CD ROM access is too slow for indexes that require multiple accesses.	Use a data-indexing method suitable for hashed entry. This allows single-seek access to any indexed key.
Hardware Selection	CD ROM access is too slow for multiuser systems.	The delivery system might as well use a PC (personal computer). (PC architecture has the largest installed base among prospective customers.)
	Only Hitachi seemed to offer a CD ROM with PC interface as well as CD ROM mastering services.	Use Hitachi products and services for the initial development.
Software Design	No DOS CD ROM driver exists that can address the entire BiblioFile database as a single entity.	Write a modular driver that allows unrestricted access to a multidisc database.
	Layered ECC (error correction coding) capability is not resident in all CD ROM drive hardware.	Write layered ECC that can be used with any manufacturer's drive.
	BiblioFile database layout unproven on CD ROM. Changes to the database layout may be needed.	Separate database access functions from user-application functions by providing a high-level data-access method that is not dependent on the database layout.

Table 3. Design constraints of the BiblioFile project.

redundant information. For the purpose of CD ROM mastering, we removed the redundant data in such a way that it could easily be regenerated by the delivery system.

The third problem in database design concerned updating. Even removing the redundant data did not reduce the database enough so that it would fit on one CD ROM disc. To publish monthly updates and to keep remastering fees to a minimum, we decided to put all indexes and the most recent data on the last disc. We could then remaster and replace only that disc.

Delivery System Hardware

Delivery system hardware was determined by the design constraints outlined in Table 3. To summarize: We saw no reason to use anything more powerful than a microcomputer in this single-user delivery system. Future plans for a multiuser system called for a distributed-processing strategy best addressed by a local-area network of microcomputers. The PC computer architecture was believed to have the largest installed base among prospective customers; and Hitachi, in mid-1984, offered the only industrial-quality CD ROM with a PC interface. Thus, our minimum delivery system configuration would consist of a PC-compatible microcomputer with 256 KB memory, monochrome monitor, single floppy-disk drive, printer, and Hitachi CD ROM drive. Ultimately, we would find 512 KB of memory to be a more reasonable minimum requirement for a high-performance CD ROM delivery system, but we chose 256 KB so that the system would be compatible with a PC terminal that is used to access a popular online system (see "Marketing Philosophy" in this chapter).

Someday it will be possible for a CD ROM publisher to be commercially successful by producing only CD ROM publications. We brought Biblio-File into a world that had an installed base of very nearly zero CD ROM disc drives. We had no desire to market hardware, but we also had no choice. We had to sell CD ROM drives along with our publication; and, once we got into the hardware business, we decided to make the CD ROM plunge easier for our customers by supplying them with a complete CD ROM system: disc, software, disc drive, and computer. We still offer our customers the total system or any part of it.

Delivery System Software

Although developing the database was fairly straightforward because we used existing software tools and resources, developing the delivery system software (the BiblioFile application program) was not. At the time, there were no programs that could do what we wanted. As a result, we determined that developing our own software would be the only solution.

We chose the C language, believing that, among available DOS languages, it provided the best combination of code transportability and low- and high-level code constructs. We also knew that we could draw from a solid base of good programmers who enjoyed working in C.

Using C was not advantageous in one respect, however: We had no C programmers on staff. Since both time and money were critical, we initially contracted (rather than hired) C programmers to develop the software system. The work was divided among them as follows:

Retrieval engine. The retrieval engine (we also called it the database driver) is a program that serves as a low-level interface between the CD ROM database and the delivery-system application programs. It activates the search routines and retrieves the results. One programmer, who was intimately familiar with the database layout, designed and coded the retrieval engine. This code was about one-quarter of the total code of the first BiblioFile delivery system.

User interface. This is the part of the BiblioFile application program that the user sees. We planned to include a user interface with functions similar to those of a comparable online publication so that it would be familiar to online system users. We assigned a separate cataloging process to each of the PC's function keys. We grouped the processes by type (for example, searching, printing, storage and retrieval) and assigned each process to a programmer for coding. But first, the user interface designer coded the BiblioFile menu (a screen that shows the user which function keys perform which processes), defined data types, and coded support routines common to all BiblioFile functions. The designer then passed these routines to the programmers who coded the BiblioFile function groups.

Search routines. This part of the user interface searches the database indexes for the words requested by the user. The search routine translates the user request into commands that the retrieval engine uses to find and retrieve the data stored on disc. The search software, which was coded by one programmer, constitutes about one-tenth of the Biblio-File application code.

Editor routines. A necessary part of a catalog-production system is the routines that let the user modify data retrieved from the database. BiblioFile's data may be thought of as a collection of generic catalog card images. Librarians must be able to edit the images to include their own call numbers and holdings information. They also must be able to enter entire new card images for data that is not found in the BiblioFile database. The BiblioFile editor lets a user edit any record fetched from the database and create new BiblioFile-format records. The editor, coded by one programmer, constitutes about one-tenth of the BiblioFile application code.

Storage routines. Storage routines allow retrieved and/or modified data to be retained and accessed by the system and to be transferred to other data-processing systems. The BiblioFile storage routines were designed to manage a magnetic-disk database of BiblioFile format data. The magnetic-disk database can be used to accumulate data for card and label production, online catalog production, and archiving. The storage routines were coded by one programmer and constitute about one-twentieth of the BiblioFile application code.

Print routines. We developed special routines to print sorted sets of catalog cards and book, pocket, and spine labels. Requirements for printed output vary from library to library and we tried to accommodate as many printers as we could. Among all delivery-system application software, the print routines were the most time-consuming to design. Both a librarian and a programmer worked on the print routine code, which constitutes about one-quarter of the BiblioFile application code.

Configuration routines. We also developed a program that lets a user customize each of the above system functions. User-defined software configuration was especially important for the print routines, but we made it available for all the functions. For example, the user can configure the editor to set up a data-entry template for new records that automatically inserts data that must be present in every record.

Timeline

BiblioFile's development goals were well defined by September 1984 and were implemented as shown in Figure 1. We wanted to finish the disc for an industry trade show in mid-January 1985, so our goal was fixed and our schedule extremely tight. Against many odds, we met the deadline.

Upon completing the BiblioFile database design in the summer of 1984, we compiled and indexed the database, stored it on magnetic tape, and sent it to Japan for mastering. Throughout this time, we continued work on the retrieval software code.

Figure 1 shows that mastering took two months. This unusually long mastering period was due to the BiblioFile disc being the first commercial CD ROM. The manufacturer faced a number of problems that it had not previously encountered on test runs. Today, manufacturers can master a disc in less than 10 days.

278

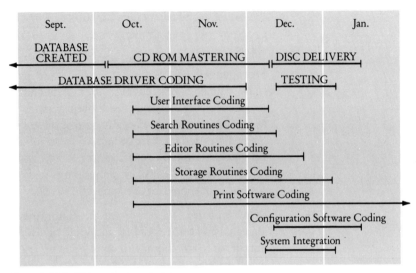

Figure 1. BiblioFile's production schedule.

After the disc was mastered, we received copies of it —handfuls at a time—for about a month. We used the first batch to test the newly finished retrieval program which was untested prior to delivery. Today, you can test retrieval software before mastering the disc with CD ROM emulation systems. Such systems typically use a PC with several high-capacity Winchester disk drives along with special software that simulates the CD ROM operating environment.

When we determined that our retrieval software was a success, we began developing the software components of the delivery system. We wanted to provide printer routines for every printer option possible. Since there are so many options, we continued writing printer routines long after introducing the product. When we finished most of the system coding we assembled all software components and hardware components into a single turnkey system.

We introduced the final product the first week in January 1985, and volume shipments to subscribers began in March 1985.

The total cost of developing the BiblioFile database and the Catalog Production System software was about $250,000, but a good portion of this money was an investment in future products. We can now produce publications of similar complexity for about $60,000.

Updating Strategy

We update monthly and remaster and replace only the last disc in a set.
Since this disc contains the indexes for the entire database, the user has a
completely updated database. That is, disc four of a four-disc set is replaced with the new edition of disc four, and both old and new data is accessible exactly as though the entire disc set has been replaced. This is a
pleasant contrast to the MARCFICHE method of incremental updates,
whereby new data (fiche) is received with its own stand-alone indexes.
With the incremental update method, the database soon becomes unwieldy, and periodic publication of cumulative indexes is necessary.

Data Security

Probably the biggest roadblock to CD ROM publishing is the problem of
data security. There are few enough publishers with 600 MB of CD
ROM-worthy data, and most of them are unwilling to release it, in its entirety, to the general public. Publishers of print and online media feel that
pirating their products simply is not worth the effort. To many of these
publishers, the thought of distributing their valuable databases in compact,
inexpensive, machine-readable form is chilling, to say the least.

The Library Corporation addressed the problem of data security in much
the same way as do publishers of print and online media—that is to say,
not at all. The reasons are contained both in the company charter and in
the nature of the CD ROM publication. The charter calls for the company
to publish inexpensive bibliographic information. The company is very
small and quite efficient. It simply is not worth the effort to try to compete against such a company, with the same data, in so narrow a market.
In addition, the entire BiblioFile publication—data, data structures, programs, and documentation—is in the public domain. Companies that
don't wish to be so daring can take heart in that little effort is required to
mark a copyrighted CD ROM database with identifiers that cannot prof-
itably be removed (the needle-in-the-haystack principle applies). It also
should not be difficult to keep abreast of the competition and to quickly
check for potential copyright infringement.

What is it about the nature of the CD ROM publication that leads us to be
so careless about data security? With a CD ROM publication, the message
varies according to the delivery-system application with which it is read.
A CD ROM publisher may enlist the support of a publication's potential
competitors by encouraging them to develop applications that use the same
data. A publisher may even work with potential competitors to design the

database so that all foreseeable delivery systems can use the data. This is the method behind the madness of releasing BiblioFile to the public domain. A number of companies use the BiblioFile discs in their applications. This fulfills the needs of markets not addressed by the services of the Catalog Production System—and it also increases the sales of the BiblioFile database.*

Pricing and Distribution

BiblioFile's price of $870 for a quarterly subscription includes a four-disc set, single-disc updates, catalog production software, users' and programmers' manuals, and frequent (about 10 during 1985) updates of the software and manuals. Then add to this price the cost of a CD ROM drive and PC (about $2500), and BiblioFile still costs less than setting up an online system.

The performance-to-price ratio and the novelty of BiblioFile were so high that substantial word-of-mouth advertising was sparked within the library community, as was disbelief among prospective customers—a disbelief that could be overcome only by demonstrating the product at trade shows and meetings. The demonstration approach to selling was new to The Library Corporation. The initial results were summarized succinctly by the company's marketing director, Linda Kolker: "After watching the BiblioFile demonstration attentively, their most common reaction was to crawl behind the computer and look for the telephone line. Once satisfied that there was no phone line, their response was uniformly positive. It is a very rewarding product to sell, but you must teach the concept before you can sell the product."

Marketing Philosophy

CD ROM is different enough from other publishing media to warrant a new marketing approach—an approach that includes potential competitors. To Brower Murphy, the creator of BiblioFile, the market was more than libraries. It was a web of bibliographic information providers, processors, and users. This market concept influenced the ultimate form and success of BiblioFile even more than design considerations.

---

*The name "BiblioFile" refers to the bibliographic database on CD ROM, while "BiblioFile Catalog Production System" is BiblioFile database and the Catalog Production System software. The Catalog Production System is one of the delivery system applications that use the BiblioFile database.

Murphy founded The Library Corporation in 1974 to publish bibliographic information. He believed that such information should be free and that access to it should be inexpensive. This belief led him to publish public-domain data—first on microfiche, then on CD ROM.

When Murphy switched from microfiche to electronic media, his role changed from that of information provider to that of system developer. He enlisted a team of programmers to help build the delivery systems for his new electronic publications. Then he placed most of this software in the public domain in an effort to motivate other companies to become CD ROM publishers and delivery-system developers. He felt that by encouraging all companies involved in bibliographic retrieval to embrace this new technology, he would help build the industry for all of them.

Subcribers also played an important part in BiblioFile's design. For a new industry to develop and grow, it must be accepted by the consumer. In an effort to stimulate this level of acceptance, Murphy let subscribers buy access to bibliographic data at an unprecedented 25 cents a megabyte, receive valuable data-processing services free, and make BiblioFile a living product by continually feeding their ideas for improvements back into the product development cycle.

Murphy's desire to create an industry through cooperation is evident in many of BiblioFile's features. For example, BiblioFile was designed to output its data in the ANSI standard format for bibliographic data—which allows it to feed its data to other bibliographic data-processing systems. The software was also designed to be compatible with existing online systems. Online publishers such as OCLC (Online Computer Library Center), whose M300 terminal has 256 KB of memory and a floppy-disk drive, determined the "low-end" PC configuration on which BiblioFile runs. M300 users can access both low-cost BiblioFile data and services and proprietary OCLC data and remote services.

A CD ROM Publisher's Business

The transition of The Library Corporation from microfiche publisher to CD ROM publisher changed our business. Once an information provider, we now provide both information and information-processing services. In learning to teach the concepts of CD ROM publishing, we discovered new business opportunities in the CD ROM market web and have become increasingly involved in joint publishing ventures. We have published and developed delivery systems for other publishers' data, and we have combined our data and talents with those of other companies to produce better products than either company could produce alone.

These joint ventures benefit everyone, but they also pose a special problem: Most of these ventures have been in association with companies that also are information providers. Although many of them have the engineering resources to do systems development on the PC, the device-handling requirements of CD ROM (notably, its enormous storage capacity) call for special file-handling techniques that are outside the expertise of most DOS programmers. Consequently, the burden has been on us to provide many delivery systems.

Since we have limited engineering resources, we have developed a DOS-installable device driver that takes advantage of the full storage capacity of CD ROM. This driver has turned the once-esoteric CD ROM drive into just another DOS disk—a turn of events that makes CD ROM more accessible to a wide variety of systems developers.

To further promote CD ROM experimentation, The Library Corporation distributes its DOS device driver, along with programmer's documentation, free program updates, and a license for unlimited copying and distribution of the driver, to any company or individual interested in developing a joint publishing venture. This DOS device driver offers substantial, but not complete, DOS support of CD ROM. The recent introduction of DOS extensions by Microsoft should make complete DOS support of CD ROM drives a reality. With this support, the cost of developing a product like BiblioFile is now about one-fifth of what it was two years ago.

About the Author

Brian Martin lives in Silver Spring, MD. He is a consultant in systems and product development. As Chief Technical Officer of The Library Corporation, he participated in developing the first commercial CD ROM publication.

A Clinical Medical Information System on CD ROM

Micromedex, Inc., has been publishing medical information on microfiche for more than a decade. In 1985 it introduced the same product, with enhancements for a personal computer, on CD ROM, becoming the first publisher to offer a CD ROM product to the medical community. In late 1985, Micromedex became a wholly owned subsidiary of Mead Data Central. The following case study is an account of this publisher's experiences as it grappled with and embraced a new technology without letting go of the old ones.

Since 1974, Micromedex has provided physicians, pharmacists, and other health professionals with clinical data to assist in patient care. The information in the databases is written and reviewed by a board of medical specialists from the United States, Canada, and other countries. It is edited by medical professionals, including physicians, pharmacists, and nurses.

The databases are marketed under the name Computerized Clinical Information System (CCIS) to hospital and industry medical personnel.* The system provides evaluated, referenced data on:

- Diagnosis and treatment of medical problems (anything from AIDS to wrist fractures) with an emphasis on critical care and emergency medicine (Emergindex System).

- Clinical drug information, including comparisons of drugs that are used for similar conditions, drug interactions and incompatibilities, adverse reactions, drugs' effects during pregnancy, dosing regimens, metabolism and excretion (breast milk, urine, and so forth), and patient instructions (Drugdex System).

---

*See pages 543-44 of *CD ROM: The New Papyrus* (Microsoft Press, 1986) for a more complete description of the Micromedex products.

- Abstracts, cumulative from 1982, of the world's medical literature relating to critical care and emergency medicine. The abstracts are formatted and indexed extensively for easy review (Emergindex System).

- Identification and treatment data for more than 450,000 potentially toxic substances. Descriptions include drugs (prescription, over-the-counter, drugs with slang names, drugs of abuse); consumer products; industrial chemicals; plants; snakes, spiders, and other venomous creatures; and many other toxic substances that can be inhaled, ingested, or absorbed (Poisindex System).

- Interactive programs that determine drug dosage, perform calculations, and create predictive graphs based on patient characteristics such as age, weight, prior conditions, and blood drug levels. Subscribers use these programs to aid in proper diagnosis and treatment.

From Microfiche to CD ROM

The databases first appeared on computer output microfiche (COM) in 1974. These microfiche editions continue to be updated and republished every quarter. Each one-year, prepaid subscription entitles subscribers to four cumulative editions.

The first computer application of the CCIS databases was marketed on magnetic tape to hospital mainframe users—primarily those with administration and data-processing departments committed to providing clinical data to physicians, not just accounting and billing services. Here again, a yearly subscription with quarterly updates was the basis for revenues. Today, magnetic tape databases continue to be healthy members of the product line, but the market is limited to institutions that have IBM mainframe systems (running under DOS, PCS/ADS, MVS, or MVS-XA).

As personal computers became more widespread in hospital departments, the market pressure for the Micromedex CCIS databases on a PC-based system increased. In 1983, using its existing programming staff, Micromedex began developing a PC application to meet this demand.

At first, the designers considered dial-up access, linking the personal computers to an online information vendor. This idea subsequently was rejected because we felt "pay as you go" dial-up access would jeopardize the existing subscription revenues. With the online approach out of the picture, the programmers turned their sights to high-capacity storage devices.

The first personal-computer-based application was developed and demonstrated to customers using a 474 MB Fujitsu Eagle disk drive. The data was downloaded from an IBM 4331 to the Eagle drive in a process that was time-consuming and required a fair amount of technical expertise. Although the system was very well received, it was immediately apparent that the hardware cost for the disk drive and tape drive would be too great for personal computer users. Updating the hard disk every quarter would also be beyond the technical capability of most Micromedex customers.

Our company was encouraged by the favorable reception of the computerized microfiche databases. We began to search for a technology that would meet the requirements we considered important: easy updating and lower hardware costs without a sacrifice in performance. At the time, the 12-inch videodisc and the 12-inch optical disc were the only media that roughly met these requirements. We experimented with both types in an attempt to find the right storage device on which to market our already-developed application. Unfortunately, the hardware costs for the 12-inch devices were prohibitive for many users, and market resistance continued to be significant.

Finally, Reference Technology, Inc. (RTI), in May 1985, premastered the Micromedex CCIS on CD ROM using the same data tapes provided for the 12-inch optical disc. The application software was ready to go, since it had been fully developed and tested using the 12-inch disc. The first customer received a system in early June 1985, complete with a CLASIX S-500 DataDrive (manufactured by Hitachi) and the Micromedex CCIS databases on CD ROM with software on floppy disks.

Why CD ROM Was the Perfect Storage Medium

Micromedex needed a delivery medium for its more than 300 MB of data that would allow electronic access from personal computers. CD ROM was the ideal medium because it provided:

- High-density storage.
- Replicability at the factory level (similar to microfiche) in a format easily updated by the least sophisticated user.
- Virtual indestructibility of the discs—important in an environment where careful handling of media is impractical and unrealistic.
- Low-cost hardware as a peripheral to a PC, particularly when compared with any other mass storage device.
- High consumer acceptance of the new technology bolstered by widespread publicity and the availability of compact discs in the audio market.
- Very acceptable performance as a computer peripheral.

Design Decisions and Supporting Rationale

Designing a CD ROM system presents a few of the standard challenges common to all systems, and several new and unusual ones. This section describes some problems associated with the development of our CD ROM system, including such issues as:

1. Understanding the user environment.

2. Defining the basic delivery system.

3. Deciding whether to find a service bureau or develop the system entirely in-house.

4. Determining an appropriate updating strategy.

5. Protecting the data.

6. Estimating costs and budgeting for a new, untested product and production method.

7. Assuring the quality of mastered discs and software.

8. Marketing and distributing a new high-tech product.

The User Environment

The targeted market for the Micromedex CCIS application is hospital-based health professionals. Unlike trained hospital librarians, physicians, nurses, and pharmacists who need clinical information do not have the time or inclination to master complicated search strategies to get the needed data. Instead, they are far more likely to reach for a medical text-book. Or, if time is available, they may ask the hospital librarian (when there is one) to search the relevant literature.

In designing and marketing information systems for physicians, pharmacists, and nurses, it is critical to consider the characteristics of the audience. Most medical professionals have little experience with computers, so it is essential that mastery of the user interface require little or no training. In many hospitals, there is rapid turnover of medical staff, residents, and interns, who have a need for information but no time to learn how to search for it. Furthermore, the critical nature of hospital activities heightens the need to retrieve information quickly.

The CCIS CD ROM development team attempted to keep the subscriber profile in mind in designing the user interface. They assumed most subscribers previously had used only books, journals, or microfiche to find answers to medical questions. Consequently, they chose a menu design that would be easy to understand, listing on every screen all the available options. They added interactive programs to aid in drug dosing or calculating possible toxicity—an attractive and valuable feature for any computerized medical information system.

Basic Delivery System

The CCIS environment consists of an IBM PC- or AT-compatible microcomputer running IBM's MS-DOS version 2.00 or later. Micromedex currently uses the RTI CLASIX S-500 stand-alone CD ROM player, with the RTI parallel "long card" (IBM AT-compatible) interface. We chose this front-loading CD ROM drive because of the space constraints in emergency departments and hospital pharmacies, two areas where the system frequently is located. The drive must fit between the PC system unit and the monitor without requiring any additional counter space or special handling.

The RTI Series 500 is a Hitachi CD ROM drive, but we chose Reference Technology's PC interface card because the Hitachi PC interface card originally was not designed to work well with the IBM AT or with the COMPAQ DESK PRO 286. RTI services the drives and also supplies software that reflects any hardware changes. Our hardware involvement is therefore minimal, and we can concentrate instead on optimizing the retrieval package.

Each subscriber must license the RTI STA/F File operating environment for CD ROM. Quarterly updates include a new release of the retrieval software, which contains changes to existing programs as well as new features, such as graphics programs, developed in response to user demand. Because of the high user demand for hard-copy support, the system includes text-printing software for most printers and graphics-printing support for IBM and Epson printers.

The user enters information at the keyboard, usually with a single keystroke.

The Service Bureau Role

As mentioned, Micromedex completed the basic design and implementation of the system in both magnetic and 12-inch optical media. We were in the position of waiting for the "perfect" delivery medium, rather than attempting to create a CD ROM application. Our technical resources in the area of computer hardware were limited. We also were anxious about marketing an information product we had spent years developing, but which lacked an appropriate delivery system. RTI, which produced our LV ROM discs, helped us in all these areas.

When RTI opened its CD ROM production facility, it began converting databases on our LV ROM tapes to the CD ROM format. Since the software and data were already in the proper format, it took only a day to demonstrate a working application. Within a week, we were able to market the same application.

We depended on RTI to support our new CD ROM product. Since our resources were limited, we needed a service bureau to provide the CD ROM hardware and computer interface and to help with system integration. In addition, CD ROM mastering was not available domestically, and RTI was willing to hand carry the database tapes to Japan and supervise the mastering process there, a process that otherwise would have taken three to five months.

Furthermore, RTI prepared our data to Hitachi's mastering specifications. It also provided a sophisticated device driver (STA/F File) that allowed file-level access to the CD ROM from MS-DOS. This enabled us to use our application with no software modifications.

Updating Strategy

Our databases are updated, republished, and distributed in their entirety quarterly, whether they are microfiche, mainframe, or CD ROM products. The medical data is time sensitive and must be distributed in a timely manner. The databases always have carried expiration dates, and subscribers return previous editions to limit medical-legal liabilities.

Before we began marketing the CD ROM product, our editing and data-production cycles were staggered so that a different database was produced each month with a maximum of two files in any one month. With both microfiche and computer tape, producing more than one database at a time is not economical. Furthermore, the databases on microfiche are marketed separately to different departments within a hospital. But this system changed with CD ROM production. Because of the high cost of CD ROM mastering and because of the capacity of a disc, bundling the databases to be mastered and sold together made economic sense.

Initially, we kept the same editorial and microfiche production schedules, but delayed mastering until all databases could be mastered simultaneously. Unfortunately, this often meant that our microfiche customers received their individual databases before the CD ROM customers received their discs. To correct this disparity, we drastically altered the production cycles so that three of the databases would be produced quarterly in all media during the same months. The fourth database was discontinued in microfiche, because it had not been successful in that medium.

The change in production cycles led to a data-processing and editorial bottleneck, which required an internal mainframe CPU upgrade after the third CD ROM update. Soon after we upgraded our system, compact disc manufacturing facilities became available in the United States, and we were able to switch from Japan to the U.S. for mastering and replication. The upgrade, combined with a more efficient manufacturing cycle, sped up processing and shipping operations enough to enable us to easily meet quarterly deadlines in all three media.

Data Security and Copyright Protection

Traditionally, online information vendors have charged for the use of their databases by monitoring connect-time and search activity. This "pay for use" philosophy has been a major stumbling block in bringing CD ROM-based products to market, because many information providers can't find a way to match the online revenues. CD ROM allows them to distribute the same database locally with unlimited use to customers who had paid for the same thing by the minute.

Fortunately, Micromedex didn't have this problem. Users subscribe to our databases, whether on microfiche, magnetic tape, or optical disc, on an annual, unlimited-use basis. However, we still face some common data-protection issues. All our databases are on the same disc, but are marketed both bundled and unbundled. Since the databases are distributed in digital format, we have some concerns about their being downloaded and copied. Currently, the volume of data and the uniqueness of CD ROM distribution itself offer some protection. Even if the data could be downloaded, much of the value of the database—the indexing system—would be lost.

Protecting access to unbundled databases is somewhat more difficult. With unbundled databases, software copy protection so greatly complicated subscriber support, and was so offensive to some subscribers, that it was discontinued after one quarterly edition. Our best method for protection is to offer attractive prices for the bundled databases. Our subscribers, which are mainly hospitals, also must sign license agreements before we install the CD ROM system. An institution is unlikely to risk an unauthorized downloading after signing such an agreement. In our relatively small market niche, where our sales force is well acquainted with each user, data theft is not a major threat.

Estimating Costs and Budgeting

Micromedex is a small company with approximately 65 employees. We brought the CD ROM product to market in June 1985, using only existing staff. As market acceptance and customer demand grew, we needed more people to help in product development, program refinement, and customer support. After three editions, we increased the hours of a part-time programmer to full-time to free another person to spend his time entirely on maintaining and further developing the CD ROM product. We created a two-person customer technical support staff that had responsibility for duplicating software; shipping out systems consisting of DataDrives, discs, and software; writing and revising installation procedures; providing technical support for trade (medical) shows; supporting the salespeople with demo systems; and answering customers' questions pertaining to system operation. We increased the field sales staff from three to nine people in an effort to more fully educate and penetrate the market in a shorter time. We also added two sales support people to schedule product demonstrations, since this new medium generated much curiosity. The production staff consists of twenty people other than programmers and technical support. Full-time editors make up 20 percent of the staff, and human-resources and finance staffs account for another 12 percent.

Production Costs

As discussed previously, at one point Micromedex needed to upgrade its mainframe CPU to handle the increased processing and merging of database production cycles required by the CD ROM delivery format. Another capital expenditure was a floppy disk duplicating device so that we could efficiently produce software for each quarterly update.

During each publishing cycle we contend with all sorts of incremental production costs. Simple things like printed labels for discs, special shipping boxes, additional shipping costs, and the floppy disks all add up quickly, and sometimes unexpectedly.

Premastering and mastering costs, which include the charges from both RTI and The 3M Company, range from $9000 to $13,000, depending on variables such as software services used, the number of tapes provided, and the quantity of discs ordered.

Marketing Costs

Introducing a product to market usually is very costly. For small companies, the process is limited by what they can afford.

The Micromedex marketing budget is geared mainly to product demonstrations at the traditional professional meetings we have always attended. The CD ROM product has sent us to a few new trade shows that focus on computers in medicine. Because our CD ROM system requires computer equipment, drives, and monitors, we now rent more space at these shows than we did. In addition, we must rent the computer equipment and bring in technical support personnel to handle setup and equipment failures—expenses we did not have previously.

We had to create new literature describing CD ROM and the new CCIS product to meet the demand for information. As proponents of a new technology, we needed to educate customers so that they would feel comfortable with a new delivery mechanism. Product literature that explains the technology while describing the product is a critical, and costly, marketing tool.

The CD ROM product also has generated new expenses from our sales department. Old and new salespeople are equipped with demonstration hardware and trained to use it. Each salesperson maintains an inventory of personal computer and DataDrive hardware, to be able to leave a system for a few days at a customer's site and still keep one.

Although the costs of marketing any new product are high, the return on investment increases as market accceptance grows. As customers and salespeople become more familiar with the new technology, the cost of education goes down and sales calls can be made more efficiently. Thus, the time and cost of marketing begin to decrease, and the profit margin eventually increases.

Product Implementation

The process for getting good results with a CD ROM-based system starts with data preparation. Because of the slow seek time of CD ROM, data structures that minimize random accesss must be developed.

The menu-oriented design of our application limits the decisions a user can make within any menu. We took advantage of this limitation in preparing data for CD ROM mastering. As we generate the databases on our mainframe computer, we calculate all possible decision routes the user can take when selecting data. We then embed these route calculations as "pointers" to the data's physical location on the disc. This considerably cuts the number of seeks required to find the data. When the user follows one of these "prerecorded" routes, the search software can jump immediately to the selected data in a single seek.

The most time spent on the CD ROM product was in development of mainframe software. Fortunately, our data existed in a highly structured electronic format before this project was started. And our Computer Output Microfiche (COM) product already included a complex indexing and cross-referencing scheme. We therefore avoided some of the problems faced by many information providers, who produce databases from phototypesetting tapes that must be structured and indexed from scratch. The bulk of our data-preparation time was spent in developing tools to generate data structures that allow one-seek searching.

We relied on Reference Technology for software support. It provided us with the CD ROM device driver, called STA/F File and STA/F Key.

STA/F File often is called a device driver, but is more accurately an extension of the MS-DOS file system. It is the software interface that translates the CD ROM file structures so they can be read by MS-DOS. STA/F File also defines the layout of files and directories on the CD ROM. STA/F Key is a program that creates and retrieves "keyed" data (see Chapter 7 for more information on keyed data). This program saved time in production by automatically creating the keyed data structures. It also shortened the time spent in developing data-generation and -retrieval software. As our software application stabilized and our understanding of CD ROM technology grew, we eventually were able to build an indexing and retrieval method specifically suited to our application. Even after producing five quarterly editions of our CD ROM product, we still find room for improving and optimizing data structures and retrieval software. Our philosophy of product development is to develop a marketable product and then "fill in the blanks."

The In-House Production Process

With our quarterly disc production, we continually update our databases following a series of well-defined steps. Approximately 45 days before the current disc expires, we begin a new production cycle. During this cycle, we build the new data files and indexes, and we record these data structures, along with the updated database, on magnetic tape.

The Service Bureau Production Process

When the data arrives at the service bureau, RTI technicians use a software system to analyze the whole collection of information (data and index files). Their goal is to establish the most efficient disc organization for minimizing access time. In our case, the system places the data and index files next to each other, since data retrieval almost always will follow an index search. The software then builds a disc directory, which specifies where all files are stored. The directory is physically located at the center of the data—again, to minimize disc access time. The software system Reference Technology uses to configure the disc is the STA/F File system; the same program later is used to access and retrieve the data.

Disc Quality Assurance

RTI coordinates all schedules with the mastering facility and delivers tapes adapted with its data-preparation process. It also accepts delivery of the discs from the mastering facility and checks their quality. All discs undergo a quality-assurance procedure that involves reading the entire surface and performing random seeks. Reading the entire surface guarantees that all data is accessible. Random seeking ensures that the disc and drive together meet maximum access-time specifications. About two hours is devoted to checking each disc.

Software Quality Assurance

When the discs are returned from Reference Technology, Micromedex runs a full quality-assurance cycle on the software and discs that will be delivered to users. Before discs are mastered, we emulate the CD ROM system on a mainframe computer using the software and data that will be mastered on disc. During this last stage, we incorporate in the software the latest updates and options and correct any indexing or minor data problems we encounter.

Marketing and Distribution

Targeted customers for the Micromedex CCIS CD ROM product were the 1500 hospitals that already had Micromedex databases on microfiche and other hospitals that had filled out lead cards at trade shows and conferences. We approached our market in a traditional manner, sending out a mailer that described the new delivery system. In our mailer, we emphasized the added value of computer control and interactivity not possible with the microfiche systems.

In response to our marketing campaign, our potential customers began voicing their concerns. To help allay some of these, we immediately initiated a number of policies to encourage user confidence in the new CD ROM delivery format. The most common concerns and their remedies were:

- **What happens if the CD player stops working? After all, this is an unproven technology.**
  We provide a hardware maintenance agreement that includes a swap-out of the DataDrive by overnight express mail (supported by Reference Technology).

- **What about data backup?**
  Microfiche is provided free to customers who request it for backup.

- **Can we network the system to another PC?**
  Although networking is not feasible, additional subscriptions within the same hospital are available at a drastically reduced price. For example, the first subscription to all the databases within an institution costs $7500 a year. Additional locations within the same facility can subscribe to the same data for $750 a year.

- **Can we subscribe to some, but not all, of the databases?**
  Users can subscribe to separate databases by paying for software that only accesses the requested databases.

Pricing

We continued the subscription pricing strategy for our CD ROM products that we established for our microfiche products. Prepaid subscriptions encourage unlimited use. This seems to contribute to the number of proponents within a hospital who will support the renewal subscription.

Sales Process

Our basic sales philosophy at Micromedex is to let the information sell itself. In calling on potential customers, our salespeople generally find it easy to capitalize on the highly credible knowledge in the databases.

However, a CD ROM product has certain technological requirements. As a result, the sales process for the CD ROM product varies somewhat from a microfiche sale. Before arranging an on-site demonstration, the salesperson needs to know the answers to questions such as:

○ Do the potential customers already have a personal computer? If so, what kind?

○ Are they aware of the costs involved in a subscription?

○ Are the funds budgeted?

○ Can we arrange for other hospital departments to participate in the demonstration?

○ Does this hospital currently subscribe to our database(s)?

To encourage migration from microfiche to CD ROM, we credit any unused portion of the customers' microfiche subscription(s) to the first-year cost of the CD ROM CCIS.

The typical sales call for a CD ROM system takes longer than a similar microfiche call for a variety of reasons.

○ Equipment must be set up and checked out.

○ Scheduling appointments takes longer. Since the subscription price for an initial location is high relative to additional subscriptions within the same facility, it is important to demonstrate the product for decision makers from various departments. Getting seven or eight people together in a hospital takes time even when an appointment has been made.

○ Since CD ROM is a new technology, there usually is a testing period. After demonstrating the database system, the salespeople generally leave the hardware and CD ROM software to allow staff who work other shifts to review the system.

Distribution

A customer who decides to subscribe is given the option to buy the DataDrive and subscription outright or to make monthly payments. At first, we did not offer monthly subscription pricing for the hardware and databases, but during our first year we found that some customers had difficulty buying the equipment outright. (This is because unbudgeted expenses, particularly capital expenditures, usually are difficult to justify during hospitals' annual budget processes.) For this reason, we decided to offer monthly subscription pricing with an option to include hardware.

Customer Support

Questions from users of the CD ROM CCIS product initially were handled by the programmers who developed the software. But after four months of selling the new CD ROM product, we found that few calls were related to search problems, even though no user's manual was distributed with the system. Instead, most calls pertained to hardware-integration issues. Incompatible printers and personal computer hardware were the major problems. This demand necessitated a customer support staff of two whose primary function was to help these subscribers sort out their difficulties. With each succeeding update, we simplified and condensed installation procedures to minimize problems associated with setting up the system.

Market Response

From the beginning, user acceptance of the new CD ROM technology was high, because it made the CCIS database accessible through a personal computer. The database's availability in electronic form has led some physicians to review the data more seriously than when it was on microfiche. In fact, a number of new subscribers did not subscribe to the microfiche system because they considered microfiche cumbersome and unwieldy.

To maintain this high level of acceptance, we have continued to improve the application software, making it easier and more efficient to use. We also added programs that let the user print any number of lines or entire sections from a document. This feature is especially important to our target market, because they often need to place copies of referenced data in a patient's chart.

The positive response from the Micromedex hospital market has encouraged the company to continue enhancing the CD ROM product and develop or license additional medical information. As CD ROM discs and players become more common, potential users will be further encouraged to invest in new hardware. However, because of the need and demand for the clinical data on the Micromedex CD ROM system, we have met only slight resistance to our requirement that customers purchase a dedicated CD ROM drive.

Comments in Retrospect

The risks inherent in having the first medical database marketed on CD ROM brought with them decided advantages. Micromedex became known outside its traditional market, which gave it more credibility within its own customer base. The motivation for Reference Technology and Micromedex to accommodate each other's particular needs and limitations was very high, since we were "in this new thing together." Users' acceptance was excellent, because they wanted the data, the system worked, and partly because people outside the computer field do not perceive the risks of a brand-new technology. For many customers, personal computers seemed new!

In the end, the delivery system is not nearly as important as the information itself and the application that lets the user get to the data. When Micromedex began marketing its Poisindex poison-information system on microfiche, many people said doctors would never use microfiche. We currently have a user base of more than 1100 Poisindex microfiche hospital subscribers in emergency departments, hospital pharmacies, and poison-control centers. Doctors, nurses, and pharmacists use the microfiche because they want the information it contains. The same principle applies to CD ROM. It is a workable medium for storing high-density data accessible from a personal computer. It is easy to reproduce and update. Data integrity is excellent, and security is good. For Micromedex, the risk was definitely worthwhile.

About the Authors

Marilyn G. Winokur is vice president of product development and operations at Micromedex, Inc., a leading publisher of proprietary medical databases since 1974. She had been managing editor of the Poisindex and Drugdex databases and administrator of the Rocky Mountain Poison and Drug Information Center, which houses and works closely with some of the Micromedex editorial staff. She has supervised the development of the Micromedex CCIS CD ROM product from its inception to the present. She earned her B.S. degree from the University of Pennsylvania.

Leonard S. Rann is director of optical systems for Micromedex, Inc. He developed the Micromedex CCIS CD ROM architecture and software. Before working on the CD ROM product, he developed the 12-inch LV ROM version of the Micromedex databases and the software to produce the Poisindex substance database for the microfiche and mainframe delivery systems.

William Thornburg is a systems engineer at Reference Technology, Inc. Before joining RTI in 1984, Thornburg designed several control systems for Electronic Processors, Inc. He received his B.S. in mathematics from Colorado State University and his M.B.A. from the University of Colorado.

Micromedex, Inc.
660 Bannock Street
Suite 350
Denver, CO 80204-4506
(303) 623-8600

Reference Technology, Inc.
5700 Flatiron Parkway
Boulder, CO 80301
(303) 449-4157

APPENDIXES

Glossary

access time: The time required to find, retrieve, and display a piece of recorded information. Access time usually refers to the longest time a storage device requires to get to a piece of information. For many CD ROM drives, access times range from 0.5 to 1.5 sec.

active display: Contents currently displayed on a screen, as opposed to screen contents being held in memory for later display if needed.

Adaptive Differential Pulse Code Modulation: See *ADPCM*.

address: The location in a computer's memory or on disc of a particular piece of information. A numeric code defines the location, describing it explicitly (the *absolute address*) or in relationship to another address, such as the beginning of a file (the *relative address*).

ADPCM (Adaptive Differential Pulse Code Modulation):   A digital sampling method that adapts to changes in signal characteristics (such as amplitude or pitch period) by correlating successive data samples. Specifically, the value of a previous sample (or samples) is extrapolated to predict the current sample using one of several predictors. Alternately, the system may use an *adaptive quantizer* (AQ) or a combination adaptive predictor (AP) and adaptive quantizer to determine sample values. ADPCM is used to reduce quantizing noise when compressing digitized signals.

algorithm: 1. A method of problem-solving in which solutions are derived following a prescribed set of well-defined steps. 2. Any step-by-step procedure for solving a specified problem.

aliasing: Distortion of digital information that occurs when the sampling rate is less than twice the maximum frequency component in the sampled signal. In images, aliasing appears as jagged edges, called "jaggies," along diagonal or curved boundaries; in sound, aliasing produces false tones.

alphanumeric: Alphabetic and numeric, usually referring to keyboard characters containing both letters and numerals.

analog: In electronics, a signal that is continuously variable (often expressed as a wave), as opposed to a *digital* signal, which is discretely variable (often expressed as pulses). Analog phenomena in nature include waves, time, temperature, and voltage. These can be expressed digitally by periodically sampling the analog components.

Analog-to-Digital converter (A/D converter, or ADC): A device that samples an analog signal at regular intervals and quantizes each sample (that is, represents each sample's value with a binary number of some predetermined length expressed in bits per word). This process, called *Analog-to-Digital conversion,* produces a digital signal that describes the original analog signal. Setting the sampling rate and the word length high enough to resolve all useful information in the signal is important. In practice, some information always will be lost.

application software: Programs designed for a specific task, such as word processing or data search and retrieval.

artificial intelligence: Computer programs that perform functions normally associated with human reasoning and learning.

ASCII (American Standard Code for Information Interchange): A code established by the American Standards Association, ASCII is a standard table of 7-bit digital representations of upper- and lowercase Roman letters, numbers, and special control characters in teletype, computer, and word-processor systems. ASCII is used for alphanumeric communication by all major software manufacturers except IBM, which uses EBCDIC, a similar code it devised. Since most computer systems use a full byte to send an ASCII character, many hardware and software companies have added their own nonstandard and mutually incompatible codes to the official ASCII 128-character set, extending it to 256 characters.

aspect ratio: The width-to-height ratio of a rectangular object or figure. In computer displays, this can refer to either the screen shape or the pixel shape. Video has a screen aspect ratio of 4:3, and film an image aspect ratio of 3:2. No common standard exists for pixel aspect ratio, though the trend is toward square (1:1) pixels.

asynchronous: In computing, a system in which the stages in a program are queued so that the completion of one operation initiates the next.

asynchronous file: A data file that must be accessed and displayed quickly but is not tied to a specific data transfer rate. For example, a text file is asynchronous; the text's usefulness doesn't depend on a specific delivery rate.

audio frequencies: Frequencies that the human ear can hear, usually 20 to 20,000 cycles per second. See also *hertz*.

audio track: A section of a Compact Disc that can be addressed separately; usually a track contains a complete musical piece.

authoring language: A high-level, plain-English computer language, often based on a computer language such as BASIC or Pascal, that enables users without formal programming skills to write computer programs. The same program generally contains both content and logic.

authoring system: A collection of authoring programs and equipment that enables nonprogrammers to write interactive programs, often working in everyday language, and without the painstaking detail formal programming requires. Using an authoring system, a person can develop a program without knowing its inherent commands and logic.

auxiliary data field: In CD ROM Mode 1, a 288-byte-long data field in a physical sector used for additional EDC/ECC error detection and correction. In Mode 2, a 280-byte-long data field available to the user.

background task: A task that a computer program performs while the primary or foreground program is not using the central processing unit (CPU), usually when the foreground task is waiting for user input. The user often isn't aware it's being executed.

bandwidth: 1. The range of frequencies (measured in cycles per second) a piece of audio or video equipment can encode and decode. Video uses higher frequencies than does audio and so requires a higher bandwidth. 2. The maximum number of information units (bits, characters) that can traverse a communications path each second.

batch processing: A data-processing method in which all data is gathered and processed or transmitted at one time, involving no interaction with the user.

BER (bit error rate): Expressed as the number of bits encountered before one erroneous bit is found (for instance, in CD ROM the BER is 1 erroneous bit in 10^{12} bits) or as a frequency of erroneous bits (for instance, 10^{-12} bits).

binary notation: A counting system that uses only two digits, 0 and 1. Whereas a decimal sequence runs 0 1 2 3 4 . . ., a binary sequence would run 0 1 10 11 100 . . .. Binary notation is used to represent numerals, letters, symbols, and other data. The binary system is suited to computers because its two values can be transmitted via an electric current as pulses that are weak or strong, on or off, and can be recorded on a magnetic storage medium as unmagnetized or magnetized.

bit: A contraction of *binary digit*, a bit is the smallest piece of data a computer can recognize. A bit is written as either 0 or 1 and represents either the on or off variation of voltage. Data bits are used in combination to form characters; framing bits are used for parity and transmission synchronization in telecommunications and CD ROM.

bit error rate: See *BER*.

bit map: A screen display in which each pixel location corresponds to a unique main memory location accessible by the central processing unit. Also can refer to images intended for display on this type of display system. See also *pixel*.

bit stream: 1. A steady binary signal that contains no start or stop element. 2. A method of transmitting a continuous character stream.

bits per second: A measure of information systems' speed of transmission, usually expressed as baud rate (usually about one bit per second).

blank padding: Blank characters immediately preceding the terminating linefeed character in data records. Records that contain only a linefeed character represent blank lines and should have no blank padding.

block: An amount of data that is moved or addressed as a single unit. In CD ROM, a block can be 512 B, 1 KB, or 2 KB.

block error correction: During CD ROM premastering, a process in which an error correction code (ECC) consisting of a string of bits is appended to each block of data (2048 bytes) to ensure that all erroneous user data will be recovered.

board: Synonymous with *circuit board* or *card*. The circuit card that holds the chips and wiring that control either some essential function of the computer's central processor or a peripheral such as a CD ROM drive. See also *interface*.

Boolean search: A search strategy using AND, OR, and AND NOT functions to combine search terms for selecting information.

bpi (bits per inch): A measure used to express a recording medium's information density.

branch: For certain computer programs, the action of jumping from one sequence to another. At a branch point, the computer selects one of two or more sequences to be played or processed next, based on data input.

browser: An application program that lets the user meander through areas of information on a CD ROM, viewing the contents.

buffer: A small part of a computer's memory that temporarily stores data. Buffers can compensate for a difference in data flow rates when transmitting data from one device to another or can hold data likely to be used in the near future.

burst error: Errors detected in consecutive data bits on CD ROMs, often caused by scratches, fingerprints, or other physical irritants to the disc. Burst errors cause most data loss in optical memory. Error correction codes are designed based on the anticipated frequency and duration of burst errors.

bus: 1. A circuit through which data or power is transmitted. 2. In a computer, a circuit board that transmits coded data in either parallel or serial mode between processors or other hardware components in a computer system.

byte: An 8-bit unit of digital data. In data processing, a byte often describes one position or one character, because most computer systems use a full byte to store an ASCII character. A byte can have 256 (or 2^8) possible combinations of 8 binary digits.

C language: A compact, high-level programming language that is easily moved from one computer to another.

cache: Generally, temporary storage for data requiring very quick access. See also *buffer.*

card: Computing term synonymous with *circuit board* (see *board*). See also *interface.*

cathode ray tube: See *CRT.*

CAV (constant angular velocity): A disk drive mechanism that spins a disk at a constant speed, resulting in the inner disk tracks' passing the reading mechanism more slowly than do the outer tracks. Sectors on a CAV disk radiate in uniform patterns from the disk's center, so they are smaller at the inner areas, with higher storage density. A floppy disk is a CAV disk. See also *CLV.*

CCD (charge-coupled device): A semiconductor device capable of both photodetection and memory, which converts light to electronic impulses. Scanners use one- and two-dimensional CCD arrays to perform the first stage in converting images into digital data.

CCITT: Acronym for the French name of the International Telegraph and Telephone Consultative Committee. Among other things, the CCITT issues the standards for facsimile, an image-transmission method. See also *facsimile.*

CD-Digital Audio: Synonymous with *Compact Disc Digital Audio* (see entry).

CD-I (Compact Disc Interactive): A technical specification for a self-contained multimedia system that allows simultaneous, interactive presentation of video, audio, text, and data. The standard, also known as the *Green Book standard,* envisions dedicated players and discs delivering pictures, sound, and text via domestic TV and audio equipment, as well as computer monitors. Proposed jointly by Philips and Sony, CD-I is expected to appear commercially in 1988.

CD-PROM (Compact Disc Programmable Read-Only Memory): A write-once CD ROM disc. Not yet available commercially.

CD ROM (Compact Disc Read-Only Memory): A version of the Compact Disc standard intended to store general-purpose digital data for personal computers. Provides 556 MB user capacity at 10^{-13} corrected BER, compared with 635 MB at 10^{-9} for the CD standard. Also known as the *Yellow Book standard.*

cell animation: A moving picture produced by displaying a series of complete screen images in rapid succession.

central processor: The "brain" of the computer, to which all of its parts are linked and where all information processing—instructions, calculations, data manipulation—occurs. Also called the CPU (central processing unit).

CGM (Computer Graphics Metafile): An ANSI standard (ANSI X3.122-1986) developed to organize the content of structured graphics metafiles. It is too early to predict whether the standard, adopted only recently, will be successful.

channel: 1. A path or circuit along which information flows. A channel for digital data carries an analog signal since digital data is encoded into voltage changes, which are analog signals. The size, or *bandwidth,* of the channel determines how much information can flow through it. A CD ROM drive has a channel bandwidth of 150 KB per second. 2. Parallel data streams stored on CD-I, especially those the user can select.

channel separation: An audio player's ability to distinguish between two high-fidelity stereo signals.

character string: Any group of characters that a computer system treats as a single unit.

check sum: A method for detecting errors that occur while transmitting data. All of the data bytes in a buffer are added together, and the resulting sum (the *check sum*) is transmitted with the buffer. When the data is received, the data bytes again are summed, and the result is compared with the check sum. If the two sums differ, then an error has occurred in the transmission.

chip: A device in which microscopic electronic circuitry (such as that forming a transistor or integrated circuit) is printed photographically on the surface of a tiny piece of semiconductor material (usually crystalline silicon).

chrominance: The color information in a full color electronic image. Requires *luminance*, or light intensity, to make it visible. Compare with *luminance*.

CIM (Computer-Input Microfilm): The process of reading microfilm data via a scanning device and then transforming it into a form a computer can use. Compare with *COM (Computer-Output Microfilm)*.

CIRC: See *Cross-Interleaved Reed-Solomon Code*.

circuit: A means of two-way communication between two points.

clock: In computers, a device that marks time and generates a periodic signal, which controls the timing of all computer processing operations in a synchronous computer.

clock pulses: Electronic pulses emitted periodically to synchronize the operation of computer circuits. Also called *clock signals*. See also *hertz*.

clock rate: The rate at which clock pulses are emitted.

C.L.U.T. (Color Look-Up Table): A selection of colors assigned a digital value and held in a table. The program decodes a color picture for display by matching the code stored for each pixel with the associated color value in the look-up table.

CLV (constant linear velocity): A disc drive (such as a CD ROM drive) that rotates the disc at varying speeds, moving data past the optical head at a constant speed. The drive must rotate the disc more slowly as the head moves from the inner tracks toward the outer perimeter. This design allows data to be stored on the disc at a constant linear density, but requires special tracking and sensing devices to slow down the disc as the head rotates. A CD ROM drive's rotational rate ranges from 500 to 200 rpm.

color coding: Representation of colors in codes a computer can understand. Common color coding methods include RGB (Red-Green-Blue), HSV, and YUV. Different color-coding schemes are used to compress images, to aid in manipulating information, or to accommodate the output devices' physical characteristics.

color standard: The way in which a color video picture is composed and transmitted. Three distinct, incompatible color standards—*PAL, NTSC,* and *SECAM* (see entries)—and some minor variations within the PAL and SECAM systems, are in use. (For monochrome, six standards exist.)

COM (Computer-Output Microfilm): A system for converting digital data into images on dry, processed microfilm.

Compact Disc: The trademark name for an injection-molded aluminized disc, 12 cm in diameter, which stores high-density digital data in microscopic pits that a laser beam can read. Conceived by Philips and Sony, it was originally designed to store high-fidelity music for which Compact Disc Digital Audio now is a standard format accepted worldwide. Because of its very large data storage capacity, the Compact Disc now is used as a text/data medium in electronic publishing (CD ROM).

Compact Disc Digital Audio: The industrywide audio standard to which all digital audio Compact Discs and all digital audio Compact Disc players conform. Sometimes called the *Red Book standard.*

Compact Disc drive: A device designed to read both digital data and Compact Discs (CD ROM or CD-I). CD-I drives will be designed to play CD-Digital Audio discs as well.

Compact Disc Interactive: See *CD-I.*

compatibility: The extent to which different types of discs can be interpreted by various players or drives. For example, all CD-Digital Audio discs are fully compatible with all CD-Digital Audio players, so any player can read and reproduce music from any disc, regardless of its manufacturer.

composite monitor: A CRT monitor that accepts composite video input. In composite video, the luminance (brightness), chrominance (color), and synchronization information are combined into a single signal. Broadcast television uses a composite video signal.

compression: 1. In the context of digital images, the process of compacting data based on the presence of large white or black areas in printed pages, engineering drawings, or other images. The CCITT digital facsimile standards contain one- and two-dimensional compression/decompression algorithms. 2. Text compression refers to any technique that saves storage space by eliminating gaps, empty fields, redundancy, or unnecessary data. All compressed data must be expanded by a reverse operation called decompression.

compression, nonrecoverable: Schemes that make data more compact by removing some information, resulting in a reconstructed image not identical to the original. With a well-designed scheme, this information loss is largely unnoticed.

compression, recoverable: Schemes for condensing data so that it can be totally reconstituted in its original form.

compression algorithms: Formulas for condensing data to save storage space. The CCITT Group III and IV standards for digital facsimile contain some of the most successful of these.

computer graphics: Line drawings, pictures, charts, and graphs created using a computer.

computer-generated information: Information a computer produces based on programmed instructions.

configuration: An electronic system's composition, particularly its physical components.

constant angular velocity: See *CAV.*

constant linear velocity: See *CLV.*

contiguous file: A file whose sectors are stored as one continuous and connected unit on a disc.

contouring: A visual effect that occurs in images digitized with insufficient *pixel depth* (see entry). Gives the image a blotchy, flat appearance.

contrast enhancement: An image-processing technique that increases the range of brightness levels in an image. Increasing contrast can, for example, enhance detail or can help correct for improper exposure in photographs.

controller: A computer or circuit board that controls the flow of data between a computer and one or more memory devices, usually tape or disk drives. Controllers sometimes also perform channel and error correction coding and decoding.

conversion: The transforming of a program recorded in one format into another format (for example, paper to microform, microform to electronic information).

CPU (central processing unit): See *central processor.*

CRC (cyclic redundancy code): A simple form of algebraic error correction code.

Cross-Interleaved Reed-Solomon Code (CIRC): The first level of error correction used in CD ROM and the only error correction needed for CD Digital Audio. Use of CIRC yields an error rate of one uncorrectable error per 10^{-9} bytes. Further error detection and correction in CD ROM systems improve this to one error per 10^{-13} bytes.

CRT (cathode ray tube): Display mechanism in a television set. The sealed glass tube is filled with low-pressure gas. An electron gun (or guns, in the case of color monitors) in its neck focuses a narrow beam of electrons that scans the screen, causing its phosphor coating to glow where hit, thus creating an image.

cursor: The pattern on the computer screen that indicates where you can enter information. Cursors of graphics displays typically are in the shape of an arrow or pointing hand; on a text display, the cursor often is an underline or highlighted character.

cyclic redundancy code: See *CRC.*

DAC: See *Digital-to-Analog converter.*

DAD (Digital Audio Disc): Usually refers to a *Compact Disc* (see entry). See also *Compact Disc Digital Audio.*

data preparation: The process of converting data on media other than CD ROM into a form suitable for delivery on CD ROM. Involves several steps, including initial conversion of data into machine-readable form, indexing, and building the files and file directories.

database: 1. A collection of digitally stored information. 2. A collection of data elements within records within files that sometimes relate to other records within other files.

database management system (DBMS): A set of programs that organize, store, and retrieve machine-readable information from a computer-maintained database.

decibel (dB): A logarithmic measure of the ratio between two powers, voltages, currents, sound intensities, and so forth. Signal-to-noise ratios are expressed in decibels.

decode: The process of transforming data into its original electronic state. Data usually is encoded to reduce storage requirements, and it must be decoded to be displayed, searched, or played.

decoding, onetime: An image-decompression technique in which an image is decompressed, or expanded, as it is transferred from the storage device and then is loaded into the image frame buffer in expanded form.

decoding, repetitive: An image-decompression technique in which an image is transferred in compressed form to the image frame buffer and is expanded during each screen refresh.

decoding hardware: In Compact Disc, the equipment required to interpret the encoded data recorded on the disc.

dedicated: In computing, a system that performs one particular job and cannot be used for any other.

delivery system: In CD ROM, the set of CD ROM and computer equipment used to deliver the information. A delivery system can involve a CD ROM drive only, a computer, or a monitor and keypad, or it can include several memory devices, a printer, and a variety of peripherals.

delta encoding/decoding: A means of reducing a signal's bandwidth by storing or transmitting only the differences between consecutive values rather than the values themselves.

designated transfer rate (DTR): The data-transmission rate a particular device-application combination requires to accurately play or present data.

device driver: Software that tells the computer how to talk to a peripheral device such as a printer or a CD ROM drive.

DGIS (Direct Graphics Interface Specification): A graphics device driver specification that Graphical Software Systems, Inc., developed for use primarily in graphics processor chips. It provides a standardized interface for application programs to use in accessing graphics functions on these chips. DGIS supports structured and bit-mapped graphics.

Differential PCM (DPCM): A data-compression technique for quantizing sound digitally in which the differences between each sample value and the next are recorded rather than the values themselves. Compare with *ADPCM (Adaptive Differential PCM)*.

digital: In computing terms, data that is generated as or translated into a series of discrete, fixed values such as digits or other characters. The opposite of digital is *analog*. Digital information is recorded in binary notation.

digital (sound) recording: 1. The recording of sound in a pattern of discrete values. In digital recording, the sound level is sampled at a frequency at least double the highest frequency to be reproduced. 2. A recording in which a numeric or digital value represents each sampled sound level.

digital tape: Tape manufactured specifically for digital recording.

digital technology: Technology based on the processing of numeric (usually binary) values. Digital technology's flexibility and consistency are greater than those of analog technology, which is based on variations of physical parameters. Digital technology also is potentially faster and more accurate.

digital videodisc: A videodisc on which digital data has been encoded in the FM format normally used to record the video signal on a videodisc.

Digital-to-Analog converter (DAC): A mechanical or electronic device that converts discrete digital numbers to continuous analog signals. See also *Analog-to-Digital converter*.

digitize: To convert analog information into digital data that a computer system can process.

Direct Read After Write: See *DRAW*.

directory: A structure specifying the exact locations, or *addresses*, of files on an electronic storage medium (such as a floppy disk or CD ROM disc).

disc geography: The layout of data on a disc. Disc geography refers to, among other things, the starting and stopping points of data segments, the interleaving factor of interleaved files, and the distribution of data that must be placed in close proximity for seamless branching and playback.

disc origination: The process of formatting the files on the disc and creating the exact disc image to be mastered for a CD ROM. Occurs at the end of the data-preparation process.

disk operating system (DOS): A microcomputer software program that controls the flow of data between the system's internal memory and external disks. VMS, MS-DOS, CP/M, and UNIX are widely used operating systems. CD ROM operating systems include Reference Technology's STA/File, TMS's LaserDOS, Digital Equipment Corp.'s Uni-File, and MS-DOS with CD ROM extensions. Most CD ROM operating systems work with the proposed High Sierra Format.

display adapter: The display system component that processes the computer data into a video signal the system's display monitor can interpret. This circuitry may be built into the computer or may be supplied via a separate card.

display buffer: Synonymous with *frame buffer.* See *buffer.*

display list: A set of structured graphics commands that the presentation device executes to draw an image on the screen. You can animate a display by having the presentation device read only changes to the list.

dissolve: A video effect in which images from two different motion sequences blend gradually to produce a gentle transition from one scene to the next.

dithering: 1. A bit-mapped graphics technique that expands the number of gray levels or colors on a display at the expense of spatial resolution. Groups of pixels are treated as a composite pixel, the brightness of which is varied by altering the number of component pixels that are illuminated. 2. A technique used to prevent contouring in digital images with limited gray scales. Analogous to creating halftones in printing, in dithering small regions of pixels are treated as a single larger pixel; the larger pixel's gray scale is altered by turning on different numbers of pixels in the cell.

document: The basic unit of retrievable data within a database. Document size varies; generally, documents should be as small as needed to efficiently index a database.

dots per inch: see *dpi.*

double-buffering: A method for temporarily storing data in two small areas of a computer's memory; one buffer is filled while the other is emptied. This technique helps maintain a steady flow of data to the display system and is especially useful in animation or other data-intensive applications.

download: The process of loading program data from some storage medium into the computer.

dpi (dots per inch): A measure of resolution—that is, the number of pixels per inch on a CRT display or scanning device.

DRAW (Direct Read After Write): Describes a recording machine that reads continuously while writing to verify the quality of the written data. This allows error-free recording in a single pass, because whenever a written sector of data contains errors it is immediately rewritten.

drive: A machine for reading from and, when possible, writing to an electronic data-storage medium (such as disk, tape, or card). The medium can be optical, magnetic, and so forth.

dropout (or drop out): A momentary loss of signal on a recorded medium. Dropouts usually are caused by defects or by dirt or other contamination of the medium.

DYUV, delta-YUV: A highly efficient color-encoding scheme for natural pictures. The human eye is less sensitive to color variations than to intensity variations, so DYUV encodes luminance (Y) information at full bandwidth and chrominance (UV) information at half bandwidth or less, storing only the differences, or *deltas,* between each value and the one following it.

EBCDIC (Extended Binary Coded Decimal Interchange Code): An 8-bit code used to represent 256 numbers, letters, and characters in a computer system. Developed by IBM and used primarily with IBM equipment. Compare with *ASCII.*

ECC: See *error correction code.*

ECC layers: Several error correction schemes can be used in combination on a disc. After a data record is encoded using one scheme, you can then re-encode it using a second scheme, improving the bit-to-error ratio. Each ECC scheme is considered a different *layer,* with each residing on top of the previous one.

EDC: See *error detection code.*

edge enhancement: An image-processing technique for sharpening the edges of objects in an image, removing blur, or bringing out obscured detail.

EFM: See *eight-to-fourteen modulation.*

eight-to-fourteen modulation (EFM): A process during CD ROM disc mastering in which each "word" of 8 data bits is turned into 14 channel bits for storage on disc. The opposite process occurs when data is read from a CD ROM disc. See also *subcodes.*

emulation: Imitation of a computing function by a system not originally designed to perform that function.

encode: To convert information to machine-readable format from an analog format or from another machine-readable format, storing it as a binary number, or code, in computer memory or on disc. Encoding often refers to transforming a bit stream into a more compact representation to conserve storage space. Encoded data must be converted to be displayed, searched, or played (in the case of audio).

encryption: Encoding computer data so that reading it requires special hardware or software.

error correction: A technique that identifies and corrects errors that occur during the recording or transfer of information. Used extensively in computer storage media such as Compact Discs.

error correction code (ECC): A method of data recovery that can fully correct the 2048-byte user data block of a CD ROM.

error detection code (EDC): Used in conjunction with ECC, EDC detects errors.

error rate: The ratio comparing the amount of erroneously transmitted information with the total amount sent.

error recovery: The process of correcting erroneous data or otherwise minimizing the damage errors cause. This may consist of correcting the errors using an ECC code, masking them by interpolation or some other means of partial reconstruction, or aborting the current operation. To implement any error recovery scheme, the error first must be detected.

ESDI: A device interface standard proposed by Maxtor (of San Jose, CA) that enables a computer to communicate and exchange data with a mass storage device, such as a small Winchester drive. The ESDI was developed to exceed the limitations of the ST506 interface, and achieve data rates above 10 MB/sec. See also *IPI* and *SCSI*.

executable (object) code: A set of instructions, or a computer program, normally written in machine language for a specific computer or microprocessor, that can be executed, or run, directly rather than via a compiler or interpreter routine.

expansion slots: Space in a main computer or other device into which circuit boards can be plugged to add functions to the basic equipment.

facsimile (fax):   1. The process by which document images are scanned, transmitted electronically, and reproduced either locally or remotely. 2. The document this process produces.

fax: Abbreviation for *facsimile* (see entry).

field: 1. In data structures, the smallest unit stored in a database. For example, in a mailing list, each record would contain one name, street address, city, state, and ZIP code; each of these items is a field. 2. In video, a scan of one-half the lines that comprise a single, complete frame on the video screen. Two interlaced fields make up one *frame*. NTSC systems use a 525-line frame, so each field contains 262.5 lines. In noninterlaced systems, the field and frame are the same.

FIFO (First In First Out) buffer: A memory buffer in which the first data to arrive is the first sent out. FIFO buffers are used when a data source provides data at a different rate than that which the data destination requires.

file: In computing, a set of related information structured in a similar manner accessed under a single name.

file format: Synonymous with *logical format* (see entry).

file inversion: An indexing method that usually indexes every meaningful word within a database.

file manager: A small computer program to handle the filing function involved in transferring certain information from the machine memory to an external storage medium (such as a disc).

file system: A method of organizing data on a disc such that an application program need not be concerned with the physical location or structure of the data.

fixed-length records: A way of organizing a database such that the data is stored in records that are all the same length.

flag: In data preparation, a sequence of characters inserted in the text to convey information about a document's structure and display. The representation of these characters in the actual database is compressed.

flicker: Usually an unwanted interruption or motion jitter in a moving screen image caused by the transition between two frames that contain abrupt changes in gray levels or colors.

focus servo: The mechanism in an optical drive that keeps the reading and/or writing light spot focused on the disc surface. The mechanism can adjust to avert the effects of surface imperfections and the jarring of the drive mechanism caused by external shocks or vibrations.

font: In printing and computerized character generators, the set of characters and special symbols available in one style and size of type.

formatting: The process of blocking user data and adding information identifying each block. The formatting information includes the data address and synchronization information, and may include error correction check sums and data, as well as a data type specification. The formatting process also creates the directory for all files on the disc.

fragment: A part of a data file.

frame: 1. In Compact Disc technology, synonymous with *sector.* 2. In image technology, refers to one screen image in a timed sequence of images.

frame buffer: Synonymous with *display buffer.* A block of memory, generally part of a display adapter, that holds an image that the rest of the display adapter circuitry will use to create a video signal. Some image-processing systems have many frame buffers that hold intermediate images at various stages of processing. See also *buffer.*

frame delta: An image storage technique that stores only information that varies from one image to the next. The technique is used to minimize the space required to store and display animated or video images.

frame grabber: Synonymous with *video digitizer.* A device that digitizes a video signal and then places the digitized signal in a *frame buffer* (see entry) to be stored or processed.

frame packet: Image data used during one frame interval.

frame rate: The rate at which images in a motion image sequence are displayed on a screen. Broadcast video is displayed at 30 frames per sec, film at 24 frames per sec.

frame rate synchronization: A technique for synchronizing the refresh rate of the display monitor with the display rate of moving images to prevent object breakup.

frequency: The number of times a signal vibrates within a given period; usually measured in hertz (Hz), or cycles per second.

Gb: gigabit.

GB: gigabyte.

GCR (group code recording): Group code is a block-oriented algebraic error correction code that enables recovery from burst errors. Used, for example, in the 6250 bpi half-inch 9-track magnetic tape on which computer data commonly is premastered for CD ROM.

giga- (G-): Prefix meaning 1 billion (10^9). The initial g is hard, as in *golf.*

GKS (Graphical Kernel System): An ANSI standard that specifies a complete computer graphics generation and storage system. Oriented toward structured graphics, it provides some support for bit maps as well. The specification (ANSI X3.124-1985) works on the program interface level rather than on an application or user level.

Green Book: Another name for the CD-I standard. See *CD-I.*

Group IV Fax encoding: A standard for image compression on facsimile machines. Group IV standard uses a two-dimensional encoding scheme related to *run-length encoding* (see entry).

hard disk: An inflexible magnetic disk with greater storage capacity than a floppy disk. A hard disk is sometimes sealed within a computer to provide a large (often temporary) memory for looking up data from several smaller, handier floppy disks before running a long or complex program. The Winchester disk is one such hard disk.

hardware: Electrical or mechanical equipment involved in producing, storing, distributing, or receiving electronic signals.

hardware compatibility: The ability of two differing pieces of equipment to perform with the same software. For example, computers of two manufacturers both might use the same plug-in module, or peripheral device.

hashing: An indexing method in which the value being searched for is used to compute the location where the data is stored. An index created in this way is called a *hash table.*

HDTV: See *high-definition television.*

header field: In CD ROM, a 4-byte area of a data sector that contains the absolute sector address (3 bytes) and the mode byte.

hertz: The standard measure of frequency or bandwidth; 1 hertz is equal to one cycle per second. One kilohertz (kHz) is 103 cycles per second. One megahertz (MHz) is 106 cycles per second. Electronic data-processing equipment operates in time to a clock, performing one act for each cycle of the clock. The faster the clock runs (expressed in hertz), the faster the equipment operates.

Hi-Fi music: The second audio level (below CD Audio) specified in Compact Disc Interactive (CD-I) standard. With a frequency range of 17 kHz, its quality is equivalent to that of an LP album. A disc can hold 288 minutes of mono or 144 minutes of stereo Hi-Fi music.

high-definition television (HDTV): Any of a variety of video formats offering higher resolution than the current NTSC, PAL, and SECAM broadcast standards. Current formats generally range in resolution from 655 to 2125 scan lines, with an aspect ratio of 5:3 and bandwidth of 30 to 50 MHz. Digital HDTV has a bandwidth of 300 MHz and its quality has been compared with that of 35mm film.

high resolution: The degree of resolution (see entry) necessary for a monitor to display clearly readable 80-column text. Computers for professional use normally employ high-resolution monitors, as will the new generation of enhanced TVs due on the market in the late 1980s.

High Sierra Group: An ad hoc standards group set up to establish nominal data format and compatibility for CD ROM. The group, including representatives from the hardware, software, and publishing industries, is named after the Lake Tahoe hotel where it first met in the summer of 1985. See also *High Sierra Group (HSG) Proposal.*

High Sierra Group (HSG) Proposal: The informal name for the first draft of a standard format for placing files and directories on CD ROM discs proposed by an ad hoc committee of computer vendors, software developers, and CD ROM system integrators. Work on the proposal began in 1985 at the High Sierra Hotel at Lake Tahoe (hence its title). Standards committees are formally reviewing the proposal as this book goes to press. Until an official standard emerges, such firms as Microware (software developers for CD-I), Microsoft, Reference Technology, and TMS are using this "common format."

horizontal delta encoding: A data-compression method that stores the changes in value of a digital signal sampled along a horizontal plane.

horizontal retrace period: Time during which a TV screen's horizontal line scan returns from the end of one line to the beginning of the next.

Huffman encoding: A data-compression scheme that uses variable-length codes, choosing the shortest codes for the most frequent values. It is used for one-dimensional data compression in the CCITT Group III digital facsimile standard.

Hz: See *hertz.*

IGES (Initial Graphics Exchange Specification): This is an ANSI standard (ANSI Y14.26M-1981) that specifies an interchange format for transferring structured graphics drawings between different systems. It is designed to allow the communication of CAD databases between incompatible systems.

indexing: The process of building data structures for an electronic database that contain the location of each word or other data item. Indexes permit the computer to rapidly locate data without searching through the full body of data. A data item is searchable only if it is indexed.

in-house: Produced entirely within a company or organization, using its resources, facilities, and expertise.

injection molding: Manufacturing process used in making CD ROMs in which molten plastic is squirted into a mold.

integrated product: In computers, a system that incorporates more than one computing function. For example, a computer with a built-in disc drive, display, and printer.

intelligent player: A Compact Disc player with extra computing facilities built in (such as a CD-I player), enabling the player and the user to interact.

interactive media: Information storage devices on which information is stored in such a way that, by means of an application program, the user participates in its delivery. The medium also may store the application program. The opposite of interactive is *linear*.

interchangeability: The ability to exchange components of a computer system for different manufacturers' models and still get performance within the system specification. All compact cassettes and cassette recorders are interchangeable, as are Compact Discs and Compact Disc players.

interface: 1. A link between two systems (such as a microcomputer and CD ROM). Generally, an interface links two components or functions that normally would not interact. Both software and hardware can have interfaces. 2. In microcomputers, interface usually describes the circuit board that attaches a particular peripheral device to another microcomputer. See also *controller*.

interlace: A technique for doubling a television image's vertical resolution by broadcasting it in two sets of alternating raster lines. The U.S. standard (NTSC) television signal, 262.5 horizontal lines 60 times/sec, is insufficient to produce a clear picture. In interlace, even-numbered lines are drawn in one pass, and odd-numbered lines are drawn in a second, so that two consecutive fields draw a single image with a vertical resolution of 525 lines/sec. The eye averages similar values in television's natural images, so the image appears clear.

interleaving: The process of breaking up and reordering blocks of data on a disc. Interleaving is employed either to slow down the data transfer rate or to allow seamless, or uninterrupted, branching from one file to another. Some applications do this by alternating data blocks from several files.

I/O (Input/Output): 1. An acronym used to signify the transfer of data between computer storage and peripheral devices. 2. The equipment or processes that transmit data into or out of a computer's central processing unit (CPU).

IPI (intelligent peripheral interface): An interface standard that enables communication between a CPU and a peripheral storage device. The IPI interface handles data rates up to 10 MB/sec and is gaining support among several large companies, including IBM. See also *ESDI, SASI,* and *SCSI.*

ISO: International Standards Organization.

jaggies: See *aliasing.*

joystick: A remote-control device for a computer that looks a lot like the gearstick of a car, often used in video and arcade games and used in some interactive video applications.

jukebox: A disc player that can hold and access several discs.

K (K Byte, KB): Abbreviation for kilobyte, which is 2^{10}, or 1024, bytes. A computer's size often is expressed according to the number of kilobytes of memory it offers, and the number is usually rounded off to the nearest 1000 bytes.

keyboard control logic: The logic circuitry built into a keyboard to interpret keystrokes and convert them to the electronic signals that control the computer connected to it.

keypad: A remote-control device such as a TV's that contains a set of keys dedicated to specific functions and, usually, a set of numeric keys.

keywords: In databases, specific values stored in fields, which are indexed and can be retrieved individually. A person's last name, stored in a Name field, is an example of a keyword.

kilobits (Kb): One thousand bits.

LAN (local area network): A network of connected electronic devices within a small area such as an office or a building.

land: The reflective area between two adjacent nonreflective pits on a CD ROM disc. In CD ROM coding, a binary one represents the transition from pit to land and from land to pit, and two or more zeros represent the distances between transitions.

laser (Light Amplification by Stimulated Emission of Radar): A device that transmits an extremely narrow and coherent beam (separate waves in phase with one another rather than jumbled, as in normal light) of electromagnetic energy in the visible light spectrum.

LaserVision: Synonymous with *videodisc* (see entry).

latency: Delay in accessing CD ROM data as the disc rotates to the desired rotational speed. Average latency for a disc drive is usually one-half the rotational period.

light pen: A remote-control device that lets the user write or draw on the screen of a cathode ray tube with a photoelectric "pen." Light pens can be used to "read" the screen surface, to input information or to modify recorded data, and to interact with a teaching or training program.

logical format: Synonymous with *file format*. Specifies the organization and locations of data files on a CD ROM, defining such things as a file's size, the directory structure for all files on the disc, and the numbers of discs in the application. The *High Sierra Group (HSG) Proposal* (see entry) is an attempt by industry leaders to standardize the logical format of CD ROMs, which have been left to the discretion of operating system developers.

luminance: The intensity, or brightness component, of an electronic image. By itself, luminance creates an image in gray, black, and white. It can be combined with *chrominance* (see entry) to create a color image.

machine code: The binary code (the pattern of zeros and ones) instruction set that is the computer's native language. High-level languages such as BASIC or C are ultimately converted into machine code within the computer. Machine code operates faster, using less memory, than high-level languages, and so is extensively used in real-time applications such as games.

magnetic media: Magnetically sensitive devices for storing and distributing information. Hard disks, floppy disks, compact cassettes, and video cassettes are examples.

magnetic tape: A recording medium consisting of a thin tape coated with a fine magnetic material. Data is recorded in the form of changing magnetic levels on the tape coating.

main channel: On a Compact Disc, the section of the data stream carrying user information, as opposed to the control, display, or other information that the subcode channels carry (see also *subcodes*).

mainframe: A large, expensive, powerful computer intended for centralized application.

master: An original recording in its final format and intended for mass replication.

media: Plural of *medium* (see entry). Media often is misused as though it were singular.

medium: In computing, a substance or object on which information is stored; usually refers either to the sensitive coating on a writable device or to the device itself (that is, the disk, tape, card, and so forth).

mega- (M-): Prefix meaning 1 million (for instance, MB means megabyte).

memory: Synonymous with *storage capacity* (see entry). Any electronic repository for data. The term often is used to describe main or internal memory, in which case it must be distinguished from backup memory. See also *Random-Access Memory* and *Read-Only Memory*.

memory control logic: Logic circuitry to control information's movement to, from, or within a computer's memory.

menu: In an interactive system, a list of options displayed for the user to select from.

menu-driven: Controlled by means of menus.

metafile: See *structured graphics metafile*.

microprocessor: 1. An integral piece of hardware, a microchip, which performs the logic functions of a digital computer. 2. A piece of hardware that houses the computing parts of a computer on one circuit board or in one set of integrated circuits. The microprocessor does not contain ports for peripheral devices or memory.

mode 1 and mode 2: These terms, when referring to the Compact Disc specifications, relate to the two main block or frame formats in which data is stored on the disc. Mode 1 provides for a level of error detection and correction beyond the Cross-Interleaved Reed-Solomon Code

(CIRC), which the CD Digital Audio standard uses. Mode 2 makes each block's total data area available for user data. The CD-I standard also employs the mode 2 format.

modem (from MOdulate/DEModulate): A device for converting information for the computer into signals that ordinary telephone lines can transmit.

modulation: A process whereby information is converted to some code and the code is made part of a transmitted signal. The opposite process is *demodulation.*

monitor: 1. In video, an electronic device similar to a television that receives and displays a nonbroadcast video signal sent across wires within a closed circuit (from, say, a videotape or disc player), but that cannot intercept a broadcast signal. 2. In computing, another name for the computer screen.

mouse: A remote-control device, rather like a toy mouse on wheels, that can be guided by hand around a smooth surface to direct a cursor on the computer screen.

NAPLPS (North American Presentation Level Protocol Syntax): Pronounced *nap-lips.* An ANSI standard for graphical communication protocol that provides a method for creating pictures and compressing them into relatively short blocks of digital data for storage or for transmission over low-bandwidth channels (such as telephone lines or blanking intervals in TV signals). NAPLPS is one of the standard protocols for videotex. The specification is found in ANSI document ANSI X3.110-1983.

National Television Standards Committee: See *NTSC.*

natural images: In video, pictures displayed on the screen with sufficient resolution and color definition to give an impression of realism, as in broadcast TV. Systems limited to animation, cartoons, graphics, or text can't display natural pictures.

NISO (National Information Standards Organization): Establishes standards for libraries, information sciences, and publishing.

noise: Interference a signal picks up every time it passes through electronic circuitry. If noise is too intense, it affects the information quality. "Static" on telephone lines or "snow" on a TV screen is an example of noise. See also *signal-to-noise ratio.*

NTSC (National Television Standards Committee): The U.S. color video standard established by the committee of the same name. NTSC is used generally to describe video systems that employ the American broadcast standard: a 525-line screen running at a rate of 60 fields/30 frames per second, and a broadcast bandwidth of 4 MHz.

OCR (optical character recognition): A method for converting printed characters to machine-readable character codes through an optical sensing device and pattern-recognition software.

OEM (Original Equipment Manufacturer): Usually refers *not* to the manufacturer of a device, but to the system integrator that resells the device as part of a system. Sometimes used as a verb, as in "Company B is going to OEM company A's drive." In this case, company A will manufacture the drive and company B will integrate it into a system.

OMDR (optical memory disc recorder): A DRAW device used to write analog or digital information to an optical disc.

online processing: A data-processing method that enables a user to enter data, then have it processed and output on request. Compare with *batch processing.*

operating system: The set of programs that control a computer and its peripherals, dictating which software can be used. The predominant microcomputer operating system is MS-DOS, while larger minicomputers may use UNIX or VMS.

optical disc: A disc read and/or written by light, generally a laser. Such a disc may store video, audio, or digital data.

optical head: The assembly in a CD ROM drive containing the components that bounce laser light off the data surface of a CD ROM disc and convert the resulting reflections into electrical signals that can be interpreted as data. The head includes a laser, lenses, prisms, a focusing mechanism, and a photodetector.

optical media: Optically sensitive devices used to store and distribute information (for example, the Compact Disc or the LaserVision disc).

optical storage: Storage of information on optically sensitive materials. These optical media (such as the Compact Disc or the LaserVision disc) have very high storage density.

OS-9: The real-time operating system on which the CD-I operating system is based.

overhead: In computer jargon, the amount of storage or other resources required to accomplish some task. For example, an index to a full-text database might increase total storage requirements by 40 percent, which would be referred to as the index's overhead.

overlay: In video, a layer of visual or textual information superimposed over the main or basic image. Overlays can simply add supplementary or complementary information or they can be used to build up visual effects.

packet: Any data that has been divided into blocks of a specified size and identified with address and use information.

PAL (Phase Alternating Line): The most widely applied of the three color standards for video. PAL was developed in West Germany and is employed in the United Kingdom and across most of Europe, Africa, Australia, and South America.

palette: In digital video, the total number of colors available for pictorial presentations.

parallel: In computing, a data communications approach that sends all the bits in a byte at one time—"abreast," as it were—between the central processor and the computer's peripherals.

parity: A method of error detection that uses a percentage of redundant data to verify the user's data.

parity bit: The final bit added to a series of bits and assigned the value required to make the sum of all bits in the sector odd or even. Often added to data to provide a very simple form of error detection and, sometimes, error correction.

parity check: A test to help determine data's validity. Specifically, this test determines whether the number of zeros and ones that the binary digits of a byte of data represent is odd or even.

partial update: In information presentation, the modification of part of the text or graphics stored in a file.

PCM (Pulse Code Modulation): The representation of continuous signals using discrete pulses (for instance, the digital representation of an analog waveform). The signal on Digital Audio discs is encoded in PCM.

peripheral: Equipment, such as disk drives and printers, that is controlled by a computer but is physically independent of it.

photocomposition tapes: Magnetic tapes produced by a special word-processing program that prepares them for computerized typesetting.

photodetector: The electronic component in the optical head of a CD ROM drive that detects the light reflected back from the disc and converts the reflections into electric signals.

327

photodiode: A device used in an optical disc player to translate variations in the light reflected off the pitted surface of the disc into the electronic signals that comprise the audiovisual and data components of the disc.

photoresist: A substance, usually a polymer, that becomes insoluble (negative-working) or soluble (positive-working) when exposed to light.

physical format: Elements of the physical structure of an optical information medium, such as its size and the arrangement of the data on it.

picture element: See *pixel*.

pit: 1. A microscopic depression in the reflective surface of a CD ROM disc. The pattern of pits on the disc represents the data that is stored. The unpitted area between pits is called a *land*. The tiny laser beam used to read back the data is reflected from the lands, but scattered by the pits. A typical pit is about the size of a bacterium—0.5 by 2.0 microns (millionths of a meter). 2. Broadly used to refer to any type of data-carrying mark in optical media.

pitch: The distance between tracks or pits on a disc.

pixel: A picture element in a video display; the minimum raster display element, represented as a point with a specified color or intensity.

pixel aspect ratio: The width-to-height ratio of a pixel. Aspect ratio is a function of the number of scan lines along the vertical axis and the number of scanning spots along the horizontal axis, along with the screen's physical aspect ratio.

pixel depth: The number of bits stored for each pixel in a bit-mapped image. The greater the pixel depth (the more bits per pixel), the wider the range of intensity levels or colors a bit map can represent. The number of possible pixel values is 2^N, where N is the pixel depth.

pixel doubling: A method of changing the aspect ratio of a display by duplicating rows or columns of pixels.

pixel thinning: A technique for reducing the bandwidth or changing the aspect ratio of an image by systematically discarding pixels.

port: A connection point on a computer system through which another computer workstation or peripheral device can communicate directly with it.

prebuffering: Sending data to a memory buffer before it is needed for display or processing.

premastered tape: A magnetic master tape that contains all data and control codes that are to be recorded on an optical master disc via laser beam modulation.

premastering: In CD ROM, a data-formatting process performed on each block of user data. The process determines the sector address and adds synchronization information. If the format is to be mode 1, 288 bytes of error detection and correction data are calculated and this data is added at the end of each sector to ensure the full recovery of user block data.

presentation system: Part of a delivery system used to process and display information received from the storage system.

productivity software: Programs for improving an individual's efficiency in performing tasks or functions. These include personal productivity tools such as software for word processing and for database programs.

Programmable Read-Only Memory: See *CD-PROM.*

Pulse Code Modulation: See *PCM.*

quantization: 1. Part of the process by which analog signals are encoded into digital form. 2. Also refers to the number of bits required to store the value of each digital sample. CD audio uses 16-bit quantization for each stereo channel, resulting in a range of about 64,000 discrete sound level values (64 KB) at each sampling point. See also *sampling rate.*

query language: In database management systems, an alternative to conventional programming languages that enables users without formal training in algorithmic thought to formulate ad hoc information-retrieval requests using English-like phrases.

radial: Along a line from the center to the outer edge of a disk.

random access: The ability to reach any piece of data on a storage medium in a very short period of time. Random access makes branching, searching, and nonlinear play possible.

Random-Access Memory (RAM): Semiconductor memory circuits used to store data and programs in information-processing systems.

raster: The area that a scanning beam of a CRT illuminates. Also, the array of scan lines that cover a display area and depict images, called a *raster scan.*

raw bit error: A data error on a CD ROM disc that is sent to the microcomputer. The raw bit error rate refers to physical data errors on the disc, not the errors corrected by the CD ROM drive's decoding and correction system during playback.

read: To acquire data from one storage device or medium and transfer it to another medium, usually the computer's memory.

read head: See *optical head.*

Read-Only Memory (ROM): Semiconductor memory circuits that contain prewritten programs or data. The content of ROM circuits is permanent, while the content of Random-Access Memory (RAM) circuits is volatile.

read/write capability: For storage devices, the ability to both write (record) and read (play back) information. Most magnetic devices can write repeatedly, read, erase, and then rewrite. Usually, optical devices are read-only, although some optical discs can be written once but not erased. Erasable optical discs currently are being researched.

real time: An operating mode under which data is received and processed and the results returned so rapidly that the process appears instantaneous to the user.

record: A collection of related fields in a database. Each record in a database of company clients might contain such information as the client's name and address, purchasing history, and credit history.

Red Book audio: See *Compact Disc Digital Audio.*

redundancy: In error correction schemes, storing the same data more than once or in more than one way so that the additional information can be used to reconstruct any data lost because of media imperfections or transmission errors.

Reed-Solomon: An algebraic code used for error correction. The Reed-Solomon codes employ redundancy and are especially powerful when data is organized into long blocks and when errors come in bursts, such as those caused by scratches on an optical disc, rather than as continuous noise. The Reed-Solomon code is part of the CIRC error correction code used to correct errors in Compact Discs.

refresh rate: The rate at which the electron beam of a CRT monitor scans the screen, thereby restoring an image or displaying a new one. A computer display typically refreshes the screen every $\frac{1}{60}$ second.

relational database: A collection of data fields within records that are connected to records within other files. The files are generally combined and searched at the time of a query.

replication: The process of making multiple copies of a CD ROM.

reseek: Occurs when a playback device's read head must perform a series of redundant disk accesses to a file to read all of its data into a memory buffer. A reseek commonly occurs if the presentation device can't store and process incoming data fast enough. If the buffer fills up, reading stops, and the disc must make at least one full revolution before reading can resume. This time lag can interrupt presentation if the buffer is small, as the buffer may empty and the presentation device become starved for data before the seek is complete.

resolution: The fineness of the detail in a video or computer display screen, measured as a number of discrete elements—dots in a scanner, pixels in a monitor. The higher the number, the higher the resolution and the better the picture.

RGB (Red-Green-Blue): A computer color display output signal and image-encoding scheme comprised of separately controllable red, green, and blue elements. RGB monitors typically offer higher resolution than do composite monitors.

RLE: See *run-length encoding.*

rotational latency (or rotational delay): Delay in access to data as a disc rotates to the proper position for reading.

RTOS (Real-Time Operating System): For effective interaction, an operating system must be able to function within the constraints of *real time* (see entry). The CD-I's OS-9-based operating system is an RTOS.

run-length encoding (RLE): An encoding technique to compress the data storing a screen image. Normally used to compress high-contrast images such as black-and-white images, run-length encoding compression stores only the transitions from black to white or from white to black and the distance between transitions.

sampling: Part of the process in which an analog signal is digitally encoded. See also *sampling rate.*

sampling rate: The number of times per second that digitizing circuitry measures an analog signal to produce a digital value. See also *quantization*.

SASI (Shugart Associates Standard Interface): Commonly pronounced *sassy*. An interface protocol that enables storage devices to communicate with microcomputers. Developed by Shugart Associates, SASI has been adopted as an industry standard for small disk drives. See also *SCSI*.

scaling: Changing the size of an image to conform to an application's display characteristics or requirements.

scan lines: The parallel lines across the video screen along which the scanning spot travels from left to right when laying down the video information that makes up the picture on the TV screen or monitor. NTSC standard video systems produce 525 lines on a screen, and PAL standard video systems produce 625 scan lines.

scanner: A device that resolves a two-dimensional object, such as a business document, into a stream of bits through raster scanning and quantization. Also called an *optical scanner*.

screen: Synonymous with *video display*.

SCSI (Small Computer Standard Interface): Pronounced *scuzzy*. An 8-bit parallel interface that connects peripherals to microcomputers. Any CD ROM drive with a SCSI can theoretically connect to any microcomputer with a SCSI, although minor implementation incompatibilities sometimes prevent this. Because SCSI is a bus-oriented interface, as many as eight systems and peripherals can be connected on one. SCSI is derived from SASI, which was renamed SCSI when the United States government adopted it, with some alterations, as a standard.

search hit: An electronic search that yields a set of documents from a database containing and/or excluding words or combinations of words set forth in the search phrase.

SECAM *(sequential couleur à la mémoire,* or sequential color with memory): The video color standard developed in France and subsequently adopted by the U.S.S.R. and its satellite states and in some parts of the Middle East and North Africa. It involves sending the three primary color signals sequentially rather than nearly simultaneously (as in NTSC and PAL systems).

sector: Generally, a data block on storage media, usually with a pre-determined length. In CD ROM, a 2352-byte data block. Every CD ROM sector contains its own error detection and correction coding and has its own unique address on the disc. The 2352 sequential bytes of a sector are divided into a sync field of 12 bytes, a header field of 4 bytes, a user data field of 2048 bytes, and an auxiliary data field of 288 bytes. The user data field usually is called a *logical sector.*

seek: To position the read head of a mass storage unit in the correct location to read a particular file or piece of information. On a CD ROM drive, this generally requires also altering the rotational speed. Because seeking data on a CD ROM is time-consuming when compared to seeking on magnetic-disk media, the number of seeks required to find the desired information is an important determinant of overall CD ROM system performance. The High Sierra Group's proposed file format and directory structure provide for opening any file on a CD ROM disc with only one or two seeks.

seek error: Data error that results when a drive's laser can't accurately locate user-requested data because of physical or mechanical problems such as vibration, disc surface irregularities, and poor laser focusing.

serial: The arrangement of data or processing tasks in a series. Often used to mean the transmission of data through a communications line.

servo: Short for *servomechanism* (see entry).

servomechanism: A tracking device that continuously follows some variable quantity, using its own feedback to maintain a constant rate, temperature, or rotation. Automated temperature-control devices are examples, as are the focus and tracking servos of optical disk drives.

Shugart Associates Standard Interface: See *SASI.*

signal: A detectable impulse, produced by voltage, current, magnetic fields, or light, by which information is communicated through wires, circuitry, microwaves, or laser beams.

signal-to-noise ratio (SNR): The strength of a video and/or audio signal in relation to the interference, or "noise," it has picked up in passing between source and destination. The higher the SNR value, the better the quality of the signal.

SMPTE (Society of Motion Picture and Television Engineers): A professional engineering society that has established a number of standards for motion picture and television equipment.

SNR: See *signal-to-noise ratio.*

software: A set of programs, procedures, and documents concerned with the operation of a data-processing system.

software tools: Programs used for developing specialized software or applications.

spindle: The part of a drive that spins the disk.

sprites: Screen images, movable under program or manual control through an input device. Sprites may be characters, cursor shapes, or specific patterns. They normally are smaller than full-screen size, and in certain cases their size is restricted.

stamper: The metal plate carrying the negative image of a glass CD ROM master disc that is used to mold polycarbonate replicants.

stand-alone systems: Internally compatible systems that perform their specified functions in conjunction with an operator or user without being connected to other equipment.

standardization: Agreement among manufacturers on technical specifications for a particular device. For example, TV signals and broadcast formats, international telephone networks, Compact Disc Digital Audio and CD ROM formats, and encoding techniques have all been standardized.

stopword: A word, having little meaning for text-retrieval purposes, that is never indexed within a database. These words are included in a database's *stoplist.* Stoplists vary, but usually include articles, prepositions, and connectors such as *the, to,* and *or.*

storage capacity: The amount of data an electronic medium will hold, usually specified in (8-bit) bytes. In this way, storage capacity can be calculated in terms of the type of information stored. The Compact Disc's 600 MB storage capacity, for example, can accommodate about 150,000 pages of typed text, about 72 minutes of the finest quality sound, or about 5000 frames of video-quality pictures.

string: A series of characters encoded numerically and stored.

structured graphics: Geometric shapes stored as a set of descriptive codes rather than as bit maps.

structured graphics metafile: Any of a number of protocols for storing certain categories of images as geometric descriptions or as subroutine calls to graphics subroutines.

subcodes: Display and disc control information stored along with audio data on a Compact Disc. The Compact Disc Digital Audio format specifies 8 subcode bits for every 588 data bits and labels them P, Q, R, S, T, U, V, and W.

synchronization field: In CD ROM, a 12-byte area of a sector that contains synchronization information. In hexadecimal notation, all bytes in this field are FF except the first and last bytes, which are 00. Also called the *sync code.*

synchronous branching: Jumping from one file or one file fragment to another without interrupting the data stream, resulting in a "seamless," or continuous, presentation.

synchronous file: A file that must be received by the presentation device at a designated transfer rate (DTR), which may or may not be the same as the actual transfer rate of the storage device. An audio file is an example of a synchronous file. If data is delivered more or less quickly than the DTR, both the tempo and the pitch of the audio material will be wrong. Special device drivers and circuitry are required to interpret synchronous files.

system software: Programs that enable a computer to function and control its own operation, as opposed to *application programs,* which perform user-specific tasks. The most common type of system software is the group of programs that comprise the computer's operating system.

track: 1. A linear, spiral, or circular path on which information is placed. Refers to optical discs as well as magnetic disks. 2. In CD Digital Audio, can also refer to a single tune or musical sequence.

track jump: The action of moving quickly from one track to another nearby.

tracking servo: The servo in an optical drive that keeps the reading and/or writing light spot centered on the information track regardless of imperfections in the medium and drive mechanism or of shocks and vibrations.

transfer rate: The speed at which data is transmitted to or from a device, especially the reading or writing speed of a storage peripheral. The data transfer rate of a CD ROM is about 150,000 bytes (150 KB) per second.

transition: 1. In film and video, the change from one image to another. 2. In facsimile, the change from black to white (or vice versa), as at the edges of letters.

turnkey system: Any packaged configuration of integrated hardware and software that is designed to accomplish a particular information-processing task. The term is applied most often to dedicated computer systems that use minicomputers or microcomputers.

typesetting tapes: Synonymous with *photocomposition tapes* (see entry). **335**

user data field: In CD ROM mode 1, a 2048-byte-long area of the data field in an addressable sector that is dedicated for storing application data.

user interface: The interface or device (such as a keyboard, hand control, or touch pad) through which the user communicates with a particular system or computer.

utilities: Programs providing special processing functions that aid in graphics tasks. These functions include saving, listing, copying, and initializing.

variable-length records: A way of organizing a database such that the sizes of records containing the data need not be uniform.

vectorize: To convert a bit-mapped image to structured graphics.

vertical blanking: When the electron beam of a CRT finishes writing information on the screen at the end of a display refresh cycle, the beam must return to the top of the screen. The beam is turned off during the interval so that it does not write incorrect information to the screen; this is known as *vertical blanking*.

vertical delta encoding: Delta encoding (see entry) applied in the vertical direction.

vertical markets: Markets that demand specialized products suited to their professional needs. The medical and legal professions are two examples of vertical markets that have their own jargons and information needs. By contrast, office management products cater to a broader, more generalized market.

video: A system of recording and transmitting primarily visual information by translating moving or still images into electrical signals. These signals can be broadcast via high-frequency carrier waves or sent through cables on a closed circuit.

video digitizer: Synonymous with *frame grabber* (see entry).

videodisc: A generic term describing an optical disc that stores color video pictures and two-channel sound along a spiral track. Uses the same optical readout principle as Compact Disc, but the discs are larger (30 cm in diameter) and double-sided, and the rotational speed and data rate are higher. The program information is analog, although the control information is digital.

voice-grade audio: Sound information of sufficient quality for reproducing the human voice; normally voice-grade audio has a bandwidth of 4 to 8 kHz.

Volume Table of Contents (VTOC): 1. In Compact Disc, subcode information in the lead-in area of the disc identifying the number of tracks and indexes, their timing, and their duration. 2. In CD ROM, an area of the disc that includes the disc name, copyright information, pointers to datablocks, sequence numbers in a multivolume set, version numbers, and so forth.

WORM (Write-Once, Read-Many): An optical disc technology in which the user may write to the disc as well as read from it.

write: To transcribe recorded data from one place to another, or from one medium to another. (Information from a computer is written *to* a disk, rather than *on* a disk.)

Write-Once Medium: A data-storage medium to which data can be written but not erased.

X-Y coordinates: Points on a plane that has been divided down (Y) and across (X) on a predetermined scale. X-Y coordinates can be used to plot a drawing on a computer screen.

Yellow Book: Another name for the CD ROM standard (see *CD ROM* entry).

YUV color system: A color-encoding scheme for natural pictures in which the luminance and chrominance are separate. The human eye is less sensitive to color variations than to intensity variations, so YUV allows the encoding of luminance (Y) information at full bandwidth and chrominance (UV) information at half bandwidth.

zoom: In video and photography, the facility to enlarge (zoom in on) or diminish (zoom out from) an area of an image.

Resources

This brief list includes many of the companies involved in CD ROM, but not all. For the most up-to-date and accurate account of products and services in the CD ROM industry, we recommend the *CD ROM Sourcebook*, published by Diversified Data Resources, (703) 237-0682.

CD-I Developers

American Interactive Media, Inc.
Laser Magnetic Storage Intl.
Philips

OptImage
The Record Group

Conference Coordinators

IEEE Spectrum
Information Industry Assn. (IIA)
Info Tech
Institute for Graphic Communication
Knowledge Industry Publications

Learned Information, Inc.
Learning Technology Institute
Meckler Publishing
Microsoft Corp.

Consultants

Academic Microbroadcasting Educ.
  Network
Alltech Communications, Inc.
American Compact Disc
Buddine & Co.
Cuadra Associates
Database Development
Database Services
Dataquest
DCM Associates
Disk Trend Reports
Diversified Data Resources
EarthView, Inc.

Electronic Trend Publications
Freeman Associates, Inc.
Heyer and Associates
Info Express
Information Workstation Group
In-Four
Info Tech
Link Resources
MicroTrends, Inc.
RMG Consultants, Inc.
Rothchild Consultants
Vision Three, Inc.
Xiphias

Interfaces/Controllers

Advanced Storage Concepts
Denon America
Densus
Digital Equipment Corp.
Hitachi
Intel

KnowledgeSet Corp.
Optical Media Services
Philips
SOCS Management
Sony
Xebec

Data Preparation/Service Bureaus

Airs, Inc.
Brodart
Compact Discoveries
Cuneiform, Inc.
Denon America
Digital Equipment Corp.
Discovery Systems
EarthView, Inc.
Geovision, Inc.
Highlighted Data
Image Conversion Technology
Info Express
Information Dimensions
International Computaprint Corp.
JVC America, Inc.

Knowledge Access, Inc.
KnowledgeSet Corp.
Laserdata
Library Corp.
MicroTrends, Inc.
Publishers' Data Services Corp.
Online Computer Systems
Optical Media Services
Quantum Access, Inc.
Reference Technology
Reteaco, Inc.
Silver Platter Information, Inc.
TMS (Time Management Systems), Inc.
Tri-Star Publishing
VideoTools, Inc.

Data Preparation Systems

Digital Equipment Corp.
Quantum Leap Technologies

VideoTools, Inc.

CD ROM Systems

Amtec Information Services
Brodart
Digital Equipment Corps.
Geovision, Inc.
KnowledgeSet Corp.
Laserdata
LaserTrack Corp.

Library Corp.
Newport News Shipbuilding
Online Computer Systems
Prentice Hall
Reference Technology
SOCS Management

Mastering and Replication

3M Corporation
Denon Digital
Digital Audio Disc Corp.
Discovery Systems
Hitachi
JVC America, Inc.

Laser Logic
Laser Video
Polygram
Sanyo
Sony

Drives/Players

Denon America
Digital Equipment Corp.
Hitachi
KnowledgeSet Corp.
Nissei Sangyo America
Panasonic Industrial Co.

Philips Subsystems And Peripherals
Reference Technology, Inc.
Sanyo
Sony
Toshiba

Image Scanners

Hitachi
National Semiconductor

Tecmar
Texas Instruments

Graphics/Text Preparation Systems

Acctex Information Systems
DataCopy
DEST
Diversified Technology
EI Corp.
Eikonix
Highlighted Data
Image Conversion Technology
Imaging Technology

Kurtzweil Computer Products
Murata Business Systems
Newport News Shipbuilding
Number Nine Computers
Palantir
Recognition Equipment
Talus Corp.
Via Video

Industry Associations

AITRC
Alexandria Institute
Association of American Publishers

Association for Information and Image Management (AIIM)

Market Surveys

Ampersand Research
CD-ROM Market Opportunities
  (Link Resources)
Disk Trend Reports
Diversified Data Resources
Electronic Trend Publications

Information WorkStation Group
Optical Data Storage Outlook
  (Freeman Associates)
OROM and CD-ROM Products Applications and Markets (Rothchild Consultants)

Publications

CD Data Report
CD-ROM Review
Computer Insider
Digital Information Group
IEEE Spectrum
InfoTech
Learned Information, Inc.
Meckler Publishing
Mini-Micro Systems

Optical Information Systems
  (Meckler Publishing)
Optical Information Systems Update
  (Meckler Publishing)
Optical Memory News (Rothchild
  Consultants)
Prentice Hall
Video Computing
Video Disc Monitor

Retrieval/Indexing Software

Acctex Information Systems
Airs, Inc.
Borland International
Box Company, Inc.
BRS Information Technologies
Compact Discoveries
Computer Access Corp.
CP International
Cuadra Associates
Digital Library Systems
Disclosure Information Group
Finder Information Tools, Inc.
Fulcrum Technologies, Inc.
Group L Corp.

Highlighted Data
Information Dimensions
Inmagic
Knowledge Access, Inc.
KnowledgeSet Corp.
Library Corp.
Macromind, Inc.
Online Computer Systems
OWL
Reference Technology, Inc.
Reteaco, Inc.
Silver Platter Information, Inc.
TMS (Time Management Systems), Inc.
Zylab Corp.

3M Corporation
225-4S-09
St. Paul, MN 55144

**Academic Microbroadcasting
Educ. Network**
P.O. Box 1247
Dickinson, TX 77539

Acctex Information Systems
131 Stewart St., Suite 600
San Francisco, CA 94105

Advanced Micro Devices
901 Thompson Place
P.O. Box 3453, Mail Stop 140
Sunnyvale, CA 94086

Advanced Storage Concepts
9600 Hillcroft, Suite 325
Houston, TX 77096

Airs, Inc.
335 Paint Branch Drive, Eng Research
    Center
College Park, MD 20742

AITRC
1212 Kinnear Rd.
Columbus, OH 43212

Alde Publishing
7840 Computer Ave.
Minneapolis, MN 55435

Alexandria Institute
3100 Airport Road
Boulder, CO 80301

Alltech Communications, Inc.
2101 Grandin Road
Cincinnati, OH 45208-3307

American Compact Disc
218 Church Road
Elkins Park, PA 19117

American Interactive Media, Inc.
11111 Santa Monica Blvd., Suite 700
Los Angeles, CA 90025

Ampersand Research
P.O. Box 1142
New Canaan, CT 06840

341

Amtec Information Services
3700 Industry Ave.
Lakewood, CA 90714-6050

**Association of American
Publishers**
2005 Massachusetts Ave. NW
Washington, D.C. 20036

**Association for Information and
Image Management (AIIM)**
1100 Wayne Ave.
Silver Spring, MD 20910

Borland International
4585 Scotts Valley Drive
Scotts Valley, CA 95066

Box Company, Inc.
63 Howard St.
Cambridge, MA 02139

Brodart
Library Automation Division
500 Arch St.
Williamsport, PA 17705

BRS Information Technologies
1350 Avenue of the Americas - 1802
New York, NY 10019

Buddine & Co.
409 Jasmine
Corona Del Mar, CA 92625

CD Data Report
Langley Publications
1350 Beverly Road, Suite 115-324
Mclean, VA 22101

CD-ROM Review
CW Communications
80 Elm St.
Peterborough, NH 03458

Compact Discoveries
1050 S Federal Highway
Delray Beach, FL 33444

Computer Access Corporation
26 Brighton St.
Belmont, MA 02178-4008

CP International
210 South St.
New York, NY 10002

Cuadra Associates
2001 Wilshire Blvd., Suite 305
Santa Monica, CA 90403

Database Development
Marine Plaza, Suite 1224
111 E. Wisconsin Ave.
Milwaukee, WI 53202

Database Services
2685 Marine Way, Suite 1305
Mountain View, CA 94043

DataCopy
1215 Terrabella Ave.
Mountain View, CA 94043

Dataquest
1290 Ridder Park Drive
San Jose, CA 95131

DCM Associates
Post Drawer 605
1265 Grove Circle
Benicia, CA 94510

Denon America
27 Law Drive
Fairfield, NJ 07006

Densus, Inc.
177 Webster St., Suite A436
Monterey, CA 93940

DEST
1201 Cadillac Court
Milpitas, CA 95035

Digital Audio Disc Corp.
1800 N Fruitridge Ave.
Terre Haute, IN 47804

Digital Equipment Corp.
CD Publishing Group
12 Crosby Drive
Bedford, MA 01730

Digital Library Systems
5161 River Road, Building 6
Bethesda, MD 20816

Disclosure Information Group
5161 River Road, Building 4
Bethesda, MD 20816

Discovery Systems
Division of Battelle
555 Metro Place N, Suite 325
Dublin, OH 43017

Disk Trend Reports
5150 El Camino Real, Suite B-20
Los Altos, CA 94022

Diversified Data Resources
6609 Rosecroft Place
Falls Church, VA 22043

Diversified Technology
8585 Stemmons Freeway, Suite 103N
Dallas, TX 75247

EarthView, Inc.
6514 18th Ave. NE
Seattle, WA 98115

EI Corp.
5797 Central Ave.
Boulder, CO 80301

Eikonix
23 Crosby Drive
Bedford, MA 01730

Electronic Trend Publications
12930 Saratoga Ave., Suite D1
Saratoga, CA 95070

Finder Information Tools, Inc.
1430 W Peachtree St., Suite 312
Atlanta, GA 30309

Freeman Associates, Inc.
(Optical Data Storage Outlook)
311 E Carillo St.
Santa Barbara, CA 93101

Fulcrum Technologies, Inc.
331 Cooper St., 4th Floor
Ottawa, Ontario
K2P 0G5 CANADA

General Research Corp.
P.O. Box 6770
Santa Barbara, CA 93160-6770

Geovision, Inc.
20 Technology Park, Suite 160
Norcross, GA 30092

Group L Corp.
481 Carlisle Drive
Herndon, VA 22070

Heyer and Associates
62 Mason St.
Greenwich, MA 06830

Highlighted Data
P.O. Box 17229
Washington, D.C. 20041

Hitachi
401 W Artesia Blvd.
Compton, CA 90220

IEEE Spectrum
345 E 47th St., 11th Floor
New York, NY 10017

Image Conversion Technology
80 Blanchard Road
Burlington, MA 01803

Imaging Technology
600 W Cummings Park
Woburn, MA 01801

Info Express
6141 NE Bothell Way, Suite 104
Seattle, WA 98155

Information Dimensions
655 Metro Place S, Suite 500
Dublin, OH 43017

Information Industry Assn. (IIA)
316 Pennsylvania Ave. SE, Suite 400
Washington, D.C. 20003

Information WorkStation Group
501 Queen St.
Alexandria, VA 22314

Info Tech
P.O. Box 633
Pittsfield, VT 05762

In-Four
885 N San Antonio Road
Los Altos, CA 94022

Inmagic
238 Broadway
Cambridge, MA 02139

**Institute for Graphic
   Communication**
375 Commonwealth Ave.
Boston, MA 02115

Intel
2625 Walsh Ave.
Santa Clara, CA 95051

International Computaprint
  Corporation
475 Virginia Drive
Ft. Washington, PA 19034

JVC America, Inc.
1621 Browning Ave.
Irvine, CA 92714

Knowledge Access, Inc.
2685 Marine Way, Suite 1305
Mountain View, CA 94043

Knowledge Industry Publications
701 Westchester Ave.
White Plains, NY 10604

KnowledgeSet Corp.
P.O. Box 51125
Pacific Grove, CA 93950

Kurtzweil Computer Products
185 Albany St.
Cambridge, MA 02139

Laser Logic
222 Railroad Ave.
Danville, CA 94525

Laser Magnetic Storage Intl.
200 Park Ave., Suite 5501
New York, NY 10166

LaserTrack Corp.
6235-B Lookout Road
Boulder, CO 80301

Laser Video
One E Wacker, 35th Floor
Chicago, IL 60601

Laserdata
One Kendall Square
Building 200
Cambridge, MA 02139

Learned Information, Inc.
143 Old Marlton Pike
Medford, NJ 08055

Learned Information, Inc.
Besselsleigh Road
Abingdon, Oxford
ENGLAND

Learning Technology Institute
50 Culpepper St.
Warrenton, VA 22186

Library Corp.
P.O. Box 40035
Washington, D.C. 20016

Link Resources
(CD-ROM Market Opportunities)
79 Fifth Ave.
New York, NY 10003

Macromind, Inc.
1028 W. Wolfram
Chicago, IL 60657

Mead Data Central
9393 Springboro Pike
Dayton, OII 45401

Meckler Publishing
(Optical Information Systems;
Optical Information Systems Update)
11 Ferry Lane W
Westport, CT 06880

Micromedex
660 Bannock St.
Suite 350
Denver, CO 80204

Microsoft Corp.
16011 NE 36th
Box 97017
Redmond, WA 98073

MicroTrends, Inc.
650 Woodfield Drive
Suite 730
Schaumburg, IL 60195

Microware Systems Corp.
1900 NW 114th S.
Des Moines, IA 50322

Mini-Micro Systems
18818 Teller Ave., Suite 170
Irvine, CA 92715

Murata Business Systems
4801 Spring Valley Road
Dallas, TX 75244

National Semiconductor
2900 Semiconductor Drive
Santa Clara, CA 95051

Newport News Shipbuilding
4101 Washington Ave.
Newport News, VA 23607

Nissei Sangyo America
1701 Golf Road, Suite 401
Rolling Meadows, IL 60008

Number Nine Computers
725 Concord Ave.
Cambridge, MA 02138

Online Computer Systems
20251 Century Blvd.
Germantown, MD 20874

Optical Media Services
P.O. Box 2107
Aptos, CA 95001

OptImage
2223 King Drive
Chicago, IL 60616

OWL
Plaza Center
10900 NE 8th St.
Bellevue, WA 98004

Palantir
2500 Augustine Dr.
Santa Clara, CA 95054

Panasonic Industrial Co.
One Panasonic Way
Secaucus, NJ 07075

Philips
P.O. Box 523
5600 Am Eindhoven
THE NETHERLANDS

Philips International
Building Hwd2
P.O. Box 218
5600 Md Eindhoven
THE NETHERLANDS

Philips Subsystems And
  Peripherals
1111 Northshore Drive, Box 204
Building 2, Suite 726
Knoxville, TN 37919

Polygram
11111 San Monica Blvd., Suite 1000
Los Angeles, CA 90025

Praxis Technologies
595 Bay Street
Suite 1050, Box 54
Toronto, Ontario
M5G 2C2 CANADA

Prentice Hall
P.O. Box 500
Englewood Cliffs, NJ 07632

Quantum Access, Inc.
1700 W Loop S., Suite 1460
Houston, TX 77027

Quantum Leap Technologies
314 Romano Ave.
Coral Gates, FL 33134

Reference Technology, Inc.
5700 Flatiron Parkway
Boulder, CO 80301

Reteaco, Inc.
716 Garden Baker Road, Suite 109
Willowdale, Ontario
M2H 3B4 CANADA

RMG Consultants, Inc.
P.O. Box 7279
Silver Spring, MD 20907

Rothchild Consultants
256 Laguna Honda Blvd.
San Francisco, CA 94116-1496

Sanyo
200 Riser Road
Little Ferry, NJ 07643

Silver Platter Information, Inc.
37 Walnut St.
Wellesley Hills, MA 02181

SOCS Management
18138 Bancroft Ave.
Monte Sereno, CA 95030

Sony
1359 Old Oakland Road
San Jose, CA 95112

STET
Corso D'Italia, 41
Roma 00198
ITALY

Talus Corp.
985 University Ave.
Suite 29
Los Gatos, CA 95030

Tecmar
6225 Cochran Road
Solon, OH 44139

Texas Instruments
P.O. Box 2909
Austin, TX 78769

The Record Group
3300 Warner Blvd.
Burbank, CA 91510

TMS (Time Management Systems), Inc.
P.O. Box 1358
Stillwater, OK 74076

Toshiba
2900 McArthur Blvd.
Northbrook, IL 60062

Tri-Star Publishing
275 Gibralter Road
Horsham, PA 19044

Via Video
4800 Patrick Henry Drive
Santa Clara, CA 95054

Video Computing
P.O. Box 3415
Indialantic, FL 32903

Video Disc Monitor
5929 Lee Highway
Arlington, VA 22207

VideoTools, Inc.
P.O. Box 339
Soquel, CA 95073

Vision Three, Inc.
2110 Hercules Drive
Los Angeles, CA 90046

Recognition Equipment
P.O. Box 660204
Dallas, TX 75266

Xebec
7650 McCallum Blvd.
Suite 2102
Dallas, TX 75252

Xiphias
13470 Washington Blvd.
Suite 203
Marina Del Rey, CA

Zylab Corp.
233 E Erie St.
Chicago, IL 60611

Suzanne Ropiequet is the editor of the bestselling book *The Peter Norton Programmer's Guide to the IBM PC* and co-editor, with Steve Lambert, of *CD ROM: The New Papyrus*, one of the first books on CD ROM technology. Suzanne started her career at Tektronix and later became one of the first employees of dilithium Press, an early microcomputer book publisher. In addition, she has conducted classes in software applications training, written technical documentation, and has been a designer and consultant in the field of interactive video technology. Suzanne is also the Speaker Coordinator for the Second International Conference on CD ROM Technology, sponsored by Microsoft Corporation.

John Einberger is vice president of software development for Reference Technology, Inc. He was instrumental in forming the High Sierra Group, which he chaired and which has proposed a logical format standard for CD ROM discs. John has worked in the computer industry for more than 18 years and holds degrees in electrical engineering, computer science, and business.

Bill Zoellick is director of technology at the Alexandria Institute, a nonprofit organization dedicated to making CD ROM information retrieval systems more widely available to users through libraries and other resource centers. Before joining the Alexandria Institute, Bill was manager of software research at TMS, Inc. He has been a key participant in the High Sierra Group, playing an active role in producing the CD ROM logical format proposal. In addition, he has written and spoken widely about a broad range of CD ROM publishing issues and is co-author of a major new textbook on file structures.

The manuscript for this book was prepared and submitted to Microsoft Press in electronic form. Text files were processed and formatted using Microsoft Word.

Cover design by Ted Mader & Associates

Interior text design by The NBBJ Group

Illustrations by Nick Gregoric

Principal typography by Jean Trenary

Text composition by Microsoft Press in Stempel Garamond with display in Futura and Univers, using the CCI 400 composition system and the Mergenthaler Linotron 202 digital phototypesetter.